The Church's Seven Deadly Secrets

The Church's Seven Deadly Secrets

Identity Theft from Within

Paul H. Jones

POLEBRIDGE PRESS
Salem, Oregon

To My Students
Whose Perceptive Questions
Make Me a Better Thinker and Teacher

Cover and interior design by Robaire Ream

Library of Congress Cataloging-in-Publication Data

Jones, Paul H., 1949-
  The church's seven deadly secrets : identity theft from within / Paul H. Jones.
     p. cm.
  Includes bibliographical references and index.
  ISBN 978-1-59815-113-8 (alk. paper)
1. Church. 2. Christianity--United States. I. Title.
  BR600.3.J66 2013
  230--dc23
                                                      2012038113

Table of Contents

List of Abbreviations

Gen	Genesis
Exod	Exodus
Lev	Leviticus
Num	Numbers
Deut	Deuteronomy
Josh	Joshua
1,2 Sam	1,2 Samuel
1,2 Kgs	1,2 Kings
Isa	Isaiah
Jer	Jeremiah
Ezek	Ezekiel
Hos	Hosea
Mal	Malachi
Ps(s)	Psalm(s)
Matt	Matthew
Mark	
Luke	
John	
Rom	Romans
1,2 Cor	1,2 Corinthians
Gal	Galatians
Eph	Ephesians
Col	Colossians
1,2 Thess	1,2 Thessalonians
1,2 Tim	1,2 Timothy
Heb	Hebrews
1,2 Pet	1,2 Peter
1 John	
Rev	Revelation

Note: All biblical quotations are taken from the New Revised Standard Version (NRSV), unless otherwise noted. Additionally, the term "First Testament" is used instead of "Old Testament," and the term "Second Testament" is used instead of "New Testament." See the more detailed discussion of these terms in the Introduction.

Acknowledgments

Although writing a book is a solitary process, it is conversational. Many voices from the past, as well as from the present, inform and influence an author's thoughts and words. Those significant others for me deserve special recognition. Colleagues at Transylvania University who either read or contributed to the manuscript during different stages of preparation include Jack Furlong, Frank Russell, John Svarlien, Carole Barnsley, Angela Hurley, Martha Gehringer, Bill Bowden, Barbara LoMonaco, and Ann Cranfill. Colleagues from the academy, church, and synagogue who offered constructive criticism include Guy Waldrop, Bill Leffler, Robert J. Miller, Phil Points, Jim Duke, Clark Williamson, Albert Pennybacker, Jerry Sumney, Amy-Jill Levine, Charles Watkins, Marc Kline, Don Alexander, Carolyn Dupont, Steve Monhollen, Dave Carr, Charisse Gillett, Larry Kant, Jan Ehrmantraut, and Carolyn Richart. Appreciation is extended to Peter Alig for his editorial suggestions. Gratitude is also expressed to members of the "Top of the Hill" adult Sunday school class and TEAM evening class at my home church, Central Christian Church in Lexington, Kentucky, with whom I shared these ideas. Former students at Transylvania also reviewed chapters. They are Ben Johnson, Turner West, Julianne Norman, Shawna Corman, Abby Newcom, Shane McGuire, Clay Turner, Logan Lloyd, Shayanna Little Jolly, Marshall Jolly, Sarah McClelland, Lindsey Robke, John Reeder, and H.B. Elam. Members of my 2012 May Term course at Transylvania read and commented on every page of this manuscript. Thanks to Alexander Aultman, Michael Cooper, Caroline Durham, Travis Feck, Daniel Ficker, Hannah Greer, Kathleen Johnston, Ryla Luttrell, Della McDonald, Trevor Million, Grant Newton,

Jordan Perkins, Bennett Rieser, Alexander Stephanski, and Derek Wilkerson.

Most of this book was written while on sabbatical leave from Transylvania University. Special appreciation is extended to now retired president Charles L. Shearer and former dean Bill Pollard for their encouragement. Support from the Kenan Fund for Faculty and Student Enrichment was most helpful.

The superb staff at Polebridge Press deserves high praise. Because of their meticulous care and exceptional dedication, the manuscript is immensely improved. I applaud Larry Alexander, publisher; Cassandra Farrin, publishing associate; Char Matejovsky, production editor; and Robaire Ream, art director.

Deepest gratitude to my wife, Merry, who reviewed sections of the manuscript, but, most importantly, encouraged and supported me. Her sacrificial love and abiding presence made the extraordinary possible.

Although I am profoundly indebted to the above people for their insights and wisdom, only I am responsible for mistakes and shortcomings.

Introduction

"Why didn't my *church* tell me that?"

If you have ever asked that question, then this book is for you.

My students at Transylvania University[1] ask me this question all the time, and after twenty-seven years of teaching undergraduate religion courses, I expect and welcome the query. On the one hand, it indicates that my classes are challenging their inherited assumptions, are threatening their Sunday School images, and are creating theological dissonance. On the other hand, it means that they are now aware of diverse voices in the tradition, are eager to explore and examine them, and are ready to grow.

Because there are few places in our society, including the church, where religious issues are discussed seriously, a huge knowledge gap exists between the lectern and the desk, the pulpit and the pew. There is also a strange silence about the church's ongoing conversation with culture, as well as about the principles and practices of biblical and theological scholarship. Consequently, many Christians cannot reconcile their belief system with modernity. Some dismiss religion as irrelevant, while others erect firewalls to defend the faith. Students, like parishioners, want to know if you can read the Bible and the newspaper with the same eyes, if you can engage the brain after entering sacred space, and if you can trust with your heart what your head rejects. Silence about the vast resources of the tradition has created church secrets that, over time, rob us of our Christian identity from within.

For the past eight years, identity theft—the illegal use of another person's name—has been the number-one consumer complaint to the Federal Trade Commission.[2] This book claims that this same crime is being committed by the church against itself. That is, the church's failure to teach its own intellectual history, whether intentional or unintentional, undermines Christian identity by denying itself the staples of the faith and thereby making it vulnerable to distortions from within and temptations from without. In short, faith formation does not happen by accident. Unless the church deliberately and willfully passes on the tradition, its mission will be gradually compromised and its members will be thoroughly enculturated.

I chose the book's title, *The Church's Seven Deadly Secrets: Identity Theft from Within,* for three main reasons. First, it has shock value—and thus appeal—by playing off of the familiar concept of "the seven deadly sins."[3] More important, the seven secrets are deadly because their concealment jeopardizes the nature and purpose of the church. No less than the faith, the function, and the future of the church are at stake. Second, the disclosure of these secrets can liberate the church from its comfortable complacency and its cultural conformity. After these suppressed ideas are exposed, the church will rediscover more enthusiastically its meaning and mission, and will regain more demonstrably its vigor and vitality. Third, the title implies a conspiracy. Although I am not suggesting a deliberate church scheme to keep certain knowledge hidden from the general public (à la Dan Brown), the dearth of theological and biblical literacy among clergy and laity alike has separated the church from its true self. Over time, both cultural and ecclesial[4] forces have unwittingly combined to convert the church's intellectual history into deadly secrets.

If you think my title is too sensational, my judgment is too harsh, and my thesis is too thin, please ponder for a moment the following statistics. According to the 2010 U.S. Religious Knowledge Survey, conducted by the Pew Forum on Religion & Public Life, "Americans are clear on God but foggy on facts about faith."[5] Although 86 percent of the 3,412 nationwide respondents believe in God, the average score was 50 percent (16 correct out of 32 questions; a failing grade in my class!). Moreover, the top scoring groups were atheists/agnostics (20.9 correct), Jews (20.5 correct), and Mormons (20.3 correct). These three groups combined total less than 7 percent of Americans. Most disturbing, White evangelical Protestants (17.6 correct), White Catholics (16.0 correct), and White mainline Protestants (15.8 correct)—the membership core of the American church—were outscored by the skeptics and despisers of religion. Even worse, "People say, 'I have a personal connection with God and that's really all I need to know.'"

Although a quantifiable religious literacy test cannot measure one's qualitative relationship with God, it can identify at least two salient concerns: the religious ignorance of Americans is (1) a civic problem that will adversely shape our role as citizens in the public square,[6] and (2) an ecclesial problem that will adversely shape our role as members of faith communities. Since religion is a pervasive and perennial force that influences history and motivates people, religious ignorance has practical consequences for both the church and the world.

The remainder of the Introduction briefly identifies the seven ways in which the church contributes to this silence and the seven ways in which the American culture contributes. It then provides the seven reasons why I wrote this book. Lastly, it explains the book's overall structure.

The Seven Church Contributions

The church's knowledge gap, which creates an unintended conspiracy of silence, is produced by at least seven causes.

One, too many church clergy are quiet about what they learned in college and seminary. Perhaps there is no trickle-down effect from pulpit to pew because some ministers feel intellectually unprepared to teach, fear controversy that could get them fired, or simply reject their teaching office.[7]

Two, too many pastors believe that religious education is dangerous. They assume that congregants are not ready to hear potentially subversive ideas, fearing that religious knowledge will create a crisis of faith at best or cause a loss of faith at worst. Moreover, "free thinkers" not only disturb the status quo but they also challenge clerical authority.

Three, too many ministers have (or take) no time to teach. Like the CEO of a small business, pastors spend much of their time on the budget, physical plant, and personnel matters. Additional hours must be devoted to sermon preparation, committee work, and counseling. Teaching and thinking often take a back seat.

Four, too many priests fail to link in any serious way early Christian intellectual treasures to contemporary experience. Some ministers act as antique dealers who solely display and dispense ancient truths, while others think of themselves as pioneers who solely chart new paths and trajectories for the future. Clinging to either extreme results in identity theft.

Five, too many parishioners and pastors perceive the church as a sanctuary or safe house from worldly threats and temptations. The church too easily becomes a community of conformity where the priest provides answers, not questions. Faith, however, is not meant to be static and stale but dynamic and open to conversation and critique.

Six, too many church leaders consider theological and biblical scholarship to be the activity of experts who live in ivory towers. They think the laity finds it unintelligible, uninteresting, and unimportant. Therefore, teaching is marginalized at best and demonized at worst (since it may take your faith away).

Seven, too many churches do not take themselves seriously. Because the mission to embody faithfully the Gospel in the world is exceedingly difficult, the church asks too little of itself and it demands too little of its members. The church, therefore, dishonors both its claim to know the ultimate meaning of life and its responsibility to interpret the message to an ever-changing world. Because its voice is either too shrill or too silent, the church unintentionally creates a vacuum that the cultural assumptions about religion automatically fill.

The Seven Cultural Contributions

As the body of Christ on earth, the church lives in the world and is therefore influenced by the dominant culture. Hence, enculturation is a persistent problem. That is, the church's identity and mission are always susceptible to cultural compromise. Listed below are seven unfortunate cultural realities that contribute to the American church's ignorance of its heritage and thus the promulgation of deadly secrets.

One, the public face of religion in America is Christian fundamentalism—biblical literalism, rigid dogmatism, and conservative moralism. Promoted by both the print and visual media, fundamentalist voices dominate the airwaves and provide predictable sound bites. Christianity is wrongly portrayed as a monolithic tradition that has spoken with the same voice for the past two thousand years.

Two, Americans are deeply religious, yet profoundly ignorant. According to Stephen Prothero in his book *Religious Literacy*, over 90 percent of Americans believe in God; more than 80 percent say that religion is important to them personally; and 70 percent pray daily.[8] Approximately half of Americans describe themselves as Protestant, one-quarter as Roman Catholic, and about 10 percent as another form of Christian. Eighty-five percent of Americans self-disclose as Christian, and 40 percent of them are "born-again."[9] However, only half of American adults can name even one of the four canonical Gospels. Most cannot name the first book of the Bible.

Only one third know that Jesus (not Billy Graham) delivered the Sermon on the Mount. A majority of Americans incorrectly identify Jerusalem as Jesus's birth place, and 10 percent believe that Joan of Arc was Noah's wife.[10] Although biblical literacy—the ability to speak intelligibly about the biblical stories and their characters—is not the only measure of cultural religious fitness, this snapshot reveals an unfit America.[11]

Three, religion in America is dumbed down. Because we educate to the lowest common denominator, our public school textbooks on religion and our public square conversations about religion are notoriously oversimplified and shamelessly uninformed. The above statistics—both Pew and Prothero—make the point.

Four, most Americans possess only an elementary school knowledge of religious writings and thoughts. Although students are expected to grow in their knowledge of mathematics, history, and the sciences, our knowledge of religion remains juvenile. God, for example, is seen by many as a supernatural Santa Claus who resides in heaven and knows when we are naughty or nice.

Five, religion in America is about the heart, not the head. Since the goal of nineteenth-century revivalism was for people to know Jesus in their hearts, religious education was too often restricted and pious ignorance was too frequently applauded. This cultural default is prevalent today. During an interview for a college teaching position, I was asked by a prominent professor what new courses I would like to teach. I suggested a class on Christian theology. The educator replied, "What would you talk about . . . students' feelings?" Such deliberate separation of head and heart encourages not only religious anti-intellectualism but also ecclesial amnesia—the genesis of church secrets.

Six, Americans live in a "prose-flattened world." Because we reside in a world of scientific and technological expertise that tends to reduce everything to quantifiable information and to verify everything by the principle of causality, religion has been outsourced to the realm of feelings—a safe haven from modernity's scorn and contempt. Life lived through these cultural lenses produces shallow speech and tepid truth.[12]

Seven, America's democratic ethos indirectly undermines religion. In our culture where all experiences are valid, the personal religious playing field is level. Christian faith is not subject to religious authority. Since everyone's feelings are true, all that matters is a pious heart.

The Seven Reasons for Writing the Book

This book is both personal and professional. The seven reasons for writing it should make that obvious.

One, I am a child of the church. I was reared in a Protestant parsonage; my father was an ordained minister; my wife is an ordained minister; and I am an ordained minister. In short, I am a Christian, unapologetically. As a person of faith, I have an obligation to learn from the past, to live faithfully in the present, and to covenant with God for the future. This book is my gift to the church.

Two, I want to grow in faith and wisdom. As a child, I was enthralled by the words of the psalmist, "O Lord, our Sovereign, how majestic is your name in all the earth!" (Ps 8:1a, NRSV). I marveled at the passage and I pondered the question: "When I look at your heavens, the work of your fingers, the moon and the stars that you have established; what are human beings that you are mindful of them, mortals that you care for them?" (Ps 8:3–4). As an aspiring adult, I endorse the words of Chaim Potok in his novel *In the Beginning*: "A shallow mind is a sin against God."[13]

Because the mystery of life captivates and consumes me, I live the questions. That is the primary reason I teach religion: I get paid to be an eternal student. Daniel Migliore expresses the journey motif of faith when he writes in *Faith Seeking*

Understanding: "As long as Christians remain pilgrims of faith, they will continue to raise questions—hard questions—for which they will not always find answers. … When faith no longer frees people to ask the hard questions, it becomes inhuman and dangerous. … Human life ceases to be human not when we do not have all the answers but when we no longer have the courage to ask the really important questions."[14]

Three, I have a lover's quarrel with the church. Because I love her, I criticize the church when I think she is wrong. According to Paul Tillich, one of the great theologians of the twentieth century, "The first word … to be spoken by religion to the people of our time must be a word spoken against religion."[15] Some readers of this book may accuse me of Christian bashing or of being angry with the church. My intention, however, is to beautify the beloved. Therefore, this book divulges the church's secrets so that its future can be assured and enhanced.

Four, I want to provide an alternative voice to fundamentalism. Since humans thirst and call out for the holy, they drink whatever is available, regardless of its quality. I want to tell the forgotten stories and expose the secrets so that the wisdom and resources of the tradition are available and accessible to all.

Five, mature religion appeals to both the head and the heart. Faith includes the whole person. According to Mark's Jesus, "You shall love the Lord your God with all your heart, and with all your soul, and with all your mind, and with all your strength" (12:30). Although faith praises and prays, confesses and cares, I believe it also thinks.

Six, thought and action are inseparable. If good ideas can lead to good behavior, then theological knowledge can deepen and enrich our relationships to God and neighbor. I quote this maxim to my students: "Thought without action is empty, action without thought is blind."[16] Because thoughts affect our attitudes as well as our actions, this book uncovers good ideas that have been buried for too long.

Seven, we are all theologians. Since everyone—laity and clergy, churched and unchurched—asks questions about the meaning and purpose of life, we are all theologians. Therefore, the issue is not whether we think about the Christian faith, but whether we do it consciously and critically. According to Clark Williamson and Ron Allen in *The Teaching Minister*, "The work of the church is to *make* the Christian witness to the gospel of Jesus Christ; the work of the theologian is to *criticize* the way in which the church makes its witness of faith, and to *think* about this witness."[17] Because I am convinced that the Christian vocation includes both thinking about and enacting the faith, the church's seven deadly secrets must be revealed to prevent the cultural assumptions about religion from filling the void and thereby achieving identity theft from within.

The Book's Structure

The seven secrets disclosed in this book do not exhaust the list of neglected ideas buried in the tradition. They do, however, represent major themes that my students and I discuss. Although the chapters are independent of one another, they are arranged to complement and reinforce one another. Therefore, I recommend that you read the book sequentially.

Chapter 1, "There is No Meaning without Context," identifies Western cultural assumptions about how we think and act in today's world. Regardless of who we are and what we do, these intellectual presuppositions inform and influence our lives. Chapter 2, "Faith Means Trust, Not Belief," clarifies the relationship of these three terms by positing that faith, like trust, is a relational category, and that belief is a cognitive category that attempts to make sense of a prior experience of the holy. "The Bible Is Not the Word of God; Jesus Is," chapter 3, addresses the biggest misunderstanding in the church today. This chapter asserts that the Bible narrates the primary witness to Jesus—the normative revelation of God in history—but it is not identical to the Word (Jesus). Because chapters 2 and 3 expose the twin temptations of the tradition, they are foundational for the subsequent discussions.

Chapter 4, "Jesus Was a Jew, Not a Christian," describes the historical origins of Rabbinic Judaism and Christianity, and declares them to be "fraternal twins." It also names the seven Christian misperceptions of first-century Judaism and concludes with the five advantages of retrieving a Jewish Jesus. Chapter 5, "Read the Bible Critically, Not Literally," rejects a literal reading of scripture, endorses a critical reading of the Bible, and posits different methods to use. Chapter 6, "Jesus's Miracles Are Prologue, Not Proof," illustrates the difficulty of interpreting an ancient book in the modern world. Since miracles play an indispensable role in the belief system of many Christians, people want to know if miracles really happened and if they prove that Jesus is divine. By exploring both the past and present interpretive contexts, these topics are clarified.

The final chapter, "My Religion and God Are Violent," investigates the disturbing and depressing association of religion and violence. It examines how the Christian tradition explains the possibility of sin (and thus violence) in the world, as well as violence committed in the name of God and by God. The Postscript offers one remedy to Christian identity theft from within by positing that corporate, or congregational, worship provides a delivery system by which the church teaches its mission and meaning, reveals the church's seven deadly secrets, and creates Christian identity formation from within.

To insure clarity of meaning, two textual details need to be mentioned. First, all biblical quotations are taken from the New Revised Standard Version (NRSV), unless otherwise noted. Second, the term "First Testament" is used instead of "Old Testament" and the term "Second Testament" is used instead of "New Testament." My intention is to convey the notion that the latter narrative does not replace the earlier one but simply continues an ongoing story. This change in terminology is my way of avoiding the dangers of supersessionism as discussed in chapter 4.

One final thought before you begin to read: The Christian tradition is an exquisite and elaborate two-thousand-year-old conversation about the meaning and purpose of life lived before God and neighbor. This book adds one more voice to that ongoing dialogue about what it means to be a Christian in the world. My hope is that it will empower you to add your voice so that we all can grow in faith, wisdom, and love.

1

The Church's First Deadly Secret

There Is No Meaning without Context

This chapter exposes *the church's first deadly secret*: "There is no meaning without context." It identifies the Western cultural assumptions and intellectual presuppositions—our mental maps of reality—that inform how we think and act in the world. Two foundational questions are addressed: How did the Western worldview of cultural relativity emerge? What are the implications for religious life today? After a brief introduction, four factors that shape our way of thinking are discussed: paradigm shift, the rise of historical consciousness, the scientific worldview, and the Copernican revolution in thinking.

Five minutes before the start of the worship service the organist informed me that she refused to play one of the hymns I had selected. Another was hurriedly chosen.

The disputed hymn was John Newton's "Glorious Things of Thee Are Spoken" which uses imagery from that day's epistle lection, Rev 7:9–17, and appears in numerous denominational hymnals. As the guest preacher that Sunday, I thought my selection, recommended by a popular lectionary resource, was both appropriate and safe.

Although I had neglected to read the notation at the top of the hymnal page, which identified Franz Joseph Haydn as the composer, it would not have told me what the organist knew: This tune is most familiar as the setting for the words of the German national anthem, "Deutschland, Deutschland über alles" ("Germany, Germany above all"). And this Sunday, May 7, 1995, was the fiftieth anniversary of the surrender of the Third Reich.

That organist taught me an obvious yet overlooked lesson— there is no meaning without context.

In a news conference on July 22, 2009, President Barack Obama responded to a reporter's question about the arrest of Harvard University professor Henry Louis Gates, who is African American, by police officer James Crowley, who is white, with these words: "The Cambridge police acted stupidly in arresting somebody when there was already proof that they were in their own home." According to a CNN/Opinion Research Corp. survey, 59 percent of black respondents said that Crowley acted stupidly compared to 29 percent of whites questioned, whereas 63 percent of whites felt that Obama acted stupidly when he replied, but only 26 percent of blacks agreed.[1] Context is everything.

As a rule, Western Civilization especially discourages, even disdains, absolute claims—even religious ones. Our Greek forebears realized that everything depended upon context. Heraclitus (540–480 BCE[2]), the first so-called relativist, observed that "seawater was good for fish, but potentially fatal for men; a blow was salutary if delivered as a punishment, but evil if inflicted by a murderer."[3]

In spite of our intellectual heritage, religious people in general and Christians in particular routinely claim that their respective tradition both professes and preserves the one and only absolute truth. For example, on Saturday, September 27, 1997, Pope John Paul II appeared at a youth festival in Bologna, Italy, with iconic singer-songwriter Bob Dylan. At the conclusion of Dylan's set, the Pope quoted and then responded to one of Dylan's epic questions:

"How many roads must a man walk down before you call him a man?" And he answered it: "One! There is only one road for man, and it is Christ, who said, 'I am the life'!"[4]

Although Heb 13:8 affirms that "Jesus Christ is the same yesterday and today and forever," *we* are not and neither are *our* interpretations. Our worldview—our mental landscape or internal map of reality—continuously changes and therefore resists absolute claims. This acknowledgement partially explains the astounding fact, according to the *World Christian Encyclopedia*, that there were more than thirty-four thousand recognized Protestant movements in the world at the dawn of this century.[5] So much for one and only one absolute version of truth.

More significant, however, than the staggering number of denominations is the historical explanation for the extraordinary explosion of different Christian subgroups. Whether we like it or not, or even recognize it or not, our cultural context shapes and determines how we think about ourselves and our world, including our religion. Because there is no escaping our particularity (our embeddedness in time and in space), all people—saints and sinners alike—possess limited and therefore provisional perspectives. The refusal to acknowledge that all human observations and interpretations, judgments and pronouncements are historically and culturally conditioned and therefore relative does not change the Western paradigm. Rather, this denial establishes *the church's first deadly secret* that must be exposed: There is no meaning without context.

The titanic collision between cultural relativity and religious certainty identifies at least two salient questions that people of faith must ask and must answer: How did the Western worldview of cultural relativity emerge? And how does this context affect religion?

During the Enlightenment,[6] a foundational shift occurred in the way our culture in general and individuals in particular thought about themselves and their religious convictions. At least four factors played a pivotal role: paradigm shift, the rise of historical consciousness, the scientific worldview, and the Copernican revolution in thinking inaugurated by the philosopher Immanuel Kant. This chapter describes these four interdependent factors and then discusses their implications for religious life today.

Paradigm Shift

Introduced by Thomas Kuhn, acclaimed historian of science, in his landmark book *The Structure of Scientific Revolutions,* a paradigm is a conceptual framework or comprehensive model by which people investigate and explain the world.[7] In science, paradigms organize objects in a field of study, while, in religion, paradigms orient people to the world. Thus, a "paradigm shift" occurs when one comprehensive way of viewing the data is replaced by another. Examples happen in the field of science when a "discovery" initiates a break with the old way of thinking about the world and introduces a new way of thinking. The Polish mathematician Copernicus (1473–1543) created a paradigm shift when his sun-centered, or heliocentric, model of the universe replaced the earth-centered, or geocentric, model proposed by the Egyptian astronomer Ptolemy (90–168). Einstein caused a paradigm shift when his model of relativity, which produced higher predictability and explanatory value, replaced the Newtonian model in physics.

Paradigm shifts also occur in other fields of knowledge. In fourteenth-century Europe, nominalism, a school of thought which taught that only physical particular objects in time and space were real, replaced Platonic realism, the prevailing school of thought which taught that universals, or abstract objects, were the true bearers of reality. This paradigm shift in philosophical thinking, which on the surface appears merely theoretical and hopelessly impractical, undermined the concept of the divine right of monarchs and paved the way for the authority of government to be derived from the people.[8] The way we think about the world has immensely practical consequences for the way we act in the world.

Regardless of the field of study, a paradigm shift changes our internal picture of the world but not the external objects in the world. Whether right or wrong, grounded in fact or rooted in fantasy, our mental constructs shape attitudes and emotions as well as spark behaviors and reactions. Because paradigms organize and evaluate the data of our lives, they power perception, and, in turn, perceptions power purpose.

Stephen Covey, in his book *The 7 Habits of Highly Effective People,* provides a vivid example of the ability of paradigm shifts to power new perceptions.

> I remember a mini-paradigm shift I experienced one Sunday morning on a subway in New York. People were sitting quietly—some reading newspapers, some lost in thought, some resting with their eyes closed. It was a calm, peaceful scene.
>
> Then suddenly, a man and his children entered the subway car. The children were so loud and rambunctious that instantly the whole climate changed.
>
> The man sat down next to me and closed his eyes, apparently oblivious to the situation. The children were yelling back and forth, throwing things, even grabbing people's papers. It was very disturbing. And yet, the man sitting next to me did nothing.
>
> It was difficult not to feel irritated. I could not believe that he could be so insensitive as to let his children run wild like that and do nothing about it, taking no responsibility at all. It was easy to see that everyone else on the subway felt irritated, too. So finally, with what I felt was unusual patience and restraint, I turned to him and said, "Sir, your children are really disturbing a lot of people. I wonder if you couldn't control them a little more?"
>
> The man lifted his gaze as if to come to a consciousness of the situation for the first time and said softly, "Oh, you're right. I guess I should do something about it. We just came from the hospital where their mother died about an hour

ago. I don't know what to think, and I guess they don't know how to handle it either."

Can you imagine what I felt at that moment? My paradigm shifted. Suddenly I *saw* things differently, and because I *saw* differently, I *thought* differently, I *felt* differently, I *behaved* differently. My irritation vanished. I didn't have to worry about controlling my attitude or my behavior; my heart was filled with the man's pain. Feelings of sympathy and compassion flowed freely. "Your wife just died? Oh, I'm so sorry! Can you tell me about it? What can I do to help?" Everything changed in an instant.[9]

Paradigms also power religious perception. Prior to the Enlightenment, Western Christians defined their place in the world by understanding themselves in relationship to God's story as revealed in the Bible. As creator and sustainer of the cosmos, God determined the natural order of things and humans accepted their ordained role. However, the Enlightenment introduced a paradigm shift where those roles were reversed. Now humans—the new arbiters of truth—decided how God would fit into *their* story. Princeton University sociologist Robert Wuthnow described this shift when he observed: "At one time theologians argued that the chief purpose of humankind was to glorify God. Now it would seem that the logic has been reversed: The chief purpose of God is to glorify humankind."[10]

Similar to the Copernican paradigm shift in astronomy, the Enlightenment paradigm shift in religion displaced God from the center of the universe and replaced the deity with human beings. God must now fit into our perceptions of the world. Absent the idea of one divine way, one absolute truth, one correct dogma, the pervasive spirit of individualism gradually eroded both communal bonds and traditional authority.[11] Because personal preference was now privileged, religious practitioners morphed into independent consumers who determined not only their level of church involvement but also their degree of theological veracity. According to Barry Kosmin, co-author of the 2009 American Religious Identification Survey, the individual reigns supreme: "More than ever before, people are just making up their own stories of who they are. They say, 'I'm everything, I'm nothing. I believe in myself.'"[12]

Although this paradigm shift in religion produced many consequences, the most important for our purposes is the rise of secularization, the possibility that life can be lived without reference to a higher being or a divine plan. This new way of living in the world is best illustrated by the concepts of compartmentalization ("Religion is just something that I do on Sunday, one activity among many") and marginalization ("Religion is important but there are other priorities in my life right now"). Stephen Carter, professor of law at Yale University, writes in his insightful critique of our society, *The Culture of Disbelief,* that "religion is like building model airplanes, just another hobby: something quiet, something private, something trivial—and not really a fit activity for intelligent, public-spirited adults."[13]

The Rise of Historical Consciousness

According to Mark's Jesus, "if a house is divided against itself, that house will not be able to stand."[14] This quotation is one way to describe the culture wars that infect today's American house of Christianity. Yet, the battle lines are neither theological nor ecclesiological.[15] Rather they involve perceptions of and attitudes toward history. One camp welcomes the insights of the Enlightenment's understanding of history and the rise of historical consciousness, while the other camp rejects them.[16]

Modernity is the term used to identify our current worldview, which for the most part endorses, explicitly or implicitly, Enlightenment contributions. The accepted presuppositions of modernity are challenged by some Christians as hostile to both God and the church. The lines of division somewhat parallel the ancient debate between Protagoras and Plato. "Protagoras insisted that 'man' was the measure of all things. Plato countered that God is the measure of reality."[17] Early Christians appropriated Plato because of his affirmation of divine absoluteness, whereas the Enlightenment paradigm shift in religion caused a return to Protagoras. The defining question for then, and now, became: Is reality measured by the divine mind expressed in revealed texts or in the human mind expressed in scientific and historical inquiry?

Regardless of one's response to the above question, the key recognition is not how one replies but the shared assumption for any reply. Luke Timothy Johnson, professor of New Testament and Christian Origins at Emory University's Candler School of Theology, states that "the greatest triumph of the Enlightenment was to convince all parties that empirically verifiable truth, in this case historical truth, was the only sort of truth worth considering."[18] The veracity and authority of religious traditions were now measured in terms of referentiality: Does the biblical account match the way that we *experience* the world? In other words, did the event really happen?

According to the Enlightenment concept of historical consciousness—perhaps the most important principle in Western thinking—all human beings are historically located and culturally conditioned. Because everyone is embodied (we are flesh and blood creatures), each person inhabits the world at a particular time and in a particular space. There are no exceptions. Tombstones identify a birth date as well as a death date, and a single person cannot occupy more than one space at a given time. Consequently, we cannot get outside of ourselves and our provisional perceptions and fully understand another person, whenever or wherever that other person lived. Gotthold Lessing, the eighteenth-century German rationalist, captured this limitation when he observed that humans can never cross the "ugly ditch of history."

The implications of this principle for historical claims in general and religious assertions in particular are enormous. Since we are historical beings whose thoughts are culturally conditioned, the attainment of an absolute viewpoint, a "bird's eye view," is impossible. We can escape neither our embodiment nor our cultural context. We are prisoners of our own provisional perspectives. Consequently, we can never speak with total confidence about either past or present historical events, let alone religious truths. There are no objective and absolute interpretations, only relative ones that are shaped by our education and enculturation. Most significant, biblical and ecclesial authority cannot claim special status or exemption. Religion cannot flee the human condition. Our canonical texts and our dogmatic statements are products of particular contexts.

Although all modern people exercise the principle of historical consciousness in their daily lives, not all Christians apply it to the tradition. To declare that all human constructs are culturally conditioned and historically located seems to undermine—at first glance—any and all Christian absolute and unique claims about God, Jesus, the church, the Bible, and doctrine. If the concept of historical consciousness is correct, then our images and interpretations of God and Jesus are culturally created and therefore limited. The Bible becomes a mediated revelation that is the literary product of both Jewish and Christian human communities and transmitted through contingent cultural expressions. Because all manifestations of the church and its pronouncements are also subject to the vicissitudes of history, both the forms and the content are relative.

On the one hand, the rejection of the principle of historical consciousness could mean that we have to accept, at minimum, the cosmology of the Bible. Yet, that is silly. When Isa 11:12, Ezek 7:2, and Rev 20:8 mention the "four corners of the earth," must all Jews and Christians join the Flat Earth Society? On the other hand, the acceptance of the principle of historical consciousness could mean that we have to reject Christianity. Yet, that too is silly. There is a huge difference between the perennial need to reinterpret the major doctrines of the church[19] and revisit the major pronouncements of the church,[20] and the wholesale denial of the Christian tradition.

The rise of historical consciousness presents not only enormous challenges but also tremendous opportunities for today's church.

The Scientific Worldview

With the gradual breakdown of the static and secure medieval worldview, the certainty of faith and the confidence in divine purpose eroded. Beginning with the Enlightenment, the modern age witnessed a growing democratic spirit and a diminishing appeal to papal and royal authority. Scriptural mandates were no longer automatically accepted. The world described in the biblical story corresponded less and less with lived experience. Suddenly our planet appeared unknown and undefined. A new way of consensus-building was needed, and the scientific method evolved. Instead of an appeal to divine activity, science employed the principle of causality—cause and effect relationship—to investigate and map the tendencies and patterns of the empirical world.

By the 1600s the old Ptolemaic (geocentric) theory that located the earth at the center of the universe was replaced by the new Copernican (heliocentric) theory that viewed the earth as only one small planet orbiting a sun in a galaxy that contained billions of stars. This astronomical assertion created a tremendous upheaval not only in the scientific community but also in the religious community. Since the church's doctrines were formulated in the Ptolemaic worldview (Adam and Eve were the "crown of creation"), this scientific shift displaced humanity from the center of God's universe.

In 1687, Isaac Newton (1643–1727) published his theories on gravitation and motion in *Philosophiae Naturalis Principia*

Mathematica, considered by many scholars to be the most influential book in the history of science. Although his treatise strengthened Copernicus's heliocentric model and advanced the scientific revolution, he warned against using his ideas to view the universe as a mere machine. "Gravity," he said, "explains the motions of the planets, but it cannot explain who set the planets in motion. God governs all things and knows all that is or can be done."[21]

Because God, for Newton, was the master creator whose existence could not be denied, his theories exchanged the traditional interventionist notion of God for a designer God who followed his own rational and universal principles. One of the unanticipated consequences of Newton's ideas was the promotion of deism, the belief that God exists and created the world but neither relates to nor intervenes in it.

The consistent application of the empirical method of causality and the confident discernment of rational principles that governed the material world slowly but surely diminished the need for scientists to appeal to divine purpose in order to explain the workings of the world. Because science answered increasingly more questions about the nature of the universe, it steadily and persistently encroached into the field of religion. The concept of "God of the gaps" was born. That is, the appeal to God was only required to explain the "gaps" in scientific theories. As scientific knowledge expanded to interpret more and more of the operations of the world, God was invoked less and less. Eventually God would be retired (deism at best and atheism at worst) since one day all things would be understood through the steady refinement of the scientific method.

Pierre-Simon Laplace (1749–1827), a mathematician and astronomer and often called the "Newton of France," demonstrated in his *Celestial Mechanics* that the "irregularities" in the universe that were thought to require God's intervention actually cancelled each other out. Consequently, the solar system was self-regulating. There is a story that Napoleon, upon meeting Laplace, commented, "'You have written this huge book on the system of the world without once mentioning the author of the universe,' and that Laplace replied, 'Sire, I have no need of that hypothesis.'"[22]

Almost a century later, Albert Einstein (1879–1955), theoretical physicist and recipient of the 1921 Nobel Prize in Physics, published *Relativity: The Special and General Theory*. In this groundbreaking tome, Einstein suggested that "neither the ground on which one stands while thinking nor the time in which one pursues a thought to its conclusion is free of ambiguity, paradox, contradiction, movement—relativity."[23] Echoing the insights of the Enlightenment's concept of historical consciousness, Einstein's theory provided another means to explain, based in empirical observation, the particularity and contingency of human thought. Because the knowing subject—the observer—cannot absolutely know the observed object, truth is always subjective and provisional.

Although Einstein rejected the idea of a personal God, he valued the depth dimension of life. In his book *The World as I See It*, he wrote:

> The most beautiful experience we can have is the mysterious. It is the fundamental emotion that stands at the cradle of true art and true science. Whoever does not know it and can no longer wonder, no longer marvel, is as good as dead, and his eyes are dimmed. It was the experience of mystery—even if mixed with fear—that engendered religion. A knowledge of the existence of something we cannot penetrate, our perceptions of the profoundest reason and the most radiant beauty, which only in their most primitive forms are accessible to our minds; it is this knowledge and this emotion that constitute true religiosity. In this sense, and only this sense, I am a deeply religious man.[24]

But for many moderns this acknowledgement was too little and too late. The empirical powers of science had already flattened the transcendent into just another quantifiable bit of datum to be examined, converted the mysterious into just another problem to be solved, and transformed the holy into just another "temporary way-station of ignorance" to be explained. The preeminent paleontologist Stephen Jay Gould revered this "prose-flattened world" when he declared, "We are because one odd group of fishes had a peculiar fin anatomy that could transform into legs for terrestrial creatures; because the earth never froze entirely during an ice age; because a small and tenuous species, arising in Africa a quarter of a million years ago, has managed, so far, to survive by hook and by crook. We may yearn for a 'higher' answer—but none exists."[25]

The acceptance of the scientific worldview by Western Civilization gradually undermined for many people not only the authority of the church but also the reason for its existence. Religion and science now competed *mano a mano* for "truth," as well as for the hearts and minds of a culture. According to science, valid statements required empirical, verifiable evidence. Yet, religion appealed to supernatural causes and divine revelations that were neither sensible nor testable. Since God resided outside the boundaries of experimental research, no one could prove or disprove the existence of the transcendent. As scientists answered more and more questions about the nature of the universe, the aforementioned "God of the gaps" emerged. God was increasingly marginalized to the edges of life and eventually retired. Science challenged not only the domain of religion but also the concept of God itself. The possibility of atheism crept into Western consciousness for the first time, in addition to the possibility that awe, wonder, and mystery would go the way of God.

The Copernican Revolution in Thinking

The Enlightenment's unwavering confidence in the ability of reason to know both ourselves and the world is best illustrated by the Copernican revolution in thinking inaugurated by the German philosopher Immanuel Kant (1724–1804). Like the scientific paradigm shift in which the Copernican heliocentric worldview replaced the Ptolemaic geocentric worldview, Kant's revolutionary theory that the mind is an "active" interpreter of the world replaced the old theory that the mind is a "passive" receptor of stimuli from the world. According to the latter epistemological[26] model, objects in the natural world are not affected by the human mind when it perceives them, since objects independently imprint themselves on the receptive mind. Thus, the brain only passively engages them. Objectivity exists since the neutral observer alters neither the perception nor the status of things in the world. Most important, objectivity means that everyone "sees" the same data the same way.

Kant's proposal negates this claim because human knowledge is always subjective and conditioned. Using modern analogies to explain Kant's theory, he rejects the idea that the mind functions like a passive blackboard that is imprinted by stimuli from the world. Instead the mind functions more like an electronic scanner at a store checkout counter: its infrared laser beam initiates contact with the bar code on the purchased item and determines its cost by matching the barcode number with the pre-assigned price storied in the computer of the cash register.

In short, the human mind is active. Like a computer, it possesses default settings that act as lenses through which the world is observed and interpreted. All knowledge is therefore filtered through these categories of the mind. Much like the experience of culture shock when traveling overseas, people are not cognizant of their operational presuppositions until they encounter alternative ways of viewing the world. That is, we take our biased worldview for granted until we are shocked into realizing that there are other valid ways of living in the world. The recognition that all perceptions are shaped by our categories, that all knowledge is filtered through our presuppositions, and that all events are interpreted through our particular lenses, converges with the Enlightenment's concept of historical consciousness. Kant's assertion that the human mind is an active agent in the world, because its enculturated[27] structures influence our thoughts and actions, parallels epistemologically the claim that all humans are embodied and thus historically and culturally conditioned.

The Copernican revolution in thinking—that the mind is active and not passive, that knowledge is subjective and not objective—is frequently called "the turn to the self." That is, all thoughts flow through the mental filters of the individual mind. People do not always "see" the same thing since our "life's experiences" shape our categories and thereby affect our perception and interpretation of what we encounter in the world.[28] Because embodied humans cannot get outside of themselves to obtain a "bird's eye view" of the world, and because all interpretations of objects and events in the world are "colored" by our experiences, the starting point for all knowledge of the world is necessarily and always the self. Regardless of the domain of inquiry—science or religion, philosophy or politics, sociology or psychology—our methodologies must acknowledge and account for inherent human biases. There is no objective point of view that either transcends or avoids this epistemological catch-22.

In the name of reason Kant ironically identified its limits. Although the human mind classifies and organizes phenomena in the world, reason cannot know God since God is not a finite object in the world. Therefore, science and religion for Kant do not contradict one another because they relate to two different realms of knowledge. Science operates in the phenomenal realm that contains objects in time and space, while religion operates in the noumenal realm that addresses "objects" outside of time and space. The latter realm for Kant not only secures the epistemological foundation for religion independent of human reason but it also avoids the reduction of both the world and the divine to the material. Religion is reestablished on the ground of morality, which requires in turn the postulates of freedom, immortality, and God.

Although reason's inability to comprehend God (not the same as saying that God is unknowable) is one of the most profound ideas that humans can know about God, Kant's bifurcation of the world into two realms of knowledge to insure the compatibility of science and religion has liabilities. In particular, his epistemological segregation of the phenomenal and noumenal realms of knowledge exacerbated both the compartmentalization and marginalization of religion introduced by the paradigm shift in religion. As heirs of Kant, contemporary Christians frequently identify science as a hard discipline that is based in fact and open to public investigation, while religion is a soft discipline that is based in feeling and open only to private faith experience. Religion is reduced to subjectivity.

Kant's Copernican revolution in thinking not only fortified the Enlightenment's spirit of individualism but it also created a new challenge for Christianity—the issue of pluralism. In a world that relegates religious beliefs and moral values to the realm of private faith, how does the church talk about, let alone make, exclusive claims? In a democratic ethos that celebrates diversity and mandates tolerance, can followers of Christ believe and do anything they want? And most important, is there objective truth independent of personal opinion?

Implications for Religious Life Today

"There are two young fish swimming along, and they happen to meet an older fish swimming the other way, who nods at them and says, 'Morning, boys, how's the water?' And the two young fish swim on for a bit, and then eventually one of them looks over at the other and goes, 'What the hell is water?'"[29]

Like the two young fish, we humans are often unaware of our surroundings, particularly our mental paradigms. Unlike the two fish, we possess the power to determine how we respond to our inherited worldview. That is, we can decide to accept the default settings of the dominant culture, to ignore them yet unconsciously be shaped by them, to adopt alternative presuppositions, or to construct new ones. However, the choice to live without an interior map of reality—an internal paradigm—is no longer an option since we now live two exiles east of Eden.

In biblical language, contemporary people have experienced a double exile—banished after creation from the Garden of Eden[30] and banished after the eighteenth century from the static and secure world of the Middle Ages.[31] The confluence of the above four factors (paradigm shift, the rise of historical consciousness, the scientific worldview, and the Copernican revolution in thinking) has ceded us a post-Eden and post-Enlightenment world.

Life in a post-Eden world means that we have lost our innocence and naivete. After Adam and Eve partook of the forbidden fruit, their eyes were opened and they became *aware* that they were naked (Gen 3:6–13). The immediacy of experience and language, and therefore the possibility of univocal and objective knowledge, vanished forever (Gen 11:1–9).[32] Chaos and confusion, multivalence and misunderstanding, are now the rule and not the exception.

Life in a post-Enlightenment world means that reason reigns supreme, that the spirit of individualism permeates every dimension of life, that secularization challenges religion, and that paradoxically "the only absolute is that there are no absolutes." Although reason is a gift from God,[33] there are no sacred subjects (God, Christ, church, or the Bible) exempt from its withering and unrelenting critique. In a society that embraces individual autonomy, personal preference determines correctness. If it works for me, it is true. According to the 2009 American Religious Identification Survey, the percentage of Americans who call themselves some type of Christian has dropped more than 11 percent in the last twenty years to 76 percent, while the percentage of Americans who claim "no religion" (atheists, agnostics, other secularists) has almost doubled to 15 percent.[34] Finally, the concept of historical consciousness has ensured the loss of a unified worldview that affirms absolute and objective truth. Since all knowledge is historically and culturally conditioned, and therefore contingent, ambiguity is an endemic property of the human mind.

The convergence of these four factors has created our current cultural context. All experiences and encounters, facts and figures, are filtered through our interpretive categories. Because there is no meaning without context, these mental lenses of the active mind are as unavoidable as the air that we breathe. Yet, the anticipated head-on collision between proponents of religious certainty and advocates of cultural relativity is avoidable. The mutually exclusive extremes of complete absoluteness on the one hand and rampant relativism on the other hand are not our only options.

A middle position is both desirable and doable after the dual dangers of absoluteness and relativism are exposed.

For many Christians the twin assertions that God exists and that Jesus is the risen Lord are non-negotiable, unequivocal, exclusive truth claims. Many evangelicals, for example, are driven by the fear that a total collapse of authority and identity will follow any compromise of a single Christian truth claim (the slippery slope of relativism): "'If we have no infallible standard,' argued the American Methodist clergyman Alexander McAlister, 'we may as well have no standard at all.'"[35] Since the church is perceived as the protector of "revealed and unchanging truth," then rearguard defensive battles against the hostile, secular culture are inevitable.

Yet, these good intentions are misplaced. What many Christians fail to realize is that the transcendent, the name that we give to that depth dimension of existence that exceeds human comprehension, is necessarily mediated in earthly forms. The raw, unmediated, uninterpreted, objective nature of God cannot be experienced or known by humans. The deity is forever opaque to humans; even in the midst of revelation God is hidden (*Deus absconditus*). Two observations follow.

First, the three Abrahamic religions (Judaism, Christianity, and Islam) affirm that God is greater than religion. Before the ineffable and mysterious divine, by whatever name, only God is absolute. All religions, including human institutions and pronouncements, are frail and fallible. That is, the Christian doctrines of God and Christ represent our best attempts to convey the reality and experience of the transcendent in our lives. To acknowledge their imperfect and contingent status simply validates the claim of human particularity; it does not invalidate the God behind the doctrines.

Second, idolatry is the theological name for elevating the finite to the level of the infinite. When Christians absolutely and exclusively claim that the Bible or the church, their thoughts or their actions, are identical to God's will then they fail to acknowledge the transcendent reality beyond the representation. By definition, an idol not only purports to be the embodiment of that which it represents but also mistakenly directs us to itself rather than beyond itself.[36] Idolatry wrongly collapses the qualitative difference and distance between the finite vehicle of revelation and the referent of that revelation.[37]

Consequently, reform and reinterpretation are Christian necessities as well as virtues, a notion with which both Roman Catholics and Protestants can agree. The Roman Catholic Council of Constance (1414–1418) called for "reform in faith and practice, in head and members,"[38] and the Second Vatican Council (1962–1965) called for an "open Catholicism" that embraced *aggiornamento*—bringing up to date.[39] Protestant reformers rallied under the banner of *ecclesia reformata, semper reformanda* (the church reformed, always to be reformed).

Because Christians are embodied, particular humans and because God is a living God unfettered by either a specific tradition or a current context, the church needs to reform. At best, Christians attempt to hold in dialectical tension our faithfulness to the Gospel and our relevance to the contemporary situation, always remembering that the truths of religion are more like poetry than prose.

We now turn to the danger of rampant relativism. For increasingly more Americans, relativism is the only logical response to the rise of secularization and historical consciousness. The epistemological assertion of an active mind, and thus subjective knowledge, affords no alternatives to personal privilege and preference. Although conservative and progressive Christians can agree that humans perceive the transcendent through different cultural lenses that account for diversity in religious beliefs, they cannot agree on the kind of claims that we can make for the transcendent. For the former, the democratization of religious beliefs and moral values undermines Christian truths about reality itself—that Jesus said "no one comes to the Father except through me" (John 14:6) and that Jesus' death and resurrection changed the world. For the latter, truth claims must be rational. Therefore, they interpret the supernatural as suspicious at best and superstitious at worst. In short, conservatives are too certain and progressives are too skeptical. The former invites idolatry, while the latter practices a reductionism that dismisses that which is incompatible with empirical validation.

However, a modest middle position is possible that avoids complete absolutism (idolatry and the elevation of the finite) and rampant relativism (subjectivism and the tyranny of the self). The premise is simple yet profound: "Conversation is our hope."[40] Similar to democracy's ongoing conversation with the citizenry, the church is engaged in a sacred and perennial dialogue with and about the transcendent. Although all baptized Christians are empowered by the Holy Spirit to participate, they nonetheless bring their imperfections to the discussion.[41] Differences and disagreements are inevitable. The Gospels, for example, narrate four distinct yet complementary portraits of Jesus: Mark's apocalyptic Son of Man, Matthew's new Moses, Luke's social prophet, and John's Word become flesh.[42] Paul's first letter to the Corinthians identifies stark divisions within the early Jesus movement.[43] Diversity is innate to both tradition and scripture.

Variations within the Bible strongly suggest that the early church did not conform to a narrowly defined concept of objective truth. On the contrary, it embraced an equitable spirit that valued the fallible and flawed contributions[44] of its members precisely because their respective experiences and thoughts were required for the process of communal conversation. Although the opinions of others were respected and honored, their ideas were not above complaint and criticism. Thus, the highest value of the church is not truth, but love.[45]

If love, not truth, is the highest value of the church, then several implications follow for the religious life. First and foremost, mystery and wonder form the core of human religion. Second, ambiguity and analogy animate our perceptions and conversations. Third, knowledge of God begins with doubt[46] and "reverent agnosticism."

In this paradigm, Christian faith can still be bold, but it now must be humble as well. Since there is no escaping our particularity, all humans live two exiles east of Eden, rendering direct knowledge of God impossible. Consequently, the church must expose its *first deadly secret* that there is no meaning without context, while it constantly and carefully thinks and talks about the holy. Indeed, our finitude and our fallibility, our sins and our self-centeredness, are the pessimistic grounds of our hope-filled conversation.

The Church's Second Deadly Secret

Faith Means Trust, Not Belief

This chapter reveals *the church's second deadly secret*: "faith means trust, not belief." It debunks the popular misunderstanding that faith and belief are identical, restores the concept of faith as a relational or interpersonal category that signifies one's trust in God, and defines belief as a cognitive or propositional category that attempts to make sense of an experience of the holy. After a brief discussion of the universal experience of faith, this chapter concentrates on the Christian experience of faith in four moves: faith in Judaism; faith in the Second Testament and early church; two historical shifts (the Protestant Reformation and the Enlightenment) and their implications; and faith and doubt.

As the weekday grocery store butcher and weekend Sunday School teacher extended his soiled hand across the counter to shake the hand of the proud high school graduate, he admonished her with these words, "Whatever you do in college, do not take a philosophy or a religion course 'cause it will turn you into an atheist."

A popular author's new book on Jesus defined faith "as the requirement of a new religion that wanted to bond its members together. To be a Christian, you had to believe that Jesus was the Messiah and that he rose from the dead."[1]

In 2008 the South Carolina state legislature voted to add a Christian license plate to the state's lengthy list of vanity plates.

The specialty tag declared "I Believe" and featured a cross su-
perimposed over a picture of a stained-glass window.

As illustrated above, most Americans, regardless of predis-
position, use the words "religion," "faith," and "belief" inter-
changeably. According to *The Encyclopedia of Christianity*, the
"term 'faith' is almost synonymous with religion."[2] Dictionaries
define religion with phrases such as "true believers," "systems
of faith," "religious beliefs," and "religious faith." In ordinary
usage, faith usually means "believing" a set of doctrinal statements to be true. Christian shorthand often truncates faith to
"believing" that God exists, that Jesus is the Son of God and
died for our sins, that the Bible is the Word of God, and that
an afterlife awaits those who believe correctly.[3] A common
expression to designate the Christian religion is the "Christian
faith," and followers of Jesus are frequently called the "faithful." Yet, Christians are just as often called "believers," that is,
those who assent to the prescribed truth claims of the tradition.
Consequently, anyone who doubts or denies these professions
of faith is a "nonbeliever."

In short, most Americans, both inside and outside of the
church, assume that faith and belief are identical. Being a
Christian means to affirm the "right" set of beliefs. Employing
a mathematical analogy, if faith = belief, then a change in the
belief side of the equation (belief minus a doubt or a denial)
automatically changes the faith side of the equation. A modification in belief means a corresponding modification in faith.
However, an altered faith, based on this analogy, can no longer
be *the* faith!

To this way of thinking, Christianity—its integrity, legitimacy, and veracity—is reduced to "correct" beliefs. This dimin-
ishment not only impoverishes the meaning of "faith" but also
paralyzes the Christian. At some arbitrary point in a person's
life, a set of specific beliefs must be declared "true" and then

frozen in time. To question, let alone change, even a single idea in one's belief system invites theological dissonance at best and religious blasphemy at worst.

Over time the church's false and frequent identification of faith with belief produced the mistake of equating faith with "believing" a set of specific doctrinal statements to be true. The traditional understanding of faith as trust, not belief, was gradually forgotten and thus became *the church's second deadly secret*.

In an effort to rehabilitate the concept of "faith" for the Christian community by restoring its original meaning, this chapter defines faith in general as an awareness of transcendence (life's depth dimension) and a positive response to it. For many historians of religion, faith is "the fundamental religious category; even, the fundamental human category."[4] Because the human person is a composite of intellect and emotion, head and heart, as the fundamental human category, faith must be an act of the total person and include all elements of one's personality.[5]

In traditional language, faith is a pathway to God or door to the sacred. This chapter presupposes that faith only glimpses the presence of God; it neither apprehends nor comprehends the fullness of God—God in Godself. Faith therefore refers to humanity's relation to transcendent reality and should not be confused with the vehicles through which faith is expressed and transmitted (prayer and praise, rituals and rites, scriptures and sacraments, creeds and constructs). Most important, faith is a relational (interpersonal) category that signifies one's trust in God's gifts of grace and salvation, while belief is a cognitive (propositional) category that attempts to make sense of a prior experience of the holy and denotes acceptance of or assent to a particular set of teachings as true to that tradition's definitive experience of the divine.

This chapter begins with a brief examination of the universal experience of faith and then concentrates on the Christian experience of faith as enumerated in scripture and tradition. Subtopics include the concept of faith in Judaism; the concept of faith in the Second Testament and early church; two historical shifts and their implications; and faith and doubt.

The Universal Experience of Faith

> God does not die on the day when we cease to believe in a personal deity, but we die on the day when our lives cease to be illuminated by the steady radiance, renewed daily, of a wonder, the source of which is beyond all reason. [6]

—Dag Hammarskjold

In spite of modern trends in Europe and North America toward secularism, "the history of (humanity) is the history of religion, and the history of religion is the history of salvation by faith."[7] Faith has characterized humankind from the Paleolithic Age[8] to the present. Contemporary scholars of comparative religion, no longer isolated geographically or excluded theologically from studying the world's myriad expressions of religion throughout time, have cited the ubiquitous human capacity to recognize and respond to a transcendent dimension of life, i.e., pagan and polytheistic, theistic and nontheistic.[9] For Wilfred Cantwell Smith, faith is "the prodigious hallmark of being human."[10] For Paul Tillich, "Where there is faith there is an awareness of holiness. . . . [The] awareness of the holy is awareness of the presence of the divine. . . . It is a presence which remains mysterious in spite of its appearance. . . ."[11] For Rudolph Otto, the "numinous"—the power or presence of the divine—is a mystery that is simultaneously fascinating and terrifying (*mysterium fascinans et tremendum*) and is found in

all religions, because that is the way in which all humans encounter the manifestations of the holy.[12] For Abraham Joshua
Heschel, faith "is a blush in the presence of God. . . . [Faith]
only comes when we stand face to face—the ineffable in us with
the ineffable beyond us. . . ."[13]

Awareness of transcendence—a reality that exceeds the mundane; a depth dimension that beckons beyond the ordinary; a
horizon of meaning that locates both the end of human vision
and the beginning of more; an acknowledgement that what
people observe and know about this world does not exhaust
its wonder and mystery—is both normal and normative for humanity. Yet, the "truths" that we utter about the transcendent
are always particular and partial. Because all human insights
into the holy are doubly mediated (all experiences of the divine are mediated by material objects and human subjects in
the world, as well as by an active and historically conditioned
mind), they are central but contingent.[14] The truth claims of
faith are necessarily conceived in ecstasy yet honed by humility.

Hence, the ultimate inquiry for people of faith cannot be
whether or not God exists. Although important for theology's
conversation with the cultured despisers and skeptics of religion, that inquiry only scratches the surface of our common
humanity. More significant for the concept of faith and more
salient for the study of civilization is whether we humans con-
template the varieties and oddities of worldly existence that
remain inexplicable and thereby point to transcendent forces
that resist reductionism and refuse quantification. Explorations
into these tastes of transcendence are expressed most frequently
and fervently in art and religion. Because the latter term is the
general name that we give to those imperfect yet enduring
collective expressions of the universal experience of faith, the
remainder of this chapter will examine the meanings of faith
and belief in the Christian religion.

The Christian Experience of Faith

> Faith is the yes of the heart . . . a confidence on which one stakes one's life.
>
> —Martin Luther

> Faith "is more of the heart than of the brain, and more of the disposition than of the understanding."[15]
>
> —John Calvin

For the Abrahamic religions (Judaism, Christianity, and Islam), faith is always and exclusively faith in God. That is, faith is theocentric, or God-centered. Christianity, though, espouses a triune God who is one. Christian faith, therefore, "is the simple trust and confidence in the benevolence of God extended to us by Jesus Christ in the power of the Holy Spirit."[16]

In Christian scripture and tradition, faith usually means "obedient trust or trustful obedience" toward the God who is revealed most fully in the Word made flesh, Jesus the Christ.[17] This makes the ultimate object of faith for Christians neither a book nor a doctrine but the personal reality of God made known in Christ. Hence, Christian faith is primarily and essentially understood in terms of personal relationship. According to Gerhard Ebeling, "Whatever unclarities remain, in one respect we have been given a clear and indisputable answer to the question about the nature of Christian faith: faith knows that it is dependent upon Jesus Christ, and confesses therefore that it is faith in Jesus Christ."[18]

The declaration of faith that Jesus is the Christ (the Greek translation of the Hebrew word for *messiah*) is the cornerstone confession of Christianity.

The Concept of Faith in Judaism

Because the early Jesus movement was initially composed of Jews who read and interpreted the First Testament to fit their pre-understanding of Jesus as the Jewish messiah, a brief examination of the Jewish concept of faith as found in that text is necessary.

The Jewish scriptures have no noun equivalent to what has come to be understood in Christianity as faith. When the Hebrew text speaks of faith and belief, it uses a variation of the verb form which implies a process. It appears that the biblical concept of faith as expressed in the Hebrew word *emunah* is derived from the root *aleph mem nun* that generally means "firm" or "steadfast," as commonly evidenced in the use of the familiar transliterated Hebrew word "amen." In the religious context, *emunah* denoted "unwavering trust and confidence in God, rather than assent to theological propositions."[19] For example, in Isa 7:9 the verb root is used twice for emphasis: "if you will not have faith [in the sense of total trust] you will not be established [be found trustworthy]."[20] The emphasis on personal relationship is also evident in Exod 19:9: "Then the Lord said to Moses, 'I am going to come to you in a dense cloud, in order that the people may hear when I speak with you and so trust you ever after.'"

Not only does the aforementioned root *aleph mem nun* mean "trust" but the root *bet tet chet* is also understood and translated "trust." Expressed most often in the Psalms, words derived from this root refer to faith in the presence and providence of God. "Those who trust in the Lord are like Mount Zion, which cannot be moved, but abides forever" (Ps 125:1) and "O Lord of hosts, happy is everyone who trusts in you" (Ps 84:12).

The Shema[21] (Deut 6:4–5) emphatically underscores the Jewish relational concept of trust in God by emphasizing the total surrender of the person to the deity: "Hear, O Israel: The Lord is our God, the Lord alone [is one]. You shall love the Lord your God with all your heart, and with all your soul, and with all your might."

Gradually over time and particularly in response to encounters with Christianity and Islam, Judaism began to understand faith as "belief in the truth of certain ideas and propositions developed." This philosophical "defense of faith" culminated with "The Thirteen Principles" of Moses Maimonides (1135–1204), which were later revised in the form of a creed.[22] The opening line for each of the thirteen statements is usually translated by the English phrase "I believe with perfect faith." However, a more accurate translation of the Hebrew, *ani ma-a-meen b'emanah sh'lay-man*—one which both reflects the intention in Hebrew as well as avoids the Christian stress on *credo* ("I believe") —would be, "I have trust with perfect confidence."[23]

A return to the meaning of faith as trust in God and to a Judaism that was more concerned with conduct (*praxis*) than with belief was championed by Moses Mendelssohn (1729–1786). He preferred to translate the opening lines of the "The Thirteen Principles" as "I am firmly convinced." Faith as "a mode of life rather than as a matter of 'I believe'" has become more and more central to modern Jewish thinkers like Martin Buber and Abraham Joshua Heschel.[24]

The Concept of Faith in the Second Testament and Early Church

The concept of faith in the early church is complicated by the fact that in the Greek text of the Second Testament the same root word (n. *pistis*, v. *pisteuo*) is used to convey both faith and belief. Hence, faith as belief often functions as a summary term to identify that to which one is converted. For example, Paul, in 1 Cor 15:1–11, reminds his readers of the message of the Gospel by using formulaic words in verses 3–4 and this prologue in verse 2b: "unless you have come to believe in vain." Again, in Rom 4:24 Paul uses the same root word to communicate the content of the Gospel: "It will be reckoned to us who believe in him who raised Jesus our Lord from the dead." Faith in the Second Testament usually means belief when the authors presume that the hearers believe in God's Word in scripture or more specifically that they "believe in God and in the life, death, and resurrection of Christ as this is known through the Scriptures and the preaching of the church."[25]

Faith in the Second Testament can also mean trust or being faithful to another. This relational understanding of faith that connotes reliability, steadfastness, confidence, as well as trust, is most evident in the writings of Paul. Repeatedly Paul makes the point that faith is both secondary and subsequent to grace. It is God's prior act of grace that solicits humanity's response of faith. In Rom 4:16, he writes: "For this reason it depends on faith, in order that the promise may rest on grace. . . ." Faith follows grace, since one has faith in or trusts in God. Although Paul's shorthand can sometimes obscure this sequence,[26] his larger theological context confirms God through Christ as the agent of our salvation. In Rom 3:24–25, Paul reiterates the good news of the Gospel when he avers that all "are now justified by his grace as a gift, through the redemption that is in Christ Jesus . . . effective through faith." Although probably penned by a first interpreter of Paul, the most eloquent and emphatic declaration that humans are saved by grace through faith is found in Eph 2:8: "For by grace you have been saved through faith, and this is not your own doing; it is the gift of God—not the result of works, so that no one may boast."

This relational understanding of faith differs significantly from the first and more propositional meaning of faith as belief. For a person to have religious faith in the sense that he believes "*that* there is a God and . . . *that* this God has done and can do certain things" contrasts sharply from the person who places her total trust in God, God's grace, and God's salvation.[27] Theologically, the distinction between "belief *about* God" and "belief *in* God" is enormous. The former implies intellectual acknowledgement and assent, while the latter implies confidence and conviction. In the latter sense, the content of faith is not a set of propositions that we believe but an absolute trust in God's love and forgiveness as revealed in Jesus and narrated in the Gospel story. Even when the canonical Gospels underscore the importance of "believing," the object of believing is usually a subject, the person Jesus. John 3:16, the ubiquitous Christian mantra, confirms this practice: "For God so loved the world that he gave his only Son, so that everyone who believes in him may not perish but may have eternal life."

Because the same root word in the Greek Second Testament is used to convey both the concept of belief and the concept of faith, its interpretation includes both a propositional and a relational meaning. However, the relational use is primary, since faith for Christians first and foremost connotes "the bending of one's whole being to God" in complete confidence and total trust. All other meanings of faith are subordinate and secondary.

As the early church gradually split into an Eastern and a Western form, one distinctive feature of the Roman Catholic Church, or Western Church, was its adoption of Latin as its official language. Whereas the Eastern Church used only one Greek root word to convey the concept of faith, the Western Church employed four separate Latin words for faith.[28]

Faith as *assensus*, or "assent," reflects today's popular meaning of faith as a person's intellectual agreement with a prescribed set of propositional truths. However, the three other meanings underscore the relational dimension of faith. Faith as *fiducia*, or "trust," highlights the biblical metaphor of "trusting in God as our rock and fortress." Christians trust in God as the foundation or ground of all being. Faith as *fidelitas*, or "fidelity," stresses the "faithfulness" of one person to another. Christians are radically centered in God because they commit themselves at the deepest level of the self. Finally, faith as *visio*, or "vision," avers faith as a way of "seeing the whole." Since all of life is perceived as a gracious gift from God, faith leads to radical trust in God.

The last three understandings of faith are critical for achieving our dual purpose of differentiating the concept of faith from the concept of belief, and of retrieving the concept of faith as trust. Faith as *fiducia* flows from a deepening and trusting relationship with God; faith as *fidelitas* emanates from faithfulness to our relationship with God; and faith as *visio* perceives God as the one who shapes our fundamental relationship to the world and others.

The development of creeds in the early church also affected the concepts of faith and belief. Initially intended to circumscribe and protect the authentic, acceptable, and appropriate teachings of the church from heretical (from the Greek *hairesis* for "choice") or unacceptable thinking, creeds actually evolved from baptismal confessions. During the second century's contentious debates over "correct" thought and practice, church leaders often appealed to these baptismal formulas to legitimate their "orthodox"[29] positions. In the subsequent centuries the content of these confessions became the syllabus for catechetical instruction before baptism.

Significant for our quest for the earliest meanings of faith and belief, creeds were originally liturgical and not doctrinal.[30] At first, they addressed matters of the heart and not the head. Although today's common understanding of creeds is that they identify the content of what one should "believe," the early church rarely, if ever, used the word *credo* to denote believing. Derived from the Latin *cor, cordis* ("heart"—a close parallel is the Greek cognate *kardia*, meaning "heart" or "cardiac"), the "I do" by which the baptized affirmed their total commitment and consecrated themselves to God, to Jesus Christ, and to the Holy Spirit (a triadic formula) really meant "I set my heart."[31] That is, the primary meaning of *credo* was "to entrust, to commit, to trust something to someone." A derivative use meant "to believe" in or about a person, and seldom did it mean "to believe" a set of doctrinal claims.

In summary, prior to the Middle Ages the referent of "believing" was usually a person, not a statement.[32] When people recited the creeds, they understood themselves to be "believing in" God and Jesus, not "believing that" certain propositions were true about God and Jesus. As a relational concept, "believing" meant to trust in, to be loyal to, or to "belove" someone. Thus, creedal affirmations confirmed one's trust (*fiducia*) in God as known in the person of Jesus, not one's belief in the theological validity of the church's assertions about God and Jesus. Furthermore, to "believe" meant to commit one's loyalty or allegiance to God and Jesus. Hence, the profession of a creed involved a form of believing and faith (*fidelitas*) that committed the total self to the God revealed in Jesus of Nazareth. Succinctly, "believing that" leads to an emphasis on correct belief, while "believing in" leads to a new and transformed way of life.

Two Historical Shifts and Their Implications

Two historical developments reordered the Christian meaning and usage of faith and belief: the Protestant Reformation and the Enlightenment. In medieval Europe, the Latin word *fides* began to be translated as "the faith" (referring to the content of what was believed) rather than "faith" (referring to the act of believing). To "have faith" meant to "hold *the* faith" as enunciated in the apostolic "deposit of faith" (the creeds), and preserved and transmitted by councils and popes. Ironically, the Protestant Reformation, which exalted the role of faith (evidenced by Martin Luther's motto of "justification by grace through faith") and elevated Luther's faith-as-trust over the Roman Catholic's faith-as-credo, solidified the prominence of faith as "right belief."[33] With the plethora of new Protestant movements, they distinguished themselves from one another, as well as from the Roman Catholic Church, by emphasizing their distinctive theological doctrines and confessional statements.[34] More and more, faith became identified with "correct belief."[35]

The rise of the Enlightenment in general and the scientific worldview in particular contributed greatly to the emphasis on faith as "believing that." As the watershed event in Western Civilization, the Enlightenment dethroned revelation and installed reason as the sole criterion to verify truth. Now scientific investigation determined the accuracy and reliability of the church's dogmatic assertions. Consequently, "belief became self-consciously the yes-or-no passport to faith. For the first time, the predominant question was not even what one believed, religiously, but whether."[36] Because faith became more and more identified with "believing that" a statement is true rather than "believing in" a person, the individual investment in what one believed escalated.[37] Religious belief now functioned as the gatekeeper for faith, and for many it became a barrier rather than a bridge to the transcendent.

In the aftermath of the Protestant Reformation and the Enlightenment, Christianity in general and the concepts of faith and belief in particular were seriously impoverished. Responding to the challenges of modernity, many Christian institutions as well as individuals equated faith with "believing that" specific statements must be accepted as correct and thereby reduced belief to "propositional believing." Faith became the silver bullet adherents invoked to validate the truth claims of the church in the face of contradictory evidence. In short, faith meant "believing the unbelievable" whenever Christian dogma and scientific knowledge clashed.

A basic lesson resulted. The permanent schism between Protestantism and Roman Catholicism did not create two separate religions. Most important, the division occurred *within* the church and therefore demonstrates that Christianity is not fundamentally a belief system. If faith were only propositional, as the historical situation was beginning to assert, then two separate religions would have evolved. They did not precisely because in practice the relational concept of faith held them together even as the propositional concept drew them apart.

In essence, faith is not subordinate to belief. On the contrary, all religious vehicles and forms are secondary to faith, just as faith itself is subordinate to, derivative from, and answerable to transcendent reality.[38] Thus, "faith is not the assent to an idea, but the consent to God."[39] At its best, Christianity, like all religions, recognizes and respects its own "higher ignorance"—its partial experience and limited knowledge of the depth dimension of life. Regardless of how many truths we may accrue, human wisdom "falls infinitely short of *the* truth."[40]

Thus, Christian knowledge of God has a relational component. Although the Word comes from God, people are not totally passive. Because the definitive form of the Word for the church is the person Jesus, knowledge of God increases as our relation to Jesus intensifies and grows. To trust in Jesus means that we are open to the ongoing discernment of God's self-disclosure in Christ. Christian knowledge of God is relational since "Christians become attentive to God's self-revelation by entrusting themselves to Jesus Christ."[41] Christian faith necessarily includes both the recognition of God's prior gift of grace in the person of Jesus the Christ and the subsequent response of gratitude. By saying yes, Christians entrust themselves completely and absolutely to God's providence and protection.

Relational knowledge of God does not, however, exclude analytical reason. That is, the Christian faith is not reducible to feeling or fantasy.[42] Since faith involves the submission of the total person, the intellect is included.[43] Paradoxically, for some people the emphasis on "propositional believing" that resulted from the Protestant Reformation and the Enlightenment diminished at best and denied at worst the role of philosophical and theological reflection in the Christian life. The perceived cultural impasse between science and religion, reason and faith, was prematurely resolved by avoiding the tough questions of epistemology and by focusing instead on Christian apologetics.[44] Thus, the weekday grocery store butcher and weekend Sunday School teacher (cited at the beginning of the chapter) admonished the college-bound student to avoid philosophy and religion courses because those disciplines would encourage people to think outside of the "Christian box" and thereby challenge traditional formulations of *the* faith.

But that attitude is counterproductive. Like the cultured despisers and skeptics of religion, both religious anti-intellectualists and contemptuous anti-religionists "de-transcendentalize" the world. As an activity of the mind, theological inquiry necessarily organizes and conceptualizes, translates and reduces transcendent reality. The "higher ignorance" of faith, however, should recognize the danger of absolutizing any human perceptions and formulations of the holy. Because our insights and utterances are always partial and provisional, our religious belief-systems should never be mistaken for transcendental reality. At best, they are approximations. Thus, we learn some truth from our theological reflection but not *the* truth. Consequently, both religious and secular absolutists commit the sin of idolatry. Although the former say yes and the latter say no to the validity of the church's truth claims, they both mistakenly assume that the human assertions are unambiguous reflections of the transcendent. Not only do they elevate the finite human declarations to infinite status but they also commit category confusion. Faith and belief are never identical.

Faith is a relational concept the equivalent of which is trust. The Christian life is first and foremost about a person's relationship to the God who is revealed in the life, death, and resurrection of Jesus the Christ. Faith then refers to the grateful and positive response of a person who either hears God's redemptive Word or encounters God's redemptive acts in history. Therefore, faith is a "first order" occurrence. Because an intimate relationship with another person is based on trust, one "knows" the other person in the sense that the other has self-disclosed a consistent pattern of behavior that elicits assurance. When we speak about having faith in a person, we profess our confidence in the person as dependable in thought and action. Since faith is a relational category, trust, not belief, is the proper synonym.

By contrast, belief is a "second order" occurrence. In our post-Enlightenment world it refers to the intentional process of "making sense" of an experience in the world. To understand a prior event means stepping back and detaching oneself from the encounter. It involves the cognitive process of reflecting upon and thereby discerning the meaning of that event. "According to [Anselm's] classical definition, theology is 'faith seeking understanding' (*fides quaerens intellectum*)."[45]

Thus, the Christian first encounters or is encountered by the risen and living Lord[46] and then proceeds to make sense of that event. If that moment of revelation elicits trust, then faith is present. Only later does the person interpret the significance of that encounter in terms of what she believes it means for her life. Faith is relational and primary, while belief denotes the subsequent intellectual process of understanding the prior event of faith.

God therefore is not a problem to be solved (like other finite objects in the world) but a mystery (transcendent reality) to be experienced. Because all faith and all belief are partial, *the* truth eludes all humans. This "transcendent truth" grounds as well as promotes the mutual respect for other human experiences of and efforts to understand the holy.

Faith and Doubt

To many contemporary Christians, doubt is the archenemy of faith. Not only is it a dirty word, but it can be corrosive. Like the imperceptible flow of water that over time smoothes river rock, doubt can slowly, as well as swiftly, erode faith. Since faith for many churchgoers is equivalent to belief, and belief identifies the bedrock truth claims of our faith, then any threat—mild or massive—to the teachings of the tradition and the reliability of the scriptures undermines our confidence and eventually our confession.

Furthermore, the Gospels disparage doubt. After Peter fails to walk on water, Matthew's Jesus[47] rebukes him, saying, "You of little faith, why did you doubt?" (14:31). According to Mark's Jesus, prayer can move mountains, "if you do not doubt in your heart . . ." (11:23), and in response to Thomas' plea for evidence of the crucifixion, John's Jesus beckons Thomas to touch him and exhorts, "Do not doubt but believe" (20:27).

Although these biblical passages seem to juxtapose faith and doubt, that is not the case. On the contrary, Thomas, the poster boy for doubt as the "evil twin" of faith, confesses in the very next line that Jesus is "My Lord and my God!" (John 20:28). Let us not forget that Peter, who not only doubts but also denies Jesus three times (John 18:17, 25–27), is the premier disciple upon whom Jesus, according to Matthew, builds his church (16:18).

Doubt is denigrated in our culture and denounced in our churches because it is thoroughly and terribly misunderstood—too often equated with unbelief or disbelief. Etymologically, however, doubt is not the opposite of belief.

Derived from the Latin *dubito* (from *duo* meaning two), doubt
signifies vacillation or irresolution. To doubt means to be of
"two minds" and therefore to stand at the "crossroads of the
mind."[48] Thus, doubt denotes an open mind as well as a refusal
to equate faith with blind and thoughtless belief. Faith is "not
believing the unbelievable" regardless of the evidence, since
faith as trust does not address scientific or historical knowledge. Rooted in "transcendent reality" as revealed in Jesus of
Nazareth, Christian faith is a *relation* to the living God—revealed yet hidden, known yet incomprehensible, accessible yet
mysterious.

All faith entails participation and separation. Revelation
of the living God as manifest in Jesus constitutes the starting point of faith and thereby grounds participation in the
Christian life. All Christians, however, are necessarily separated
from God and Christ. As finite creatures, we neither apprehend
nor comprehend the fullness of the holy. Therefore, faith is
never "certain," since our separation ensures an "in-spite-of-
element" intrinsic to faith itself. Thankfully, the worldly forces
that separate humanity from God do not have the last word.
The good news of the Gospel is that God continuously loves us
in spite of the powers and principalities (Rom 8:38–39). Thus,
the "certainty of faith" (which is existential) emanates from
our participation in the life of God, while the "doubt of faith"
emerges from our separation from God.[49] "Faith is certain in
so far as it is an experience of the holy. But faith is uncertain in
so far as the infinite to which it is related is received by a finite
being."[50] Hence, the life of faith is inevitably and essentially
characterized by both risk and courage.

Doubt, therefore, should elicit profound expressions of
humility and hope. Because faith is anchored in the ineffable
mystery of the living God, our gratitude is predicated on honest humility. Full of wonder and awe, Christians should be
courageous but not cocky. Sure in our own faith-grounding

experiences, Christians should be open to alternative expressions of the holy in confidence and in celebration. Because faith is professed by fallible and finite human beings, certainty in matters of faith is grounded in a higher hope. "Now faith is the assurance of things hoped for, the conviction of things not seen" (Heb 11:1). Thus, the Christian should embrace doubt as a welcomed companion on the journey of faith, a companion who provokes more than corrodes and keeps us honest, humble, and hopeful.

Conclusion

> If God held all truth in his right hand and in his left the everlasting striving after truth, so that I could always and everlastingly be mistaken, and said to me, "Choose," with humility I would pick the left hand and say, "Father, grant me that. Absolute truth is for thee alone."[51]
>
> —Gotthold Ephraim Lessing

Humans walk an existential tightrope between two ends—cynicism and certainty. On the one extreme, many cultured despisers and skeptics of religion are not only cynical of transcendent reality but they also refuse to believe that there is anything out there worthy of astonishment and awe, respect and reverence. On the other extreme, many Christians are not only certain of transcendent reality but they also refuse to believe that there is a pervasive enigma to life that erodes confidence in unqualified and unambiguous observations and formulations of the holy. Thomas Merton, a Trappist monk, dismissed the latter when he wrote:

> This is of course the ultimate temptation of Christianity! To say that Christ has locked all the doors, has given one answer, settled everything and departed, leaving all life enclosed in the frightful consistency of a system outside of which there is seriousness and damnation, inside of which there is the

intolerable flippancy of the saved—while nowhere is there any place left for the mystery of the freedom of divine mercy which alone is truly serious, and worthy of being taken seriously.[52]

For all of us, perplexity and paradox characterize human life. The former provides depth and dimension, passion and power, while it concurrently robs us of easy answers and divests us of total control. The latter provides tension and truth, bafflement and beauty, while it concurrently robs us of simple contradictions and invites us to transform the extremes of cynicism and certainty into a higher reality. Neils Bohr, the Nobel laureate in physics, observed that "the opposite of a correct statement is a false statement. But the opposite of a profound truth may be another profound truth."[53]

Human beings have always been a question to themselves.[54] Because we seek purpose and meaning, the history of humanity is the history of religion and the universal experience of faith. Although all three Abrahamic religions affirm a God-centered faith, Christianity discerns most decisively the personal reality of God in the life, death, and resurrection of Jesus the Christ. Thus, faith for Christians is relational. As followers of Jesus, Christians marvel at the mysterious and accordingly accept their perceptions and expressions of the divine or transcendent reality as partial and provisional.

The church's second deadly secret is that faith means trust, not belief. The false and frequent identification of faith with belief produced the mistake of equating faith with "believing" a set of specific doctrinal statements to be true. Our exploration into the original meanings of faith and belief has discovered that both terms were understood as relational concepts until the Reformation and the Enlightenment. Now most Americans, both inside and outside of the church, assume that faith and belief are identical. In order to retrieve the concept of faith as trust, this chapter has argued that the Christian life is first and foremost about a person's relationship to the God disclosed in Jesus the Christ. Faith, therefore, is the response of trust and acceptance of God's unconditional and prior acceptance of us. Hence, faith is a "first order" occurrence, while belief is a "second order" occurrence. A person first encounters or is encountered by the risen and living Lord and then proceeds to make sense of that event. If that moment of revelation elicits trust, then faith is present. Only later does the person interpret the significance of that encounter in terms of what she believes it means for her life. Faith is relational and primary, while belief denotes the subsequent intellectual process of understanding the prior event of faith.

The restored concept of faith as trust, and not belief, has liberating implications for the Christian life. On the one hand, it minimizes rearguard strategies to defend the church's truth claims against the cultured despisers and skeptics of religion. On the other hand, it maximizes the vision and vitality that arises from contemplation of the varieties and oddities of worldly existence in general and the life, death, and resurrection of Jesus the Christ in particular. As the church grows more cognizant of its "higher ignorance," it must unapologetically reform its thoughts and practices from within and unequivocally celebrate its conversations with people from without.

3

The Church's Third Deadly Secret

The Bible Is Not the Word of God; Jesus Is

This chapter discloses *the church's third deadly secret*: "the Bible is not the Word of God; Jesus is." It responds to two salient questions: Why should the Bible have authority? Why is it called the "Word of God"? After a brief introduction, this chapter explores the many meanings of the phrase "the Bible is the Word of God" by examining the historical origins and development of the Word of God theology, by describing the challenges of the Enlightenment, and by explaining a fourfold typology of responses. It concludes with a theological answer to the question: Is the Bible the Word of God for Christians?

The pastor began the service with these words: "Good morning, brothers and sisters. It is always a joy to see the Lord's people in the Lord's house on this Lord's Day, eager to hear and study the Word of God."

When the chair of the church worship committee distributed to the group the Christmas bulletin cover that depicted an open Bible next to a poinsettia, one member remarked, "Christmas celebrates the birth of Jesus, not the Bible."

As my wife waited for a doctor's appointment, she read the following statement in an office magazine: "Not only is the Bible truth, it is absolute truth. As an airplane pilot needs reliable instruments because his perceptions can prove fatal, so mankind needs God's Word."[1]

With over 6 billion copies sold in two thousand languages and dialects, the Bible is the undisputed bestselling book of all time. Although the reasons are many, two are obvious: Christianity is the world's largest religion (approximately 2 billion adherents or almost one-third of the world's population) and the Bible is authoritative for faith and practice in the life of the Christian community. With the publication of the Gutenberg Bible in the 1450s and Martin Luther's assertion of *sola scriptura* (scripture alone) in the 1510s, technology and theology converged to assure unprecedented readership.

Today, in the American culture and church, several unwarranted and unexamined assumptions about the Bible exist, such as that God is its author, salvation is its end, and truth is its trademark. Shielded from error by the doctrines of inspiration and inerrancy, the Bible is the absolute authority for the community of faith. Hence, "the Bible says" ends all debates, dissipates all doubts, fortifies genuine faith, and establishes correct belief. Because so many contemporary people believe that the Bible is God's inerrant and infallible Word,[2] the distinctive Christian claim that Jesus[3]—not the Bible—is the Word of God has been virtually silenced and thereby become *the church's third deadly secret.*

But why should the Bible have authority, and why is it called the "Word of God"?

Chaos erodes human confidence in the cosmos. Even a momentary lapse of order breeds doubt. Thus, we mortals—individually and collectively—seek stability and crave certainty. We want oracles that can answer all of our questions. We incessantly yearn for a word from the divine, the bedrock source of authority upon which we can construct our pathway to paradise and build our highway to heaven. As the privileged font of wisdom that presumes divine authorship and discloses the mind of God, the Bible has been covered in jewels and carried in processions, flaunted in worship and sworn on in court.

Since humans hunger for the holy, many Christians intuitively attribute ultimate status to the Bible and instinctively call it the Word of God.

Because God's revelations to humanity are repeatedly and regularly associated with speech, the expression "Word of God," or "Word of the Lord,"[4] holds an unparalleled place of importance in both Judaism and Christianity. Although the latter frequently refers to the Bible itself as the "Word of God," in scripture the phrase usually denotes speech from God or from one of God's emissaries.

In the First Testament, God speaks and thus creates (Gen 1:3, 6, 9, 11, 14, 20, 24, & 26). The Ten Commandments or Decalogue (The Ten Words) originates in speech (Exod 20:1–17). As spokespersons for the divine, prophets repeat the words of God (Isa 1:2; 6:8–10). In the Second Testament, Jesus proclaims the word (Mark 2:2) and the gospel message is called the "word of God" (Acts 4:31; 1 Pet 1:23–25). Eventually, Jesus himself is declared "God's Word" in the flesh (John 1:1, 14).[5]

Beginning with the eighteenth-century Enlightenment, "waves of critical consciousness" endangered, if not engulfed, all authorities. Fearing the slippery slope of relativism, many in the Protestant church assumed that biblical authority required the Bible to have the "last word."[6] If the origin of the Bible, they reasoned, was not supernatural but human—the recorded responses of two ancient communities to their respective experiences of the holy—then biblical authority, as well as Christianity, was threatened. Remove one foundational doctrine from the ecclesial "house of authority" and it would eventually collapse. For those Christians, the assertion that the Bible is the Word of God now functioned as the church's theological firewall against assaults from without and from within.

This chapter explores the myriad meanings of the phrase "the Bible is the Word of God" by examining the historical origins and development of the Word of God theology, by describing the challenges of the Enlightenment, and by explaining a fourfold typology of responses. It concludes with a theological response to the question: Is the Bible the Word of God for Christians?

The Word of God Theology

Because the Bible neither dropped from heaven in the King James Version nor was created in a single moment in time, its historical origins are critical to the Word of God theology. In the case of the Christian Bible (which contains two testaments), both the Jewish and Christian communities contributed to its final form. The church inherited from the Jewish people an emerging canon[7] or authoritative writings that are now called the "First Testament" or the "Christian Old Testament." According to the book of Exodus, the divine presence is revealed decisively in the events of the Hebrew exodus from Egypt and the giving of the Ten Commandments to Moses on Mount Sinai. Although the Christian community reinterpreted the Jewish scriptures in light of the new revelation in Jesus the Christ, it nonetheless insisted that Jews were legitimate heirs of God's promise.

Most scholars agree that the formation of the Jewish canon, which required the transition from its original oral form to its current literary form, was precipitated by the crisis of the Babylonian exile in the sixth century BCE. That is, writings were created by that community to preserve its history and identity in response to traumatic social and religious upheaval. Because texts are portable (important for a people who were frequently displaced; hence the term Diaspora[8] Judaism) and reproducible (more easily than a city, temple, and monarchy), the canon has enabled the Jews to survive through the millennia.[9]

The canonization process (selection of which books were included in the Hebrew Bible) probably began in seventh-century BCE Judah with the Deuteronomic Reformation under

King Josiah (640–609 BCE). In response to the decline and fall of the Assyrian Empire, Jewish workers removed from the Temple all traces of foreign influences. According to the narrative of 2 Kings 22, "the book of law" was discovered during the restoration in 622/621 BCE. Most scholars believe that this document was the Code of Deuteronomy, currently found in chapters 12–26 of the book of Deuteronomy. The publication of this text by Josiah marks the first serious step toward the creation of an official Jewish canon.

The destruction of Jerusalem and the Temple by the Babylonians in 587/586 BCE provided the impetus for additional writings. During the exilic period (586–538 BCE), two major histories of Israel were completed: the Deuteronomistic History (the books of Joshua, Judges, Samuel, and Kings, as well as Deuteronomy) and the Priestly History (major sections of the first four books of the Pentateuch,[10] or Torah). The prophetic corpus was also finished. Thus, the exile occasioned the creation of what the Second Testament calls "the law and the prophets" (Matt 7:12, 22:40; Luke 16:16; Acts 13:15; Rom 3:21), the first two divisions of the tripartite First Testament. The third section, the Writings, was finalized around 100 CE.[11]

After the defeat of the Babylonians by the Persians in 539 BCE and the subsequent return of some of the exiled Jews beginning in 538 BCE, the Hebrews moved closer to becoming a people of the book, where the locus of divine presence was associated with written literature.[12] During the Second Temple period (516 BCE–70 CE), the concept of inspiration (speech or behavior under the direct influence of God) arose. When the era of the living prophets ended with Malachi in the middle of the fifth century BCE, those charismatic attributes associated with a person's discourse or conduct were transferred to the texts, which now mediated God's message. With the Roman destruction of Jerusalem and the Temple in 70 CE, the Pharisaic-Rabbinic party oversaw the finalization of the Jewish canon that possibly occurred at the Council of Jamnia around 90 CE.[13] Thus, the early Jesus movement, which began around 30 CE, inherited authoritative writings which were still in flux and would not be consolidated until the second century.

The identification of scripture as the "Word of God" can be traced to the First Testament. In the prophetic writings, God's presence is directly linked to words or speech. More than two hundred times, the prophetic texts use the expression "word of the Lord" (see Isa 1:10 & Jer 20:8b), as well as the formulas "thus says Yahweh" and "the declaration of Yahweh." The book of Deuteronomy emphasizes God's words when Moses communicated "the words of the Lord" in the form of law (Deut 5:5). God's sovereign acts of creation in the first chapter of Genesis are also linked to God's speech (Gen 1:3, 6, 9, 11, 14, 20, 24, & 26). The author of Psalm 19, for example, directly connects creation with the words of God in verses 1–4 and indirectly connects the law with them in verses 7–11.[14]

Since the early church cited from and alluded to many Hebrew texts, the early Jesus movement understood their authoritative writings to be the Jewish scriptures. However, the decisive focus of divine revelation for them was now centered in Christ, not in books. The Christian use of scripture, therefore, shifted from an emphasis on God's activity in the past to the present. A new cosmic age had dawned, and new authoritative texts would narrate this story. With the death of eyewitnesses and the delay of Jesus' anticipated return to earth (the *parousia*, or second coming), as well as the community's needs for uniform worship and instruction, practical reasons drove the creation of Christian writings. Although the Second Testament canon was not finalized until the fourth century,[15] inspiration was a necessary but insufficient attribute. That is, other criteria like apostolic witness (authorship) and liturgical (public worship) use played a more important role, since inspiration did not cease with these specific writings. Most important, inspiration was a gift to the whole church and not limited to particular writers at one specific time in history.[16]

In the Second Testament, Word of God theology is developed in at least four ways. First, the phrase "word of God" deliberately echoes themes from the First Testament. In Luke 3:2, this expression carries a reference to the prophets. God's word in creation is also mentioned in numerous passages, such as Heb 11:3; 2 Pet 3:5, 7; and John 1:1. Second, in Acts (4:29, 31) and in the Pauline corpus (1 Cor 14:36 & 2 Cor 2:17), word of God simply means the Christian message. Third, as an act in which God is at work, preaching encompasses the word of God (1 Cor 1:18–2:5 & Rom 9:6). Specifically, Jesus proclaimed the word of God (Luke 5:1; 8:21; 11:28). And fourth, in the Gospel of John, Jesus is the Word of God who participates in the being of God and is the self-revelation of God (1:1–18). For John, the messenger (Jesus the Word of God) and the message (Jesus is the Word) are one.[17]

The identification of Jesus as the living Word was expanded by the early church to inform not only its understanding of scripture and proclamation but also its theological and liturgical life. As the tradition evolved, the two major branches of Christendom emphasized different dimensions of the common claim that Jesus was the living Word of God. In the Eastern Orthodox Church, the focus on Jesus as Logos (John 1:1–18) highlighted the incarnation as a theophany (God made manifest) in human form that leads to our divinization. In the Western tradition, Augustine and others stressed Jesus the Word as God's personal gift of grace to humanity that leads to faith. Later, the Roman Catholic Church underscored both the need for scripture to be interpreted commensurate with the tradition and the presence of the Word in the sacraments, especially Christ's eucharistic presence.[18]

However, the Western church and Word of God theology suffered a permanent rift because of the Protestant

Reformation in the sixteenth century.[19] In medieval theology, scripture and tradition were understood to "co-inhere." That is, the two ecclesial sources could not disagree since they both derived their authority from Christ, the living Word. Yet Martin Luther (1483–1546), the major figure of the Protestant Reformation, severed this connection. After disagreements and debates with the Roman Catholic Church, he eventually denied the authority of the church and popes, and asserted scripture as the "firmer foundation and surer guide" and thus the norm for faith and practice. His appeal to *sola scriptura* (scripture alone) became a rallying cry for the protesters (Protestants) and an enduring characteristic of the movement.

Although Luther never systematically defined his view of biblical authority, he nonetheless regarded both the books of the Bible and their authors as inspired. Consequently, he called the Bible the "Word of God." Yet the words of scripture were not equivalent to *the* "Word of God." That primary designation was reserved for Christ alone. Hence, the authority of scripture was grounded in the One to whom the Bible bore witness. Jesus was the incarnate Word of God in perfect human form, while scripture was the incarnate Word of God in imperfect linguistic form. For Luther, the Bible was "the cradle" that held Christ.

John Calvin (1509–1564), the French Reformer who preached and taught in Geneva, agreed with Luther's elevation of the word of scripture over the word of the church. Nevertheless, he added a key insight by stressing the "internal testimony of the Holy Spirit" which self-authenticated the Word's truth in human hearts. By the seventeenth century, many Protestant theologians not only absolutized their claims about scriptural authority but they also derived their propositional or doctrinal truths from the text. Protestantism was well on its way to becoming a "Bible-centered" tradition.[20]

In response to Protestantism, the Roman Catholic Church convened the Council of Trent (1545–1563). Although there was agreement that the authority of the church should prevail over the Protestant assertion of scriptural primacy, the Council affirmed both modes as sources of revelation when it declared that the pure gospel was "contained and handed on *in libris scriptis et sine scripto traditionibus* (in written books and unwritten traditions) and that both were to be received and venerated *pari pietatis affectu ac reverential* (with equal feeling of piety and reverence)."[21]

Despite their theological overlap, Roman Catholicism and Protestantism assigned distinctive roles to the Bible. First, they read a different canon. In opposition to Luther's preference for the First Testament favored by Jerome (ca. 342–420) and the Second Testament, the Council of Trent approved the longer canon (established by the Council of Hippo in 393) that included the First and Second Testaments, as well as the deuterocanonical or apocryphal books.[22] Second, they read the Bible differently. The Council reaffirmed that no scriptural interpretation should be "contrary to that sense which holy mother Church has held and now holds" for "it is her office to judge about the true sense and interpretation of Scripture."[23] Protestants, however, extolled the freedom of the individual to interpret the Bible commensurate with individual conscience informed by the Holy Spirit. This "democratic" methodology directly challenged ecclesial authority. Third, they disagreed on the role the Bible played in worship. For most Protestants, scripture reading and preaching anchored the service, while for Catholics the eucharist centered the Mass. Fourth, they disagreed on the personal use of the Bible. To many Protestants, the Bible is a devotional book—the primary vehicle to know God and thereby ground one's spiritual life. Although Catholics study and meditate on scripture, Protestants routinely identify themselves as "Bible believers" who attend "Bible-centered" churches. Consequently, challenges to the authority of scripture occasioned by the Enlightenment were more severe for Protestantism.

These differences notwithstanding, we may conclude that the Christian tradition's Word of God theology can be summarized in four statements. One, the Word is uniquely and decisively revealed in the person of Jesus—his life, death, and resurrection. Because God became flesh in Jesus of Nazareth, the incarnation inaugurates the new humanity. Two, the Word is historically particular. Beginning with the events of God's self-disclosure in the life of the Hebrew people and culminating in the central events of Jesus' life, the Word is revealed in specific times and places. Three, the Word is relational. The communion of God and Jesus (the incarnate Word) grounds the relationship of Christians to God and to one another. Four, the Word is ultimately and essentially about God. The good news of the Gospel is that Jesus is the Word made flesh through whom God loves and redeems the world.[24]

The Challenges of the Enlightenment

Immanuel Kant's famous maxim "Dare to know" accurately reflects the Enlightenment paradigm of elevating the role of reason and empowering the individual to challenge authority. No longer exempt from cultural critique, church authority in general and biblical authority in particular were contested. Post-Reformation Protestantism, which felt the threats most intensely, fought battles with humanists from without and with factions from within. Theology, "conceived as a science of systematically ordered truths," grounded itself in the Bible, which was interpreted as a "book of revealed truths." The stakes could not have been higher. Since the doctrines of inspiration and inerrancy secured biblical certainty, the challenges of the new scientific worldview, as well as the rise of historical consciousness and biblical scholarship, were profound and protracted.

Although the development of a new scientific paradigm[25] did not directly challenge biblical authority and the claim that the Bible is the Word of God, it altered the cultural ethos. The appeal to the principle of causality to explain phenomena in the world minimized claims of divine purpose. Empirical reductionism flattened the transcendent into just another quantifiable bit of datum to be explained. In short, religious affirmations of supernatural causes and divine revelations were no longer plausible. Charles Darwin clearly drew the battle lines in 1859 with the publication of *The Origins of Species*, in which he asserted that all life evolved over time from common ancestors through the process of natural selection. In response, American fundamentalism emerged at the beginning of the twentieth century to defend the "ancient faith of the church" and to champion biblical authority, inspiration, and inerrancy. According to these modern Christian apologists, "the Scriptures not only contain the word of God, but are the word of God; hence all their elements and all their affirmations are absolutely errorless."[26]

The Enlightenment principle of historical consciousness, which postulated that all human beings are historically located and culturally conditioned, directly challenged any ecclesial claim for absolute truth.[27] Since all interpretations are subjective and all religious expressions are temporal, both our canonical texts and our biblical explanations are particular and provisional.

Because this new method of reading the text treated the Bible like any other historical document, it threatened Christianity's conventional view of biblical authority.[28] Subject to the rigors of the historical-critical method, the Bible was demoted from salvation history to mortal history. Practitioners of this new approach to biblical hermeneutics (method of reading) liberated the text from the shackles of ecclesial domination, retrieved the submerged voices in the biblical writings, and explained the origins of textual discrepancies and contradictions. Biblical traditionalists were horrified! For them, the appeal to myth over miracle and legend over literalism denied divine authorship and undercut church confidence. Not only did the new biblical scholarship obscure the true and plain meaning of the text, but it also questioned the church's claims that the Bible was divinely inspired, infallibly accurate, and immutably valid for all times. To advocates of the new method, however, the concept of historical consciousness no longer permitted an individual or an institution to declare a final and fixed meaning for any text. Since the Bible, like any historical writing, is particular and provisional, its message for the present generation is never identical to its past messages. Meaning unfolds diachronically (over time). The Bible speaks a new word to the church in every new situation.

A Fourfold Typology

The shaking of the Christian foundations caused by the challenges of the Enlightenment produced numerous theological responses concerning biblical authority.[29] Because many trajectories are available, a representative fourfold typology is most useful. At one end of the spectrum are those persons who deny altogether the biblical writings as authoritative scripture. For many reasons, these people regard the erstwhile sacred texts as historical sources and/or religious classics, but not Holy Writ. At the other end are those persons who continue to defend the biblical writings as inspired and inerrant, truthful and trustworthy. The latter theologians epitomize the biblicist (the Bible is inerrant and infallible, and therefore interpreted literally) or propositional (the Bible reveals doctrinal truths) model. In the middle, we find two positions.[30] The right-of-center position modifies the biblicist model "by displacing the locus of revelation from the canon of scripture as such to specific events, figures, concepts, or subsets of texts."[31] Karl Barth's claim that scripture as narrative discloses Jesus as an agent of salvation is an excellent example. The left-of-center position severs the connection between biblical content and revelation by locating scriptural authority in its power "to occasion new occurrences of revelation and new experiences of redemptive transformation." David Kelsey's functionalist model that understands God to be active in scripture to shape identity, but not to reveal propositional truths, is an ideal illustration.[32] Since the first, or historicist, position denies the authority of scripture and consequently does not develop a Word of God theology, a brief description and critique of the remaining three positions will follow.

The Biblicist, or Propositional, Model

For advocates of the inerrancy and infallibility of scripture, there are only two mutually exclusive ways to ground biblical authority: human experience or divine truth. The former permits no standard since the individual determines the veracity of the text, which leads then to religious relativism. The latter, however, assures objective truth due to the Bible's divine origin.[33] Consequently, this approach is the only one that safeguards biblical authority.

According to the biblicist model, scripture is "authoritative because it expresses the mind of God, the very words of God."[34] Since the content of scripture is irrevocably and unambiguously tied to divine revelation and inspiration, its truth, which is propositional, is without error. This claim is valid, in the words of Jack Cottrell, because "biblical statements are the testimony or word of someone we have reason to trust, namely, GOD HIMSELF. Here is the heart of the conservative view of biblical authority: The Bible is entirely true and thus authoritative because it is the Word—indeed, the very *words*—of God."[35]

The assertion that "The Bible is the Word of God" encapsulates for this model a core biblical teaching and a fundamental truth of scripture. Through the act of revelation, the nature of God is disclosed and "the body of divinely given truth" is communicated in the form of words. Inspiration, as the supernatural influence empowered by the Holy Spirit upon the prophets

and apostles, guarantees flawless transmission. Thus, inerrancy
can be attributed to the writings, since an all-knowing and all-
powerful God would not allow errors. "Revelation and inspiration," proponents argue, "are the *reason why* the Bible can be
called the Word of God, and inerrancy is the *result* of its being
the Word of God."[36]

Parenthetically, supporters of this model usually quote 2
Tim 3:16 to proof-text their claim: "All scripture is inspired
by God and is useful for teaching, for reproof, for correction,
and for training in righteousness. . . ." Even if we ignore the
circular nature of the argument, this verse is irrelevant for at
least two reasons. One, the term "scripture" refers to the First
Testament, and not to the Second Testament, since the latter
was not yet completed, let alone canonized, when this letter
was written. Moreover, the Greek for "sacred writings" (*hiera
grammata*) found in the previous verse is the term used by
Greek-speaking Jews to refer to the First Testament and the
word for "inspired" (*theopneustos*) found in this verse is used
only here in the Second Testament. Two, verse 16 addresses
the "nature of scripture *for the purpose of aiding the Christian
life.*" That is, the statement is making a religious claim about
the value of the Christian gospel, not about the nature of scripture itself.[37]

Although the undeniable strength of the biblicist/proposi-
tional model is that it takes the Bible seriously, at least five diffi-
culties exist. One, the Bible contains errors.[38] In the beginning
there were two, not one, creation stories[39] and in the end Jesus
died on two different days.[40] Because this model insists that
the Bible is the inerrant Word of God, the possibility of errors
embarrasses its advocates at best and invalidates its affirmations
at worst. Moreover, the doctrines of inspiration and inerrancy
compel proponents to defend a docetic[41] (ahistorical) text.
Unlike the embodiment of God in Jesus, the Bible is treated
like a supernatural document immune from the problems of

historical conditioning and contingency. As the repository of timeless truth, these sacred writings are not only free from error but forever applicable in all areas. Both of these claims mistakenly assume a static worldview and deliberately ignore the transmission of the gospel message in fragile "clay jars" (2 Cor 4:7).

Two, according to most advocates of the biblicist model, inspiration and inerrancy apply only to the original writings or "autographs" and not to our oldest manuscripts or current copies.[42] Since we do not possess the exact documents written by the authors, the inerrancy assertion is both irrefutable and irrelevant. It is irrefutable because one cannot demonstrate the existence of errors in a nonexistent text. It is irrelevant because one cannot read an unavailable text. Defenders nonetheless allege that today's copies are sufficiently accurate and trustworthy.[43] Regardless, our current Bibles are neither originals nor inerrant.

However, additional problems persist. If God can inspire the composition of errorless writings, then surely God can also inspire inerrant copies. Furthermore, an inerrant text requires an inerrant interpretation; otherwise the text is useless and the point is moot. Yet for millennia, God has used errant copies of scripture as well as errant teachers and preachers of scripture to communicate the Word with humankind. Are inerrant autographs even necessary?

Three, the biblicist model patterns itself after the Hebrew prophets. That is, God inspired the individual authors of each biblical book just like God inspired each individual Hebrew prophet. Today, this comparison is untenable. The vast majority of scholars agree that we do not know the identity of the biblical authors or even the number of authors for a given book. Contemporary scholarship renders "obsolete the model of inspiration which understands the production of each Biblical book to be the result of the inspired work of an inspired author."[44] At minimum, the locus of inspiration must encompass the communities that produced these writings.

Four, this model declares that the Bible is "level" or equal in all its parts since the words of scripture are the very words of God. Few Christians, however, want to defend the biblical stories of bigotry and slavery perpetuated in the name of God. Fewer still want to condone the violent acts of God[45] or endorse the intellectually implausible narratives[46] in both testaments. Critical judgment and moral reflection must accompany our reading of the Bible.[47]

Five, the affirmation that the Bible is the Word of God confuses the relationship between God and scripture by conflating the two. Because this model places so much emphasis on Holy Writ, it tends to collapse God into the text. To study scripture is tantamount to "probing the mind of God." This identification commits the heresy of bibliolatry (worship of the book).

Barth's Narrative Model

To Karl Barth (1886–1968), one of the premier theologians of the twentieth century, the Bible is stippled with stories that preserve the content of revelation. Distinct from the biblicist model, however, revelation for Barth does not divulge divine propositional truth. Rather, it discloses the "self-manifestation by God in historical events."[48] Thus, the authoritative quality of scripture resides in the narrative's ability to make available to the reader a person's identity as disclosed in their behavioral patterns.

Like a historical novel, the Gospels recount the "identity descriptions" of Christ, who is "God with us" (Immanuel, or Emmanuel). The character of Jesus "comes alive" as the text describes the history of his acts in which his identity unfolds. Barth makes four points. One, the acts of Jesus constitute his identity and do not simply illustrate it. Two, Jesus' intentions and their enactments are interdependent. His intentions are to live in "unbroken fellowship with God" and "to help man in his conflict 'against the power of chaos and death which oppresses him.'" His acts usher in the Kingdom of God in history. Three, the crucifixion is "the paradigmatic enactment" or perfect example of Jesus' intention. Four, Jesus' intentions and actions are marked by "sovereign freedom." Most important, he freely determines his own destiny, especially the cross.[49]

For Barth, the Bible is more interested in the patterns of Jesus' personhood than in details or doctrines. The Gospels can, therefore, be casual about specifics precisely because their purpose is not historical reliability or reconstruction. Their authority resides in their witness to the reconciliation accomplished in the life of Christ and most decisively revealed in Jesus' crucifixion and resurrection. Thus, the written words of scripture function as the Word of God as they witness to the Word of God incarnate.[50]

These insights ground Barth's major contribution to the Word of God theology—his threefold meaning of the phrase "Word of God": (1) the revealed, incarnate or living Word of God is Jesus the Christ; (2) the written Word of God is scripture; and (3) the proclaimed Word of God is the church's preaching of the Gospel.[51] Like three concentric circles, these forms are separate but interrelated. Although the innermost circle is the revealed Word of God in Christ, access to this circle occurs by the second circle, the witness of scripture. In turn, this witness is mediated by the preached Word of the church, the outer circle.

While the whole Bible provides access to God's self-disclosure in history, the Gospels provide God's decisive self-revelation in Jesus the Christ. Theologically significant, revelation does not communicate facts about God but, rather, God's presence to humanity. Therefore, the biblical texts are not authoritative by any inherent property they possess, such as being inspired or inerrant. Scripture is authoritative because it both narrates and invites the community of faith into a new way of living in the world with God and with others. The Bible is "inspired" in the sense that by the promise and grace of God the ordinary human words of the biblical writings are transformed into the Word of God. In turn, the text renders Jesus present and thereby occasions an encounter with the risen Lord, who can transform the divine-human relationship.

The strengths of Barth's model are twofold. One, the Bible is taken seriously. As the narrative that discloses God's identity as revealed in the history of the Jewish people in general and in the life of Jesus of Nazareth in particular, Barth affirms biblical authority and avows the Bible as the Word of God. Two, his model avoids the embarrassment engendered by textual contradictions and inconsistencies, since revelation is about "identity descriptions" and not propositional truths.

The weaknesses are also twofold. One, this model privileges the Gospel words and deeds of Jesus at the expense of other sections of the Bible. Not only is the First Testament depreciated, since its importance lies primarily in its anticipation of the messiah, but the overemphasis on Jesus endangers a theocentric reading of the Bible. "God with us"—the connective theme between the First and Second Testaments—includes but is not exhausted by Jesus. God also dwells with the Hebrew people. Two, narratives do not totally exclude propositional truths. While the Gospel writers who reported Jesus' life, death, and resurrection were more interested in fashioning confessional portraits then in providing biographical details, the uniqueness of Jesus involves both theological and propositional truths.

Kelsey's Functionalist Model

To David Kelsey, retired professor of theology at Yale Divinity School, Christian scripture assumes the Christian church.[52] The Bible becomes Christian scripture only when "*it functions to shape persons' identities so decisively as to transform them.*"[53] Furthermore, biblical writings operate as scripture when they are used *"in the context of the common life of [the] Christian community."*[54] To call a text "scripture" is, therefore, to acknowledge how it functions and what it does for the people of God.

Succinctly, scripture is indispensible to the life of the church because it preserves and transmits, shapes and informs, a particular way of living in the world. Distinct from Barth's narrative model, Kelsey's functionalist model is focused less on a person and more on God's activity in and through scripture. Christian identity is formed as God encounters the community of faith in its reading and interpreting of the biblical texts. Although the Bible is the church's book, Christianity is not a religion of the book. On the contrary, the lordship of the living Christ and the presence of the Spirit preclude the elevation of the text. Consequently, scripture is different from tradition. Scripture names that which the church uses to sustain her self-identity; tradition—either the process of "handing on" the gospel, or the content "handed on"—identifies the nature and purpose of the church. Therefore, the expression "Word of God" when applied to the Bible "is a way of drawing attention, not to 'what God is using the Bible to *say*,' but to 'what God is using the Bible *for*,' viz., shaping Christian existence."[55]

This model offers at least two distinct advantages. One, it takes history seriously. The power of God through the entire Bible to shape and transform individual and corporate lives appeals to neither divine intervention nor supernatural inspiration. More important, redemption occurs in history. God's saving activity occurs through a historical text, not in spite of it.[56] Two, it takes the church seriously. Although any text can transform its reader, the Bible as scripture transforms lives within the context of the Christian community and for Christian existence in the world. That is, Christian identity formation occurs because the church uses the Christian scriptures in its life and witness.

At least two weaknesses affect this model. One, it struggles to articulate biblical authority. Although it unapologetically calls the Bible the Word of God when referring to God's use of the text to shape identity, this approach reconceives the concept of authority in functionalist terms. Two, it struggles to retain the traditional language of inspiration. Because any work of art can transform human experience, there is nothing distinctive about the Christian claim for biblical inspiration.

Conclusion

We are now prepared to answer our initial question: Is the Bible the Word of God for Christians?

Our examination of the historical origins and development of the Word of God theology yields two constants: (1) the Word is uniquely and decisively revealed in the person of Jesus; and (2) the Word is ultimately and essentially about God. Grounded in the prologue to the Gospel of John (1:1–18), reiterated by Martin Luther and the Council of Trent, and reaffirmed by Karl Barth and David Kelsey; Jesus, God's Word in human form, is for Christians the normative self-disclosure of God in history. Because God's revelations are associated with speech, the Bible can also be designated the Word of God in human words. However, the Christian tradition is explicit—the person Jesus trumps scripture and is, therefore, the ultimate authority for the church.

Employing these twin theological principles to guide our response, the two end positions of our fourfold typology are dismissed respectively as irrelevant and illegitimate. Because the first, or historicist, position classifies the Bible as exclusively a historical source and/or a religious classic, it denies biblical authority altogether and therefore does not develop a Word of God theology. Although biblical content may be helpful for the scholars' reconstruction of the historical Jesus, this model proves irrelevant to our question. The biblicist or propositional model, the fourth position, unequivocally affirms Jesus as the true revelation of God, but its unqualified elevation of the Bible as an equivalent manifestation of the Word of God proves theologically illegitimate. Although advocates of the biblicist model insist on this affirmation, since it secures for them the Bible's divine origin and its inerrancy, this identification collapses God into the text and thereby commits the heresy of bibliolatry (worship of the book).

Both middle positions, however, are exceedingly helpful. Karl Barth contributes a key insight via his threefold Word of God theology, which correctly and concisely summarizes the tradition's theological principles. Yet, his overemphasis on Jesus can obscure our theocentric (God-centered) thesis. Consequently, Kelsey's model proves more valuable. He affirms both the church as the context where scripture functions to shape Christian identity and the role of God to use the Bible to transform human existence. Because history is taken seriously, the three interrelated doctrines of inspiration, inerrancy, and infallibility are dispensable. For Kelsey, the Bible, like Jesus, can occasion an encounter with the living God through the power of the Holy Spirit.

We are now ready to determine whether the Bible is the Word of God for Christians. Based upon the preceding discussion, the answer is *both* no and yes—in that order! Initially, the response is no. For Christianity, Jesus the Christ is the ultimate authority for the church. Both the Gospel of John and the tradition testify that Jesus is the Word of God in the flesh. He is the normative revelation of God in history.

However, the answer is also yes. The Bible is the Word of God in a secondary or derivative sense. Because the Bible narrates the primary witness to the Christian definitive revelation of God in history and occasions redemptive encounters with the living God in Christ through the power of the Holy Spirit, it merits unique status in the tradition. Most important for Christians, as a witness the Bible points away from itself (thereby avoiding bibliolatry) and toward Jesus, the incarnate manifestation of God in history. Biblical reliability resides, therefore, in the reality to which it points and not in itself. Christians trust absolutely in God and in Christ.

Succinctly, the Bible heralds the Word of God, but it is not identical to the Word. That is, the Bible for Christians derives its authority from its primary witness to Jesus. It should never be mistaken for the Word itself. Most people do not equate a biography of a person, regardless of its quality or thoroughness, with the actual person. Elevation of a book to that rank would diminish the person. Theologically, the Christian tradition must never domesticate God by claiming that the ultimate mystery of life can be reduced to a book. The absolute identification of the normative Christian revelation (God in Jesus) with the narrative vehicle (the Bible) that witnesses to that person commits the heresy of bibliolatry and unwittingly creates the "fourth person of the Trinity." Christians can call the Bible the Word of God only when they mean that the Bible is God's secondary revelation in human words. Christian faith is ultimately trust in Christ as the one who most fully discloses in history the identity of God. In reading, studying, and interpreting the Bible, Christians also trust that God encounters the church, transforms its existence, and shapes its identity.

In conclusion, *the church's third deadly secret* is that the Bible is not the Word of God for Christians—Jesus is. As the professed Christ, he is first and foremost the Word of God. This liberating truth, now exposed, frees the church from defending the Bible as inerrant and infallible. Nonetheless, the Bible can be designated the Word of God, but only in a secondary sense. As the historical witness in human words to God's decisive self-disclosure in Jesus, the Bible derives its authority from the person it discloses—Jesus the Christ, the Word of God in human flesh.

The Church's Fourth Deadly Secret

Jesus Was a Jew, Not a Christian

This chapter uncovers *the church's fourth deadly secret*: "Jesus was a Jew, not a Christian." It asserts that, after the Holocaust, the integrity of Christianity demands a revised theology of Judaism, which necessarily begins with a revised portrait of Jesus. After an extended introduction, this chapter undertakes this revisionist portrayal of Jesus in three steps: it presents a description of the first-century context; it offers and refutes seven basic Christian misperceptions of Judaism; and it proposes five advantages of a Jewish Jesus.

Jürgen Moltmann, a prominent German Protestant theologian, tells the following story in his autobiography, *A Broad Place*:

On 22 May 1978, our first [Jewish-Christian] dialogue took place before a conference of Protestant clergy in Niefern [Germany]. The subject we had been given was a demanding one: "Jewish Monotheism and the Christian Doctrine of the Trinity." When the dean introduced Pinchas Lapide as the only Jew in the room, Lapide jumped up and cried, "I am not the only Jew in the room; the other one is hanging on the cross over there," and he pointed to the crucifix on the wall. The dean and the clergy present visibly collapsed; they had never thought of that.[1]

The identity of Jesus is not obvious, even to theologians. Recall the omnipresent portraits of Jesus that adorn the exterior walls of our Sunday School classrooms, as well as the interior walls of our religious imaginations. Those formative images often depict a blond, blue-eyed, northern European Jesus,[2] whose facial features contrast sharply with those of the first-century Semitic people of the Middle East. Why is that?

There is no doubt that the religious identity of Jesus for twentieth-century Germany included a racial component, and consequently both Christianity and Jesus were intentionally divorced from Judaism. In 1934 Bishop Ludwig Müller, appointed by Hitler as head of the German Protestant Church, declared that there was "no bond between them [Christianity and Judaism], rather, the sharpest opposition."[3] A catechism published by a pro-Nazi Protestant institute in 1941 asserted that "Jesus of Nazareth in the Galilee demonstrates in his message and behavior a spirit which is opposed in every way to that of Judaism. . . . So Jesus cannot have been a Jew."[4]

Although contemporary Christians may dismiss Moltmann's story as a German aberration that remains from the deliberate efforts of Nazi Germany to replace the Jewish Jesus with an Aryan Christian Jesus,[5] that explanation conveniently ignores two millennia of the Christian "teaching of contempt."[6]

There is, however, a basic *theological* reason Christianity severed Jesus from Judaism: a Jewish Jesus threatened the identity of Christianity in general and of Jesus in particular. If Jesus were only a Jewish teacher, then both the originality of his message and the distinctiveness of Christianity would be undermined. Although the fourth ecumenical council at Chalcedon in 451 decreed that Jesus was fully human and fully divine in one person, the precarious balance between the human particularity of Jesus and the divine universality of Jesus was too paradoxical to preserve. Grounded in a certain reading of scripture and encased thereafter in Christian thinking, from the tradition's beginning Jesus' divine attributes started to supplant his human attributes.

In short, the church's elevated language about Jesus disembodied him. Because of his intimate relationship with God, Jesus soon began to hover above history as a spiritual being. Shorn of his particularity—his rootedness in time and space—he only appears to be human, that is, the heresy of docetism (Jesus seems or appears to be human but he is really a divine being). As a fully divine person who is mystically united to God, Jesus neither needed nor desired the religious resources that connected the Jews to the holy. Consequently, the Christian tradition gradually yet deliberately separated Jesus from his humanity[7] and thereby purged him of his Jewishness. The historical fact that Jesus was a Jew, not a Christian, became *the church's fourth deadly secret* as the Jewish Jesus faded from Christian memory.[8]

The issue of whether Jesus was a Jew is not academic. According to Jaroslav Pelikan, it is inherently practical.

> For the question is easier to ask than it is to answer, and it is easier to avoid than it is to ask in the first place. But ask it we must: Would there have been such anti-Semitism, would there have been so many pogroms, would there have been an Auschwitz, if every Christian church and every Christian home had focused its devotion on icons . . . of Christ not only as Pantocrator [Almighty, or Ruler of All] but as *Rabbi Jeshua bar-Joseph*, Rabbi Jesus of Nazareth, the Son of David, in the context of the history of a suffering Israel and a suffering humanity?[9]

In a post-Shoah[10] (from the Hebrew word for catastrophe, it is substituted for the more traditional term "Holocaust") world, Christian anti-Semitism[11] in general and a non-Jewish Jesus in particular can no longer be explained away as an accident of history, a misfortune of theology, or a regrettable result of sociological factors. John Gager posits this question at the beginning of his book *The Origins of Anti-Semitism*.

> The experience of the Holocaust reintroduced with unprecedented urgency the question of Christianity's responsibility for anti-Semitism: not simply whether individual Christians had added fuel to modern European anti-Semitism, but whether Christianity itself was, in essence and from its beginnings, the primary source of anti-Semitism in Western culture.[12]

Tragically, it took the death of six million Jews to force Christians to *own* their theological and historical complicity. In the words of Father Edward Flannery, author of the classic history of anti-Semitism *The Anguish of the Jews*, "It became evident that a revised Christian theology of Judaism was imperative, not for the defeat of anti-Semitism alone but for the integrity of the Christian message as well."[13] And a revised Christian theology of Judaism *must begin with a revised portrait of Jesus of Nazareth.*

Before we begin our reinterpretation of Judaism and Jesus, key terms and concepts must be clarified. Then, three sections outline this revisionist project: First, a brief description of the first-century context is presented; second, a summary of seven basic Christian misperceptions of Judaism is offered and refuted; and third, five advantages of a Jewish Jesus are proposed.

Two preliminary comments are necessary. First, we need to be exceedingly careful about the use of the terms "anti-Judaism" and "anti-Semitism." Most early Jesus followers were Jews[14] and thus the early disputes were mainly intra-Jewish. Just as the fiercest name-calling in the Israeli Knesset (legislature) today over who is a Jew would not be labeled anti-Jewish or anti-Semitic, the debates between emerging Rabbinic Jews and developing Christian Jews were primarily in-house arguments. Because the term "anti-Judaism" identifies a religious or theological position, its use is appropriate because of the Gentile presence in Pauline Christianity. However, the term "anti-Semitism" is a modern concept denoting a racial[15] prejudice and should not be applied to conflicts of the first century of the Common Era.

Second, the "formal" separation of Christianity from Judaism is traditionally dated around the middle of the second century CE.[16] By this time the canonical books of the Second Testament were composed, the traditions of *adversus Judaeos* (against the Jews) and the "Jew" as religious other had begun, and both disastrous Jewish wars with Rome (66–70 and 132–135 CE) were over. Moreover, in 135 CE, Emperor Hadrian outlawed the practice of the Jewish religion in general and Sabbath-keeping in particular. "To avoid this Hadrianic legislation, some Gentile Christians followed the lead of the Bishop of Rome by adopting the Day of the Sun, instead of the Sabbath, in order to show separation from the Jews and identification with the Roman society."[17] Furthermore, Justin Martyr's dialogue with Trypho, a Jew, written around 160 CE, indicates that by then these respective heirs of the tradition of Israel identified themselves by the separatist designations "Jews" and "Christians."

Members of the Jesus movement were initially perceived by Romans as Jews and were therefore entitled to the same protection that the empire afforded all Jews. By the end of the first century of the Common Era, however, the separation had begun. At that time, this minority Jewish sect was predominantly a Gentile religion that understood itself as the "true Israel." Thus, at a critical time in their identity formation, early Jesus followers faced a "double jeopardy." On the one hand, most Jews rejected their claims that they were the "true Israel," that Jesus was the expected messiah, and that Torah observance did not extend to all Jesus followers.[18] On the other hand, most Romans perceived them as non-Jewish, since most Jesus followers were Gentiles who worked on the Sabbath, ate pork, and did not require male circumcision. Members of this sect were appropriately labeled by Romans as religious outsiders who lacked ancestral traditions. In short, Gentile Jesus followers were unpatriotic[19] (because they refused to worship the emperor) and unprotected.

Caught in a vise grip between Jewish rejection and Roman hostility, "Gentile Christianity" had to defend itself in a world where a new religion could not possibly be true and an exclusivistic cult could not possibly be protected. Consequently, this emerging community, for public relations and political gain, had to explain how their movement was not novel but a legitimate heir to the promises of Israel. This indispensable act of self-definition not only required a strong sense of group identity that would ensure survival, but it also necessitated the creation of the Jew as religious other.[20]

The First-Century Context

Because the decisive Christian revelation of God in history occurs in the form of a person, the incarnation must be taken seriously. Therefore, the particular time and place of the life of Jesus of Nazareth cannot be ignored. In the words of Paula Fredriksen and Adele Reinhartz, "first-century Judaism was first-century Christianity's context and its content, not its contrast; . . . this Judaism was not Christianity's background, but its matrix."[21]

The distinction between a background and a matrix is not merely semantic. On the contrary, the use of the term "background" implies a passive backdrop, not unlike the photographer's interchangeable scenery screens that can be switched without impacting the subject of the picture. A matrix, however, is interactive. There is a world of difference between being in front of a photographer's screen of a desert and actually being in the desert. The former has no effect on the person, while the latter does. Judaism is not an interchangeable background for Jesus; it is his home.

The ubiquitous Christian misperception that Judaism of the late Second Temple period (the time of Jesus) is the "mother" religion of Christianity—a not so subtle form of supersessionism[22] (Christians replace the Jews as God's chosen people because Christianity is the fulfillment of biblical Judaism)—informs many descriptions of the first century of the Common Era. But since the late 1940s, with the discovery of the Dead Sea Scrolls and other Second Temple manuscripts, this traditional interpretation is no longer tenable. Instead of portraying Judaism as monolithic and static, historians now see it as diverse and dynamic. Both Jewish and Christian scholars talk about "multiple Judaisms" during the first seventy years of the Common Era.[23] Indeed, the Jerusalem Talmud[24] cites twenty-four sects at the time of the destruction of the Temple.[25] Because the historian Josephus, writing at the end of the first century, identifies only four Jewish sects (Pharisees, Sadducees, Essenes, and the Fourth Philosophy),[26] the variety within both the Jewish and early Christian communities has been long forgotten.

Most important for our purposes, the formative period of both Rabbinic Judaism and Christianity occurred within a religious context devoid of orthodoxy. This time of religious instability is a direct consequence of the destruction of Jerusalem and the Second Temple by the Romans in the year 70 CE. Absent its cultic center—the Temple, the priests, and the sacrificial system—Judaism had to reform itself. This unprecedented period of identity crisis locates the religious milieu that produced both Rabbinic Judaism[27] and Christianity.

Thus, the formation of present-day Judaism (Rabbinic Judaism, which was influenced by Pharisaic Judaism[28]) and Christianity (a minor Jewish sect that separated from Judaism[29])

occurred *simultaneously*. Because these were the two predominant forms of Palestinian Judaism that survived the Jewish-
Roman war, during the last third of the first century CE they
competed for leadership in the Jewish community. They also
verbally sparred over the "correct" interpretation of texts and
ultimately clashed over the future identity and direction of
Judaism without its cultic center. According to Jacob Neusner,
any religious system that appeals "as an important part of its
authoritative literature or canon to the Hebrew Scriptures
of ancient Israel" is Jewish.[30] Both Rabbinic Judaism and
Christianity[31] qualify and therefore must be understood as legitimate heirs of ancient Judaism. The emergence of Rabbinic
Judaism as the normative form of post-Second Temple Judaism
does not deprive Christianity of its Jewish roots any more
than the birth of Christianity deprives Rabbinic Judaism of its
legitimacy.

The realization that Rabbinic Judaism and Christianity share
a common heritage permits a significant shift at the level of root
or foundational metaphor. Viewed as two distinct religions, the
traditional interpretation characterizes Judaism as the "mother"
of Christianity. That is, Judaism birthed Christianity, and by in-
ference, the child (Christianity) superseded the parent.

However, Jewish-Christian relations as understood within
the revisionist context developed in this chapter affords a very
different interpretation of historical origins. Rabbinic Judaism
and Christianity are born of "the same womb"—the period
after the destruction of Jerusalem and the Temple by the
Romans. Consequently, the more accurate root metaphor is
"fraternal twins."[32] Both Jewish sects jockeyed for post-de-
struction prominence by responding to the same set of identity
and survival questions. Because they offered divergent visions
of how post-Second Temple Judaism should evolve, their
rivalry must be understood as intra-Jewish polemics. In the
words of Alan Segal, "The time of Jesus marks the beginning of

not one but two great religions of the West, Rabbinic Judaism and Christianity. . . . As brothers often do, they picked different, even opposing ways to preserve their family's heritage."[33] Succinctly, Rabbinic Judaism and Christianity are different *Jewish* responses to the demise of ancient Judaism and the crisis engendered by the devastation of Jerusalem and the Second Temple in 70 CE.[34]

This interpretive matrix illuminates the context and content of both the intra-Jewish debate and the eventual separation of Jesus followers from Judaism. In the year 49 CE, Emperor Claudius ordered all Jews to leave Rome. According to the Roman historian Suetonius, the emperor expelled them because "the Jews constantly made disturbances at the instigation of Chrestus." Although the spelling is nontraditional, this reference to *Christos* (Christ) is instructive in at least two important ways. First, it reveals that tensions existed within the first-century Jewish community in Rome over the identity and significance of Jesus, and, second, Romans viewed the followers of Jesus as "indistinguishable" from other members of the Roman Jewish community.[35]

This imperial "indistinguishability" is referenced in the Second Testament. According to Acts 18:15, the Roman proconsul Gallio in Achaea (Greece) dismissed charges by the Jews against the Apostle Paul with these words: "since it is a matter of questions about words and names and *your own law*, see to it yourselves . . ." (italics added). Although this Second Testament book was most likely written in the decade of the 80s, an inscription found at Delphi, Greece, pinpoints Gallio's term of office from May of 51 to May of 52 CE. It is not until the year 64, when Tacitus writes in the *Annals* about Nero's indictment of the "people called Christians" (since they follow "Christus") as the arsonists who started the great fire that ravaged Rome, that we have the first recorded mention of the Jesus movement in a non-Christian source.

Ironically, first-century Judaism was usually tolerant of outsiders, as evidenced by the numerous references to pagan Judaizers who attended synagogue, but it was frequently intolerant of diversity among insiders. In the words of Paula Fredriksen, "battling with each other over the correct way to be Jewish was . . . a timeless Jewish activity, and at no time more so than in the late Second Temple period, precisely the lifetime of Jesus and of Paul."[36] Yet, these debates, she continues, "coexisted with consensus." Agreements about the essentials of Temple, Torah, monotheism, election, and covenant served as preconditions for the spirited disagreements over their meaning and emphasis. Thus, the headwaters for the eventual separation of Christianity and Rabbinic Judaism are the sectarian disputes internal to Judaism itself.

At the risk of oversimplification,[37] two salient issues distinguished the post-Second Temple Jesus movement from the larger Jewish community: Torah observance and Christological confession. As membership in the church (especially through Paul's influence) became increasingly Gentile, observance of the Mosaic Torah as the hallmark for a righteous life diminished. Table fellowship was widened to include pagans. Dietary regulations were relaxed. Circumcision was unnecessary. These liberal attitudes toward the Torah challenged the dominant Jewish view that observance of the Law was obligatory. In addition, the defining characteristic of these Christian Jews was the claim that Jesus was God's unique agent of salvation.[38] This affirmation of Jesus as the long-expected Jewish (apocalyptic[39]) messiah was rejected by the majority of Jews since the messianic age for Christian Jews no longer coincided with the arrival of the messiah.[40] Because Judaism believed that the coming of the messiah and the coming of the redeemed world (without suffering and evil) would occur simultaneously, and given that there was no evidence for a redeemed world, Jesus could not be the expected messiah.[41]

Since the early church's interpretation of both Torah and Christology was rooted in ancient Judaism, initial followers of Jesus still understood themselves to be Jewish—yet members of a "superior" form of Judaism. That is, the principal impulses behind the growth and development of the early Jesus movement were positive and did not require a correspondingly negative view of Judaism. On the contrary, the "early Jewish believers in Jesus were not fleeing *from* a religion that they disliked, but rather turning *to* a new revelation."[42] The community of Christian Jews professed that the God of Israel had sent Jesus of Nazareth, God's only son, to save the world and that faith in him as the messiah or Christ was the requirement for salvation.

This subordinating polemic[43] or superior revelation[44] was at first an internal issue within Judaism. However, as the church filled with more and more Gentiles, and its original Jewish context was lost, the tendency to criticize Pharisaic Judaism increased. The majority of those who now heard and retold the Gospel message were not Jews. Therefore, the story of Jesus was no longer understood as a polemical struggle for renewal within Israel but as Christian slander against Judaism. If God had to send God's only son to redeem the world, something must be wrong with Judaism. The tendency to find fault with Judaism stipples the pages of the Second Testament.[45]

The employment of this subordinating polemic is most evident in the church's treatment of the Septuagint (the Greek translation of the Hebrew Scriptures which the early church used) as a book of prophecy/prediction of the coming of the messiah that is fulfilled in the Second Testament witness to Jesus. This hermeneutic, or method of reading, is most evident in the structure of the Christian canon. After the Marcionite[46] controversy of the second century, the church affirmed once and for all its Jewish heritage by incorporating the Hebrew Bible into its scripture. However, the placement of the prophetic section varies. In the Septuagint there are four divisions: the Torah, Histories, Wisdom, and Prophecies, (which begin with the Twelve Minor Prophets and ends with Maccabees). In today's Jewish canon, or TaNaK,[47] (which consists of three divisions: the Torah, the Prophets, and the Writings), the Prophets are located in the middle of the Hebrew Scriptures—between the Torah or Pentateuch and the Writings.[48] In the Christian canon, however, the second half of the Prophets,[49] or the literary or writing prophets (Isaiah, Jeremiah, Ezekiel, and the Twelve Minor Prophets), are located at the very end of the First Testament. Malachi, the last prophet in the Book of the Twelve Minor Prophets, leads directly into the Gospels of the Second Testament, which narrate the fulfillment of Jewish prophecy in the good news of Jesus. Thus, Mal 4:5, the second to the last verse in the final book of the Christian First Testament, reads: "Lo, I will send you the prophet Elijah before the great and terrible day of the Lord comes." This theme is picked up by the Synoptic Gospels when they portray John the Baptist as an Elijah figure who prepares the way of the Lord.[50] Matt 11:13–14 confirms this link by announcing, "For all the prophets and the law prophesied until John came; and if you are willing to accept it, he is Elijah who is to come." The Christian canon deliberately rearranged the order of the First Testament prophetic books (in the Septuagint and the Hebrew Bible) to validate Jesus as the anticipated Jewish messiah.

Seven Christian Misperceptions of Judaism

The denigration of Judaism resulted not only from a perceived superior revelation but also from a perceived superior Jesus. Because Jesus was necessarily unique,[51] the Christian claims for him separated Jesus from his Jewish context and thereby devalued Judaism and Jesus' Jewishness. The tendency of the early church to define Jesus over and against Judaism—to use

Judaism as a negative foil—is still prominent in contemporary Christian discourse.

Of the many church mischaracterizations of first-century Judaism, seven basic misperceptions are endemic to the Christian popular imagination.[52] *One,* Jewish Law was impossible to follow and a burden on the people; thus, Jesus came to free us from the Law. Many Americans interpret the Jewish Law through the Protestant (Lutheran) lens of grace versus law. According to the Apostle Paul, this trajectory claims, the works of the Law do not bring right standing before God: "For 'no human being will be justified in his sight' by deeds prescribed by the law" (Rom 3:20). Because the Law cannot save, God sent Christ. "But now, apart from law, the righteousness of God has been disclosed . . . the righteousness of God through faith in Jesus Christ for all who believe" (Rom 3:21–22a). Moreover, the commandment of love fulfills the Law: "The commandments . . . are summed up in this word, 'Love your neighbor as yourself.' Love does no wrong to a neighbor; therefore, love is the fulfilling of the law" (Rom 13:9–10). Hence, the grace of God is revealed in Jesus and nullifies the burden of the Law.

This selective interpretation is myopic at best and wrong at worst. It is myopic since it ignores the inclusive words of both Paul and Jesus. For example, in both Rom 7:7 and Gal 3:21, Paul praises the value of the Law: "What then should we say? That the law is sin? By no means!" and "Is the law then opposed to the promises of God? Certainly not!" More important, Matthew's Jesus extols the virtues of the law when he asserts, "Do not think that I have come to abolish the law or the prophets; I have come not to abolish but to fulfill" (5:17). It is wrong since Jews at the time of Jesus did not perceive the Law as a burden. According to the opening verses of Psalm 1, "Happy are those who do not follow the advice of the wicked, or take the path that sinners tread, or sit in the seat of scoffers;

but their delight is in the law of the Lord, and on his law they meditate day and night."

Succinctly, laws are both good and necessary. On the one hand, they enable people to negotiate the world with minimum risk and injury, and, on the other hand, they uphold societal standards, as well as protect the weak and the poor. Moreover, God so loved the world that God gave Moses Ten Commandments by which the community can know God's will for the human family.[53] And Jesus intensified God's directives in the Sermon on the Mount.[54] The Law mediates God's will for the world; Jesus upheld the Law and expects no less of his followers.

Two, Jews anticipated a "warrior messiah" who would defeat Rome, and since Jesus was the "prince of peace," he was rejected by the Jews. This representation is false for at least three reasons. First, there was no single Jewish messianic expectation. As the Dead Sea Scrolls[55] attest, Judaism at the time of Jesus was richly diverse, including different messianic expectations. The Manual of Discipline provides the first unambiguous evidence that the Jewish people of Qumran expected not one but two messiahs. Second, there were various Jewish responses to Rome. Although Jewish military revolts against Rome shape our memories, nonviolent resistance also occurred, such as a five-day successful sit-down strike at Caesarea Maritima in 26 CE to protest images of the emperor in Jerusalem and an appeal to the Syrian legate Petronius in 41 CE to reject the proposed placement of a statue of Caligula in the Temple.[56] Third, the caricature that the God of the First Testament is a bloodthirsty proponent of war, while the God of the Second Testament is a merciful advocate for peace, is wrong in two ways: It ignores that there are also images of a bloodthirsty God in the Second Testament[57] and it violates monotheism by espousing two different gods instead of the one God who is revealed in both testaments. Moreover, images of a loving and caring God punctuate the pages of the First Testament.[58] In conclusion, this second misrepresentation relies on selective texts and actions.

Three, Jewish culture was misogynist, but Jesus was a feminist. Because contemporary Christians expect Jesus to treat women fairly and justly, we often contrast Jewish "bad" treatment of women with Jesus' "good" treatment of women.[59] According to Rabbi Jose ben Jochanan of Jerusalem in the second century BCE, men should "not prolong conversation with women." Rabbi Hillel in the first century BCE permits divorce according to the Mishnah[60] if your wife "merely spoiled (your) food" and Rabbi Akiva, one of the earliest founders of Rabbinic Judaism, approves divorce according to the Mishnah "if (the husband) finds another woman more beautiful." In contrast, Jesus speaks with women (John 4), travels with women (Luke 8:1–3), and forgives women (John 7:53–8:11).

Not only does the above trajectory ignore, on the one hand, progressive rabbinic statements on women and, on the other hand, Second Testament texts that subordinate women to men (Eph 5:22–23; Col 3:18; and 1 Pet 3:1), but this interpretation also ignores less favorable treatment of women by Jesus. For example, he appoints no women as disciples, as well as reinforces traditional gender roles (Luke 8:1–3; 10:38–42; 17:35–36; 18:29). Although there is much to celebrate about Jesus' interaction with women, it is misleading to elevate his sensitivity to feminist issues by constructing negative stereotypes of Jewish treatment of women.

Four, Jews were obsessed with ritual purity, yet Jesus rejected purity-based laws. Two comments are crucial.[61] First, all people who lived around the Mediterranean Sea at the time of Jesus practiced purification rituals so that the major markers of human *chan*ge were kept out of sacred places where the *changeless* deities dwelled. For Jews, people became impure through contact with "life cycle" events, such as childbirth, menstrual blood, semen, abnormal flows from the genitals, and corpses.

Since most Jews became impure (childbirth, sexual intercourse, and care for the dead were virtues) and all were equally impure (nondiscriminatory), ritual purity laws were both essential and positive. Second, Jesus practiced them, too. He not only affirmed the Temple as God's dwelling place (Matt 23:21) but also accepted purification (Mark 1:40–45 and Luke 17:11–14). Furthermore, there is no biblical evidence that he opposed the purity system.

There is no question that the death and resurrection of Jesus altered the way his followers interpreted existing Jewish purification boundary lines (Rom 14:14). Therefore, new patterns were established: the Jesus community became the new Temple (1 Cor 3:16–17); social groupings were reconfigured (Gal 3:28); Jesus' death was the sacrifice of the Passover lamb (1 Cor 5:7); and Jewish rituals were adapted (baptism and breaking of the bread/eucharist/Lord's Supper[62]). The coming of Jesus did not liberate humans from boundary making, but his coming did inaugurate a different pattern of boundary markings.

Five, the Jewish Temple domination system oppressed the poor and women, as well as promoted social divisions between insiders and outcasts, whereas Jesus opposed the Temple structure. For evidence one need look no further than Jesus driving the greedy money-changers out of the Temple (Mark 11:15–17; Matt 21:12–13; Luke 19:45–46; John 2:14–16). Because the Temple was the cultic center of an exploitive religious system, it required cleansing if not destroying (a later Christian interpretation in John 11:48).

Yet, the Gospel texts indicate that the problem is neither exploitation nor domination, but everyday business. According to John, Jesus thunders: "Stop making my Father's house a marketplace!" (John 2:16b). For the Gospel writers, the issue is situational, not structural. Although the Temple system, like any religious institution, can become corrupt, there is no scriptural evidence that Jesus thought the Jerusalem Temple was. On the contrary, books of the Second Testament routinely place Jesus, his family, and his followers in the Temple.[63] Christians need to rethink the importance of the Temple for both Jesus and the early church. James Carroll suggests, "What Jesus is to me— 'the sacrament,' in the great phrase of the Catholic theologian Edward Schillebeeckx, 'of the encounter with God'—the Temple would very likely have been to [Jesus]."[64] For Jews, including Jesus, the Temple located the decisive and normative presence of God in the world.

Six, Jews are clannish and xenophobic, but Jesus practiced inclusivity and universality. Building upon the social divisions created by the Temple system, most Christians assume that Jews are ethnocentric and exclusivistic. They welcome insiders but loathe outsiders. Because they are the "chosen people," Jews self-righteously avoid Gentiles or non-Jews.

This stereotype is not only contrary to Gospel descriptions but also to Jewish practice. In Luke 7:1–10, Jewish elders ask Jesus to help the centurion's servant. Timothy is introduced in Acts 16:1 as the son of a Jewish woman and a Greek man. Moreover, "God-fearers,"[65] or Gentiles who admired Judaism but did not convert, were prevalent in synagogues. Social contact between Jews and Gentiles was not forbidden by Law. On the contrary, the

> Jewish texts *Seder Eliyyabu Rabbah* and *Seder Eliyyabu Zuta* [written sometime after the third century CE] insist: "The Prophet Elijah said, 'I call heaven and earth to witness that whether it be Jew or Gentile, man or woman, manservant or maidservant, the Holy Spirit will suffuse each in proportion to the deeds he or she performs.'"[66]

Although contemporary Christians frequently condemn Jews for sticking together, that observation is valid for most minority groups—especially a persecuted minority. More important, that judgment is based on a partial reading of the biblical text. Christians are quick to affirm Jesus as universal since his death and resurrection achieves salvation for all people. The Great

Commission in Matt 28:19 is often quoted: "Go therefore and make disciples of all nations [Gentiles], baptizing them in the name of the Father, and of the Son and of the Holy Spirit." Yet, this universal theme is also found in the First Testament. The great promises of God to Abraham underscore inclusivity: ". . . and in you all the families of the earth shall be blessed" (Gen 12:3). Through the Jewish people, God's universal love is spread.

And *seven*, the Second Testament is not talking about Jews per se but about "Judeans." Sensitivity to anti-Jewish prompts in the Gospels that encourage readers to project negative stereotypes onto contemporary Jews has encouraged alternative translations of the Greek word *Ioudaios*.[67] Used more than seventy times in the Gospel of John (usually to convey a sinister view of the Jews), but only five to six times per Synoptic Gospel, this term has been rendered by various translators as "Jewish authorities" or "the Judeans." The former deflects attention away from the Jewish people in general by identifying only those Jews who either argue against Jesus or plot his death, while the latter emphasizes the geographical and not the ethnic or religious identity of the people.

Both proposals, however, achieve the opposite effect of their intended purpose. Instead of reducing anti-Jewish triggers, they accentuate the problem by severing Jesus from Judaism. He is no longer a Jew but a Judean or a Galilean. Divorced from his religious heritage, Jesus becomes a Christian at best or a de-historicized divine figure at worst. The best solution is no solution. Keep the traditional translation; Jesus is a "Jew."

In the above seven cases, "Jesus is made relevant either by projecting a negative stereotype of Judaism or by erasing Judaism entirely."[68] Neither is acceptable.

Five Advantages of a Jewish Jesus

As demonstrated in the previous two sections, Jesus must be interpreted within the matrix of first-century Judaism. Moreover,

we can be confident about his practice of Torah commandments. Jesus of Nazareth dressed like a Jew (wore *tzitzit* or
"fringes" according to Matt 9:20 and 23:5, and Mark 6:56),
kept kosher (as did his followers, otherwise Acts 10:9–16
and 15:1–29 make no sense), observed the Sabbath (Mark
2:27 and Luke 6:6–11), taught utilizing parables like a Jew
(Luke 15:11–32), prayed like a Jew (Matt 6:9–13 and Luke
11:2–4), taught sitting down like a rabbi (Matt 5:1 and Mark
9:35), and even died like countless other Jews at the hands of
the Romans.[69] Both the rhetoric and reactions of Jesus reside
within first-century Jewish culture.[70]

There are at least five advantages when Christians reclaim a
Jewish Jesus.[71] *First,* the re-contextualization of Jesus—locating Jesus within the matrix of first-century Judaism—inaugurates the "re-Judaization of Christianity." That is, the origins of
the Jesus movement must also be located within the matrix of
first-century Judaism. Later generations of Jesus followers, who
were Gentiles and unaware of the original historical context,
heard the conflict stories in the Second Testament[72] as disputes
between Christianity and Judaism and not as intra-Jewish
debates. The Jewishness of Jesus and his earliest disciples was
forgotten and lost. The subsequent "teaching of contempt"
must now be replaced with the teaching of respect that includes
historical accuracy.

Second, a Jewish Jesus takes seriously the incarnation: "And
the Word became flesh and lived among us" (John 1:14). In
short, Jesus of Nazareth is a particular person who lived at a
particular time and in a particular place. To ignore that "fact" is
to undermine a basic tenet of Christianity. The retrieval of Jesus
the Jew reaffirms a basic Christian confession.

Third, to re-contextualize Jesus is to set Jesus within Israel's
story. In general, the church must rethink its perception of
both testaments. In particular, it must construct a hermeneutic,
or method of interpretation, that honors the First Testament
in its own context, as well as in the context of the early Jesus

movement. Although this rereading of the scriptures may dis-
orient some Christians, more importantly it will underscore
the theocentric or God-centered foundation of each tradition.
Not only are both religious communities rooted in the one
and same God, but the Holy One transcends the specific interpretations of both Judaism[73] and Christianity. The retrieval
of a Jewish Jesus can liberate God from a form of idolatry or
human captivity.

Fourth, the recovery of the Jewish Jesus and the re-Judaization of Christianity reduce anti-Semitism by declaring once and
for all that historical Christian hatred of the Jews is not essential
to the formation of the Jesus movement. *Jesus of Nazareth was
a practicing Jew who was NOT responsible for either the vitriolic
intra-Jewish polemics of the Second Testament or the anti-Jewish
interpretations of the later church.*

Specifically, a Jewish Jesus decreases anti-Semitism by clari-
fying for Christians the meaning of the Jewish *no* to Jesus as
the messiah. Because the world will be redeemed, according
to Judaism, when the messiah comes, the continued presence
of suffering confirms the absence of the messiah. And both
communities acknowledge this absence when they yearn for
the messiah. Traditionally Jews await the first coming, while
Christians await the second coming. Therefore, the Jewish *no*
to Jesus reminds Christians that our messianic expectations are
unfulfilled, or not yet. Jesus has already lived and died. As risen
Lord, however, we anticipate his *parousia,* or second coming.[74]
When Christians forget this eschatological hope, we mistakenly
posit unconditional claims about salvation. The good news of
the Jewish *no* to Jesus is that it prompts Christians to avoid
absolute assertions, as well as to welcome alternative religious
expressions of grace and peace.

Fifth, the retrieval of a Jewish Jesus compels Christians to
travel roads not previously taken. For both Jews and Christians
the respective levels of historical and theological illiteracy are

appalling, and, in the case of some Christians, lethal. The indispensable first step to expose *the church's fourth deadly secret* that Jesus was a Jew, not a Christian, is to relocate Jesus within his first-century Jewish context. Subsequently, the church must retell the Gospel story in light of the Jewish matrix of Jesus, reinterpret the ecclesial tradition in reference to the root metaphor of fraternal twins, and reeducate Christians in terms of historical origins and intra-Jewish polemics.[75] These initial attempts at respect should include serious and thorough dialogue between Jews and Christians, as well as joint efforts to heal the world (*tikkun olam*[76]). Only then will God's vision for the human family be advanced and will Christians learn to love their (Jewish) neighbors as they love themselves.

The Church's Fifth Deadly Secret

Read the Bible Critically, Not Literally

This chapter exposes *the church's fifth deadly secret*: "read the Bible critically, not literally." It acknowledges that many Americans read the Bible literally because they believe that God is its author. Yet the Bible is perhaps the most misunderstood book in America. One explanation is the strange silence in both the culture and the church about alternative ways of reading scripture. After an introduction, this chapter addresses this silence in four moves: it presents a critique of literalism; it advances the necessity of a critical reading; it posits the value of literary methods; and it proposes religious implications of a critical reading.

True Story. A Sunday School teacher asked her kindergarten class to listen to the birth story of Jesus according to Matthew and then draw a picture of what they heard.

As the teacher circulated through the room, she noticed that one child was drawing an airplane with four people on board. Curious about the identity of the passengers, the teacher asked the student who each person was.

"I'm drawing the flight to Egypt," the child replied. "And the passengers are Mary, Joseph, and baby Jesus."

"But who is the fourth person?" inquired the teacher.

"That's Pontius the Pilot."

Although this interpretation may be creative and cute, it nonetheless illustrates that literalism does not work. To hear Matthew's story of the "flight to Egypt" as literally true—as historically reliable and contextually relevant—results in humor at best and nonsense at worst. Why then is the literal interpretation of the Bible so popular and pervasive?

To many Christians, a literal reading of the Bible is both natural and logical. It is natural because readers assume that the Gospels, for example, are eyewitness accounts detailing the exact words and deeds of Jesus of Nazareth. It is logical because God authored the texts at most or inspired them at least. Moreover, literalism is enormously appealing since its unequivocal and unambiguous interpretations offer clear and concise answers to life's questions, as well as confidence and comfort that "God provides." In a May 2008 Gallup poll, 30 percent of the respondents agreed with the phrase, "the Bible is the actual word of God and is to be taken literally, word for word."[1]

Although literalism has traditionally been a viable and venerable method of interpreting the scriptures,[2] the average person did not start reading the Bible until the sixteenth century. With the invention of the printing press and the availability of vernacular translations, Protestant Christianity specifically became more democratic and individualistic, and therefore more fragmented. Yet a shared assumption prevailed. Marcus Borg calls it "natural literalism," the belief that the "Bible is read and accepted literally without effort."[3] Because God allegedly authored the book, it was not only trustworthy and authoritative but it was also uniquely and universally true. Christians, therefore, took for granted that literalism was the one and only way to read the scriptures.

However, the rise of the Enlightenment in general and historical consciousness in particular changed forever the hermeneutical[4] landscape of Western culture. Natural literalism was no longer self-evident. It was now a conscious choice. In response to this challenge to both biblical authority and interpretation, Protestant fundamentalism emerged at the dawn of the twentieth century as a late but leading form of American popular religion. Insistent that the Bible was the inerrant and infallible Word of God, fundamentalists espoused a literal, and therefore true, interpretation of scripture.

Yet many Americans, according to the cited 2008 Gallup poll, do not read the Bible literally. Although fundamentalism provides certain and comprehensive interpretations, there are compelling and convincing alternative methods of reading scripture. Why then are our churches and our culture strangely silent about them?[5]

According to Michael D. Coogan, a leading biblical scholar and Director of Publications for the Harvard Semitic Museum, there were four great Western intellectual revolutions in the nineteenth and twentieth centuries: Marxism, Darwinian evolutionary theory, Freudian psychology, and biblical criticism.[6] Although most educated Americans have either heard of or know something about the first three cultural transformations, few are familiar with the fourth—biblical criticism. Its claim that the Bible is a collection of historically and culturally conditioned documents has had little impact on the way most Americans today interpret these writings. Regrettably, most people both inside and outside of religious communities still read the Bible naively and pre-critically. Coogan cites two persistent and prominent causes: (1) clergy fear that the results of biblical scholarship could challenge biblical and ecclesial authority, as well as undermine faith and belief, and (2) scholars are reluctant or unable to communicate effectively the positive results of biblical scholarship to the church laity, as well as to the general public.[7]

Ironically, the Bible is the most widely purchased, the most highly revered, the most frequently read, *and* the most completely misunderstood book in America today.[8] Why? One contributing reason is *the church's fifth deadly secret* that the Bible should be read critically, not literally. This chapter addresses this pervasive and pernicious silence in four steps. First, a critique of literalism and the divine oracle model that sanctions this interpretation is presented. Second, the necessity of a critical reading in general and the importance of historical criticism in particular are advanced. Third, the limitations of the historical approach and the value of literary methods that privilege the role of the reader are posited. And fourth, religious implications of a critical reading of the Bible are proposed.

A Critique of Literalism

In our culture, literalism rules. Whether we call it a confessional, devotional, or pious reading of the Bible, most Americans presume that the Bible is the inerrant and infallible Word of God that should be interpreted literally. Those assumptions are so widespread that they persist even among those who do *not* accept the authority of the Bible. Although the degree of literalism may vary (from a "hard form" that affirms only the literal-factual interpretation of the whole Bible from the creation story in Genesis to the return of Jesus in Revelation, to variations of a "soft form" that permit occasional metaphorical or figurative readings while nevertheless insisting that the major events are historically accurate and the doctrinal assertions are theologically true), five basic principles ground a literal reading of scripture and the divine oracle[9] model that justifies it.[10]

The first principle is that the Bible is a divine product. Because God authored these writings, the scriptures are divinely inspired and therefore sacred. Consequently, Christians call this book the "Holy Bible" and the "Word of God." Second, the Bible conveys the direct and expressive will of God. Since God is the author and whatever God wills to communicate God can bring to expression, an identity exists between the divine voice (the content of God's message) and the vehicle of God's expression (the Bible). This identity both grounds and names this model of reading scripture—the divine oracle model[11] of biblical interpretation. Third, the Bible constitutes a single genre. Although the text is composed of diverse pieces of literature (histories, laws, psalms, Gospels, letters), when read as a seamless literary unit the Bible narrates a single, continuous coherent story of salvation history. For Jewish readers, the Hebrew Bible recites the story of Israel, while for Christian readers, the Bible tells the story of Jesus. Fourth, as the repository of divine revelation that is both uniform and universal, the Bible is level. That is, God accurately and coherently speaks in all parts of the text. Because every passage in scripture fits logically within God's larger pattern of divine speech as recorded in the entire book, God's voice resonates consistently and equally throughout the writings. Consequently, what God says in one place in the text relates to and reinforces what God says in other places in the text. As a sourcebook of divine revelation, the Bible contains propositional truths that are self-contained and not context dependent. Hence, passages can and should be used to proof-text one another. This particular method of intratextual interpretation necessarily assumes that all passages have equal value and thus are level. Fifth, the cumulative force of the above four principles confirms the Bible as the divine oracle. As a direct revelation from God, the biblical text and the divine voice are identical—the words of the oracle are the exact words of the deity. Therefore, this model of biblical interpretation undeniably and unambiguously links the unique status of the Bible with a literal interpretation. Because God can speak only the truth, the Bible's truth can be interpreted only literally.

The following five observations undermine, however, both the viability of a literal interpretation of the Bible and the claims of the divine oracle model. First and foremost, a literal reading needs an original biblical manuscript—a definitive text with definitive words. Yet it does not exist. Scholars possess only late copies of copies, which vary tremendously in quality.[12] Although 5,700 manuscripts of the Greek Second Testament have been catalogued, there exist "more differences in our manuscripts than there are words in the New [Second] Testament."[13] In addition, there are seven thousand copies (from small fragments to large productions) of the Greek Bible, but only around ten contain the entire Bible. All ten of these are now defective (missing pages), and only four predate the tenth century. Finally, scholars know of about ten thousand manuscripts of the Latin Vulgate,[14] as well as versions in other ancient languages. In spite of these abundant sources, academics estimate that there are between 200,000 and 400,000 variants or differences in the manuscripts. Second Testament scholar Bart Ehrman, a specialist in textual criticism, concludes, "[We] can't say what the words *mean*, if we don't know what the words *were*."[15]

However, even an original manuscript would pose problems for a literal interpretation. Both Hebrew and Greek biblical texts were written with minimal punctuation marks and without breaks between words and sentences. Even worse, ancient Hebrew did not use vowels. Two consonants side by side could signify different words.[16] Moreover, there are over four hundred biblical words, known as *hapax legomena* (Greek for "something said only once"), that experts are not sure how to translate since these single word occurrences cannot be compared to other usages for meaning.[17]

Second, a literal interpretation requires a reading from the original language. Translations are inadmissible. Yet the overwhelming majority of biblical literalists read neither ancient Hebrew nor Greek and therefore rely on a vernacular or native language translation. The problem is that every translation, by definition, is an interpretation. When a manuscript is translated from the original language into the target language, decisions must be made that compromise both the integrity and meaning of the original words. Any person who has taken an introductory foreign language course knows this dilemma. Furthermore, Jesus' native tongue was Aramaic.[18] Although scholars debate how much Greek he knew, the Second Testament was written in Greek.[19] Therefore, the biblical Greek words of Jesus are not the authentic Aramaic words of Jesus! If we have no original manuscript, and we read from a translated version of an imprecise text, literalism is impossible to defend.[20]

Third, a literal interpretation presupposes a consistent and coherent storyline because it asserts that the Bible constitutes a single genre. Yet discrepancies that can be neither reconciled nor rationalized plague the Gospels from the birth stories to the passion.[21] For example, in the Gospel of Matthew Jesus' hometown is Bethlehem (2:22–23), while in Luke it is Nazareth (1:26–27). For Mark (6:17–18) and Matthew (14:3–4), John the Baptist baptizes Jesus and is then imprisoned, yet for Luke (3:20) John is imprisoned immediately before Jesus is baptized. The cleansing of the Temple in the first three canonical Gospels, also called the Synoptics,[22] (Mark 11:15–19, Matt 21:12–17, Luke 19:45–48) occurs at the end of Jesus' earthly life and functions as the trigger event for his arrest, but in John (2:13–22) it occurs at the beginning of his three-year public ministry. In the Synoptics, Jesus dies during the festival of Passover (Mark 15:6, Matt 27:15), while in John he dies the day before Passover or the day of Preparation (John 19:31). These contradictions illustrate that the four canonical Gospels do not provide a shared storyline of the life of Jesus.

The common and usually unconscious solution for most readers is to conflate the four narratives. That is, harmonize the multiple Gospel stories into one single story. Christians do it all the time. At Christmas the crèche or nativity scene includes

Magi or wise men from Matthew's story and shepherds from Luke's story.[23] The two very different accounts are combined. At Easter the "seven last words of Jesus" (actually the seven last sayings attributed to Jesus) on the cross are taken from all four Gospels.[24] Again, the texts are blended.

In its wisdom, the early church canonized four separate Gospels; not one. Although Tatian, around 170 CE, produced the *Diatessaron* ("through the four") that wove the four narratives into a single, harmonious story, the church did not promote it and most moderns do not know it. Unfortunately, Tatian's impulse to conflate continues today. Most important, the authorization of four distinct Gospels (with their contradictions) not only undermines the claims of the divine oracle model that a consistent and coherent storyline of Jesus exists but it also undercuts the claim of identity between the divine voice and the biblical text.

Fourth, a literal reading necessitates selectivity. Because of contradictory passages, as well as changes in our cultural context, choices and therefore compromises must be made. For example, nearly all Christian literalists worship on Sunday (the first day of the week) but feel free to work on the Sabbath (Saturday, or the seventh day of the week), thus violating the fourth commandment (Exod 20:8–10 and Deut 5:12–14). Few Christians are snake handlers (Mark 16:18), and even fewer cut off an offending hand (Mark 9:43). If parents executed their insolent and rebellious children according to the directive of Deut 21:18–21, none of us would be alive! The litany of problematic texts is endless.[25] Since no one takes the *entire* Bible literally, those who claim that they do, do not apply the principle uniformly. There necessarily exists a gap between their rhetoric and their actions.

The fifth and final observation is subtle yet salient. Both Judaism and Christianity are literary religions. Without stories and scriptures, these traditions would not exist. However, language conceals as well as reveals. Although words are the vehicles by which humans give expression to their inner worlds and outer experiences, language alone inadequately and inaccurately captures, let alone conveys, these meanings. There is usually something left unsaid or unexpressed, as well as something misspoken or misunderstood. Words simultaneously shout "is" and whisper "is not." They reveal and conceal.

Because the mystery and ambiguity of human language permeates every speech act from inception and transmission to reception and interpretation, religious communities and their canons are also affected. This observation includes both bad news and good news.

First, the bad news. The perennial danger or bad news of any text-driven tradition is the inclination to absolutize the "said" and to ignore the "unsaid." Regrettably, published documents in themselves promote the false confidence that humans can embody the ethereal in words and in writings, and thereby confine and control the transcendent. This dangerous tendency can lead to unreflective hubris and unrealistic certainty. Prejudice and intolerance, hatred and violence too often follow.

The good news is that religious language is inherently metaphorical. At their best, faith communities acknowledge and affirm the qualitative distance between the creator and the creature. Consequently, human encounters with the divine only glimpse the depth dimension and therefore never exhaust its meaning. Our perceptions and our pronouncements are then partial and provisional. That is why sacred writings frequently use metaphors and images, symbols and myths to communicate their truth. Like poetry, religious language instinctively resists any one-to-one correspondence between the word and its referent. As an acknowledgement of the "more" beyond the observable, transcendence cannot be flattened into factuality or domesticated into one-dimensional platitudes. Although symbols evoke thought, human utterances about the divine are rooted in mystery and wonder. Although holy texts demand interpretation, their potency and power reside in the dynamic dance between the inscribed ink and the empty spaces on the printed page.[26] This symbiotic relationship mirrors on a micro level the human and divine relationship on a macro level. The divine oracle model in general, and a literal interpretation of the Bible in particular, lose this insight by claiming too much for the text and too little for the deity.

In conclusion, literalism ironically yet unintentionally subverts the very source of authority that it professes to affirm. In practice, the ubiquitous assertion "the Bible says," intended to end debate by announcing unassailable and absolute truth, is nothing more than a biblical version of chance. Individual words, phrases, or verses lifted from their original context demean both the integrity and interpretation of the Bible.

For the above five reasons, a literal reading of the Bible is self-defeating. Moreover, the theological consequences are dangerous. Although the literal hermeneutic, or method of interpretation, unequivocally and unapologetically values the text, the inherent principles of the divine oracle model treat the book as if it were God—the sin of bibliolatry. In the words of Phyllis Trible, "To appropriate the metaphor of a Zen sutra, poetry is 'like a finger pointing to the moon'. . . . [To] equate the finger with the moon or to acknowledge the finger and not perceive the moon is to miss the point."[27] And faith, as an indispensable corollary to literalism, shifts from a relational to an intellectual category. It no longer means trust in God or Jesus, but "believing the unbelievable."

A Critical Reading of the Bible

The church and the Bible need each other. The church is dependent on the Bible for its life and witness,[28] while the Bible is dependent on the church for its origins and its ongoing ability to speak. Although a literal reading of scripture seems on the surface to be the most desirable means of honoring and preserving this foundational interdependence, the above critique demonstrates the opposite. Because texts are mute, they neither speak for themselves nor interpret themselves. They cannot tell us their meanings or how to read them. Only people can give voice to the text and derive understanding. In short, books must be read and interpreted by humans.

Two rules need to guide the interpretation process.[29] The first rule is that readers must make a serious attempt to *understand the text*. This assertion means that we do everything possible to allow the text to speak in its own voice. If we wish to understand the text, we must devote ourselves to the task of insuring that we read meaning out of the text (exegesis) rather than read our prejudices and preferences into the text (eisegesis). As interpreters, we humans are masterful ventriloquists who can easily deceive ourselves into thinking that we are listening to the text when in fact we are simply hearing the unspoken presuppositions already embedded in our minds. As serious students, we want to maximize the voice of the text and minimize our own voices. We want to increase understanding and decrease misunderstanding.

The second rule is that all readers must engage the text *critically*. Because of Enlightenment insights, especially the rise of historical consciousness and the Copernican revolution in thinking inaugurated by Kant,[30] we now know that all interpretations are historically and culturally conditioned. Neither a naive nor a pre-critical reading of the text will suffice. Objective or neutral readings are illusory since all interpretations are inherently biased. The only viable alternative is to read the text critically. Contrary to popular misunderstanding, a critical reading does not demean or denigrate the Bible by finding faults within the text. More important, its purpose is to restrain the readers' urge to impose modern presuppositions onto ancient writings (as in the child's interpretation of the Flight to Egypt).

Since a critical reading values the text more than the beliefs of its contemporary readers, it addresses human bias by interpreting the text in a disciplined manner while acknowledging and criticizing one's own perspectives. Hence, a critical reading is an exercise in humility because advocates of this method attempt to minimize their pre-established agendas and maximize the meaning of the text on its own terms.

Two basic assumptions follow. First, the scriptures were composed by the Jewish and Christian communities and are not simply a divine product. Consequently, these collections of documents are subject to critical investigation like any other piece of human literature. Second, both of these communities are located in history. Since there is no meaning without context, readers of the Bible must attempt to understand its original historical and cultural context before determining its relevance for today.

Historical Criticism[31]

Despite the insidious illusion in our electronic age that information is devoid of context, neither writers nor readers live in a vacuum. No student of history would reconstruct the life of Abraham Lincoln or Martin Luther King, Jr., by focusing on his words and works isolated from his cultural context.

This axiom also applies to biblical interpretation. Historical study of the Bible is imperative since it affirms the historical particularity of revelation, the historical incarnation of biblical figures,[32] and the historical embodiment of the biblical writers. Although the historical study of the Bible presents risks, avoidance or abstention invites disaster. A text without an explicit context leaves the door wide open for making the text say whatever the reader wants. Eisegesis—reading our prejudices into the text—prevails. Sacred scripture needs a better hermeneutic.

The goal of historical criticism is to uncover the text's meaning in its original historical context. By attempting to understand the text's origins (author, date, place, occasion, context) and sources (if any), as well as the text's meaning, historical criticism seeks to understand what the biblical authors meant when they wrote to their audiences. Only after the reader answers the question, "what did the text mean then?" can he or she justifiably take up the subsequent question, "what does it mean now?"

Historical criticism is the preferred approach of most non-literalist biblical scholars today.[33] In contrast to the divine oracle model, this specific method employs the term "historical" to emphasize the conviction that the Bible must be understood primarily within its historical context. Although the divine character of the text is neither rejected nor affirmed, theological assumptions that could predetermine or predispose one's interpretation are irrelevant. The term "criticism" highlights two interrelated tasks: the biblical reader must (1) reconstruct the history of the Jewish people and the early Jesus movement, and (2) address the perennial problem of eisegesis.

For historical criticism, authorial intent as disclosed in the text has priority. That is, the meaning of any composition unfolds as the reader seeks to understand the text as it relates to its author, its context, and its reader. Unlike the divine oracle model in which God is the presumed author, this method assumes that the text has been written by individuals embedded in historically located communities. Although the text has a "life of its own" beyond the writer and the writer's social setting, interpretation begins by trying to discern authorial meaning.

Initially, the field of biblical scholarship was divided into "lower" and "higher" criticism. The former applied to the scholar's first and fundamental task to determine, as best one

can, the original wording of the text, while the latter applied
to all the other forms of biblical criticism. Because textual
criticism is foundational for the other approaches, the following description of five general methods of historical criticism
begins with it.[34]

1. Textual criticism attempts to reconstruct the original
wording of the text in order to establish a reliable, restored
manuscript for ongoing study. Because there is no original
manuscript or autograph, the only biblical writings that we possess are copies of copies that contain both scribal errors (textual
corruptions) and additions (interpolations). Therefore, textual
evidence must be weighed by evaluating known copies of the
text, as well as by comparing the possible wording options to
each other. For example, most scholars believe that the Gospel
of Mark ended at 16:8 and that verses 9–20 are a later addition to the manuscript. Also, the story of the woman caught in
adultery (John 7:53–8:11) is an interpolation.

2. Source criticism determines the sources on which a biblical writing is based, or from which a biblical book has been
compiled. The operating assumption is that some of the biblical
texts are the product of both oral and written transmission that
combined various sources to comprise the present book. For
example, most scholars espouse the documentary hypothesis
to explain the development of the Pentateuch. That is, four
separate sources, combined and revised over several centuries,
were edited to form the first five books of the Bible as we now
have them.

3. Form criticism recognizes both the stages of development (prehistory) of a text and the literary forms, or genres,
of a text. For example, the two different versions of the Ten
Commandments, or Decalogue (Exod 20:1–17 and Deut
5:6–21), probably reflect different stages of use and development within their respective communities. In addition, both
testaments contain a wide range of literary genres. The First

Testament includes narratives, legal material, wisdom sayings, prophetic announcements, and psalms (which also contain sub-genres), while the Second Testament includes Gospels (which also contain subgenres), letters, a (purported) history, and an apocalypse. Most important, this analysis realizes that the form of a text provides a salient clue not only to its meaning but also to its context, or life situation (*Sitz im Leben*[35]).

4. Redaction criticism investigates how the editing or redact-ing process by the text's final author and/or editor reveals that person's motives. Relying on the findings from the two previ-ous criticisms to determine both the stages and the sources of a text, this method is particularly useful for the study of the Synoptic Gospels. Since most scholars believe that Mark is the earliest canonical Gospel and serves as a source for both Matthew and Luke, a comparison of parallel passages helps us to see how Matthew and Luke have edited Mark. For ex-ample, the baptism of Jesus story found in Mark 1:9–11, Matt 3:13–17, and Luke 3:21–22 contains significant differences. The brief Markan account is inflated by Matthew to include a protest by John (Matt 3:14–15). Because Jesus' baptism was probably an embarrassment to the early community (if Jesus was sinless and superior to John, why was he baptized by John?), Matthew's supplement provides his response. Luke solves one of the dilemmas by having John imprisoned (3:20) before Jesus is baptized.[36]

5. Canonical criticism expands the interpretive trajectory from the historical context of the text to include the canoni-cal context of the biblical writings. At least two implications follow.[37] First, readers have expectations for the biblical books that may or may not have been anticipated by the authors. As normative for synagogue and church, these texts are now read by faith communities and individuals not only from different times and places, but also with different religious and ethical agendas. Second, specific texts are not read in isolation but in

relation to the other biblical books. For example, the placement of the books in their canonical order affects interpretation. The Christian version of the First Testament places the
writing prophets at the end of that Testament and immediately
before the Gospels so that their prophecy is fulfilled in Jesus.

In conclusion, these five methods of historical criticism are
intended to uncover the text's meaning by providing informed
responses to the following set of questions:

1. Who wrote the book or spoke what is written in the
   text?
2. When were the contents composed?
3. Where was the book written or message delivered?
4. To whom was it originally addressed?
5. Why was it written, or what was its purpose?
6. What sources did the author use?
7. What did the author actually write and what was added
   later?

These questions underscore the essential role that the method
of historical criticism plays for readers who want to understand
the Bible.

The Limitations of Historical Criticism and the Value of Literary Criticism

Forged on the anvil of Enlightenment rationalism, historical
criticism provides modern readers of the Bible with methods to
ascertain the meaning of a biblical text in its original historical
context. Yet two prominent limitations persist.[38] First, historical criticism's primary interest in the texts as historical sources
too often prevents them from being read as literature. That is,
the predominant focus on authorial intent and historical context precludes an examination of the biblical texts as autonomous writings independent from their own histories and their
authors' purposes.

Second, historical criticism does not presuppose the theological truth of the Bible. Although the divine character of the text is not automatically rejected, these methods of historical criticism are not interested in the agency of God in history but what the human authors meant. In short, historical criticism brackets certain issues. Because this avoidance may be understood to dismiss the religious dimension of the text as incompatible with modern sensibilities, the theological content may be ignored at best and denied at worst. Regrettably, this omission prohibits many historians from asking a foundational question: What kinds of experiences created these religious communities and in turn motivated the writing of these texts? This section formally addresses the former limitation, while the chapter's conclusion briefly comments on the latter limitation.

Literary Criticism

As a broad and loose term, literary criticism represents a fundamental shift in the way scripture is understood as text. Distinct from both the divine oracle model that views the Bible as the vehicle of divine speech and the historical methods that view the text as sources for the reconstruction of authorial intent and historical context, literary criticism generally operates with the assumption that readers produce meaning. Thus, the text itself is the reader's sole focus.[39] What is said in the text is simply the "voice of the text." The reader does not look behind the text to discern either the voice of God or the voice of the author. Because the text has its own voice, the message and meaning of a text inhere within the words themselves.

This basic assumption of literary criticism recognizes that books by themselves are inert and inactive. Readers alone produce meaning. All of the previous methods primarily read the text in order to understand author and context while ignoring the reader. The divine oracle model equates authorial intent with God's will and hence the context of the text is construed almost exclusively in theological or doctrinal terms. Historical methods pursue authorial intent by interpreting context in explicitly historical terms. By contrast, literary criticism perceives both author and context as properties of the text. Consequently, the reader replaces author and context as the central element to which the text relates. Succinctly, interpretation only involves the reader and the text.

Three distinctive features characterize most literary methods. First, the text is treated as ahistorical, and thus is atemporal. Rather than seeing the text as the product of divine or historical causality, most literary critics view the text as a finished product. Textual comparisons are therefore couched in literary terms rather than historical ones. Most important, the meaning of a text is not understood diachronically (unfolding "through time," or in linear time) but synchronically ("with time," or in a single moment in time). Attention to time and history only occurs when the voice of the text requires it. Second, the text is regarded as autonomous. Because the text has its own voice and its own life separate from its historical context, it can be interpreted as if it were independent of its historical setting and its author's intent. The text not only stands by itself but it also provides internal clues on how to interpret it. Third, the meaning of a text is understood aesthetically. Since texts intrinsically possess meaning, the locus of meaning shifts from the past to the present. For literary critics, the only relevant question for biblical interpretation is "what does it mean now?"

Although literary criticism includes a broad range of approaches that focus on various intrinsic aspects of the text, only two methods will be described below.[40]

1. Narrative criticism explores how the story of the text (narrative) constructs meaning and fashions reality for the reader. Two elements of the narrative are analyzed: the story (what is told) and the discourse (how the story is told). Story involves how the combination of events, characters, and settings cre-

ates a plot, while discourse involves how the author shapes the story to convey a specific ideology or perspective. Narrative critics study biblical stories to ascertain how the text's rhetorical strategies persuade the reader to adopt the author's version of reality, as well as how the reader understands the story and comprehends its meaning.[41]

2. Reader-response criticism focuses on how a text is received by its reader, not how it originated or how it is arranged. Because the reader plays a prominent role in the "production" or "creation" of meaning, this method "approaches biblical literature in terms of the values, attitudes, and responses of readers."[42] This shift in emphasis permits an openness to the Bible as religious literature and to how the reader's religious convictions influence the experience of reading scripture. Thus, the religious concerns of both the text and the reader are respected.[43]

This discussion of the various ways to read the Bible would be incomplete if it did not recognize challenges posed by disenfranchised readers. Because the Bible has played and continues to play a major role in the creation and validation of oppressive structures of existence, diverse and distinct approaches have been recently developed that can be classified under the rubric of "ideological criticism." These methods would include feminist theology,[44] black theology,[45] and liberation theology, or socioeconomic criticism.[46] Although these hermeneutics differ tremendously, they all agree that traditional theology is too parochial and that traditional biblical interpretation is too insensitive to the marginalized.

This extensive list of approaches by which one can read the Bible critically is not presented to intimidate and frustrate the reader. Christians are not called to be biblical experts but to live biblically literate lives. Therefore, Christians need to learn about these critical methods because they need to value the voice of the Bible more than their own voices. Consequently,

serious readers need to use biblical dictionaries[47] and commentaries[48] (that do employ multiple methods and thereby
minimize bias) to supplement interpretations. Although a critical reading is definitely preferred to a naive reading, the results
of historical-literary readings of the Bible do not by themselves
produce a full understanding of the text. These methods are
constructive techniques that allow the text to speak in its own
voice and thereby expand and enrich the ongoing conversation
between scripture and the interpreter. The ultimate purpose,
however, is to listen, learn, and live accordingly.

The Religious Implications of a Critical Reading of the Bible

From Christianity's inception, books have been central to the
church's faith and practice. Whether they narrated the stories
of Jesus and the apostles, provided instruction in what to believe and how to live, offered courage and hope in times of
persecution, or imparted guidance for worship and governance,
books were indispensable.[49] Therefore, it was inevitable that
authoritative writings emerged by which the community defined, transmitted, and sustained itself. Once the Bible was established, the subsequent and salient question was how to read
and interpret it. This chapter has argued that one contributing
reason for the strange silence in our society about modern
methods for reading the text is *the church's fifth deadly secret*
that the Bible should be read critically, not literally. Now that
we have examined and rejected literalism and the divine oracle
model, presented the merits of a critical reading as practiced
in both historical and literary approaches, it is time to identify
four religious implications of a critical reading of the Bible.

First, the Bible is the church's book and therefore sacred
scripture.[50] It is sacred because these writings are the authoritative witness to the normative revelations of God in history. Like
a sacrament, these human manuscripts herald the redemptive

presence of the divine. It is scripture because this text is the foundational document for Christian identity and vocation. Although the Bible imparts communal Christian identity, it is more important that the biblical story itself discloses God's identity, which in turn challenges our false familiarity—the assumption that just because we are acquainted with God and the Bible, we automatically understand. Bible reading concurrently reveals our vocation, or calling by God, to conform our memories and hopes to the biblical narrative. Since the Bible is the church's conversation partner that both questions our presuppositions and lures us toward new life, best interpretations are made within the community of faith, where both the tradition is valued and critical methods are available.[51]

Second, biblical "truth" presupposes trust. Demonstrated by our critique of literalism, the first casualty of a critical reading of scripture is factual truth. The biblical story contains contradictions and inconsistencies. Two extreme and often emotional reactions must be avoided: re-entrenchment and relativism. The former defends "fact fundamentalism" by insisting that the biblical story is objectively and literally true. This option is untenable. The latter endorses "uncritical subjectivity" by insisting that the biblical story means "whatever you say it does." Although this option is popular today, not all interpretations are equal. What is significant is that Christian truth is not identical to historical truth because religious truth points to the transcendent that is revealed in but not limited to history.[52] Moreover, there is no neutral ground by which an observer can claim objectivity. Faith, therefore, is always a joyful and courageous risk. It is trust. Religious truth resides then within the community's story of God's presence with them, and stories are only falsifiable or verifiable from within themselves. Yet the biblical story contains many stories. As the Word of God, the Bible speaks with one as well as many voices. Because God's story is singular and several, it is a difficult read. Thus, a critical and communal reading of the Bible is essential not only to clarify religious truth for today but also to live faithfully and trustingly within its story—to call it home.

Third, a critical reading of the Bible must be supplemented by historical imagination, which is not the same as fantasy. If one of the goals of the Christian life is to live within the biblical story, then we are called to be "insiders,"[53] not biblical experts. As story, scripture is elastic. Imagination then enables the reader to move beyond the results of historical and literary criticism to envision "a new heaven and a new earth." On the one hand, imagination frustrates the tendency of religious communities to codify and thereby absolutize truth—to reduce mystery to the mundane, symbols to sentences, and poetry to prose. On the other hand, history tethers imagination and prevents it from becoming free-floating fantasy. As the witness of a particular community's experience of God in history, the Bible both anchors and activates historical imagination.

Fourth, "conversation is our hope."[54] Humans converse and chat, confer and consult, because we are innate and inveterate talkers. Although we speak about everything under the sun, we are obsessed with meaning and purpose. We perennially ask questions and therefore participate in the ongoing conversation about life. Through the centuries, the epicenters of that conversation are religious communities that inevitably transcribe some of those conversations and subsequently designate some of those writings as canonical. For Christians, the ultimate conversation is about the God revealed in Jesus of Nazareth. The Bible, as the community's primary witness, is then our principal partner in conversation.[55] Because that continuous conversation is sacred, the church needs to teach biblical literacy and living beyond the literal.

6

The Church's Sixth Deadly Secret

Jesus' Miracles Are Prologue, Not Proof

This chapter discloses *the church's sixth deadly secret*: "Jesus' miracles are prologue, not proof." Because miracles play an indispensable role in the belief system of many Christians, it illustrates the difficulty of reading an ancient book in the modern world. After an introduction, this chapter explores this complicated and controversial topic in four steps: it examines the challenges of the Enlightenment; it describes the Greco-Roman and Jewish contexts; it presents the Gospel portraits of Jesus the miracle-worker; and it posits some implications for the religious life.

"The Miracle on the Hudson." Those laudatory words, spoken on January 15, 2009, by New York governor David Paterson, captured America's fascination with US Airways flight 1549. Less than two minutes after its takeoff from New York City's LaGuardia Airport, the plane struck a flock of large Canada geese, which knocked out both of its engines. Horrified yet mesmerized, Americans watched as the pilot, Chesley "Sully" Sullenberger, guided the 75-ton jet to a safe splashdown in the middle of the Hudson River with 155 passengers and crew members on board. Everyone escaped serious injury.

ABC sportscaster Al Michaels counted down the final seconds of the USA's improbable 4–3 1980 Winter Olympics men's ice hockey victory over the heavily favored Soviet Union team with these now famous words, "Five seconds left in the game. Do you believe in miracles? YES!" Although Coach Herb Brooks' squad went on to win the gold medal when it defeated Finland, this Davidesque triumph was immediately dubbed the "Miracle on Ice."

The use of the term "miracle" (derived from the Latin *mirari*, "to wonder at") to describe both dramatic rescues and extraordinary achievements is common in our culture. In a five-day period, *USA Today* headlines declared the rescue of Nick Schuyler, who clung for forty-six hours to a capsized boat in the Gulf of Mexico, as "a miracle, doctor says," and the twenty-three-hour operation for seven-year-old Heather McNamara, in which six vital organs were removed and then restored after a tumor was cut out, as a "miracle surgery."[1]

Events that defy explanation and dumbfound experts are often identified as "miraculous" by theists in general and Christians in particular. The German literary giant Goethe (1749–1832) spoke for many when he wrote in *Faust*, "Miracle is faith's dearest child." According to C.S. Lewis, the British apologist, Christianity cannot escape the presence and profundity of miracles.

> One is very often asked at present whether we could not have a Christianity stripped, or, as people who ask it say, 'freed' from its miraculous elements, a Christianity with the miraculous elements suppressed. Now, it seems to me that precisely the one religion in the world, or, at least, the only one I know, with which you could not do that is Christianity. . . . [You] cannot possibly do that with Christianity, because the Christian story is precisely the story of one grand miracle, the Christian assertion being that what is beyond all space and time, what is uncreated, eternal, came into nature, into human nature, descended into His own universe, and rose again, bringing nature up with Him. It is precisely one great miracle. If you take that away there is nothing specifically Christian left.[2]

Embedded in the foundational story of the church and testified by the throngs of infirmed who travel to Lourdes, France, and other places for miraculous cures, Christians affirm a God who intervenes again and again in human history. According to a 2004 Fox News poll, 82 percent of Americans believe in miracles,[3] and, according to a 2008 Pew Forum U.S. Religious Landscape Survey, 79 percent "agree that miracles still occur today as in ancient times."[4]

Yet the literal interpretation of biblical miracles, reaffirmed by Protestant Reformation theologians,[5] was challenged by both the Enlightenment's scientific worldview and the rise of historical consciousness. Supernatural theism, which espouses a God separate from creation ("Our Father, who art in heaven") who periodically intervenes in worldly affairs, was now problematic. Since the universe was understood to operate as a closed system of matter and energy according to natural laws, God was no longer required. Neither past nor present interventions passed the rigorous test of rationalism. Christian scholars, like George E. Ladd, rebutted:

> The uniqueness and the scandal of the Christian religion rests on the mediation of revelation through historical events. Christianity . . . is rooted in real events in history. To some people this is scandalous because it means the truth of Christianity is inexplicably bound up with the truth of certain historical facts. And if those facts should be disproved, Christianity would be false. This, however, is what makes Christianity unique because, unlike other world religions, modern man has a means of actually verifying Christianity's truth by historical evidence.[6]

For many Christians, the biblical testimony is indisputable and undeniable—Jesus' miracles certified him as the divine Son of God.[7] Moreover, he performed them to "prove that God is like no one else, that He has complete control of creation . . . [and] that He can do miracles in our lives as well. If the miracles did not occur, then how can we trust anything the Bible tells us, especially when it tells us eternal life is available through Christ?"[8]

Regrettably, these Christians have reduced the challenge of the Enlightenment to a simple selection between modernism and literalism. Even the renowned biblical scholar, Rudolf Bultmann (1884–1976), was misguided when he wrote: "It is impossible to use electric light and the wireless and to avail ourselves of modern medical and surgical discoveries, and at the same time to believe in the New Testament world of demons and spirits [miracles]."[9]

Christians are not forced, however, to choose between an ancient cosmology and the modern worldview. That is a false choice which leads to theological schizophrenia—employing a "modern mind" while inhabiting the everyday world but using an "ancient mind" while inhabiting the faith world. The concept of a "natural law" that is "violated" by a miracle is a contemporary way of thinking[10] and should not be imposed on the biblical depiction of Jesus' wondrous deeds. Rather, present-day readers must recognize and respect the differences between current categories and first-century ones. Therefore, the salient question we need to ask about Jesus' miracles is not "Did they happen?"[11] but "What is their *meaning* in the context of the biblical narrative?"

According to the Gospels and the early church, Jesus performed miracles. As this chapter demonstrates, Jewish prophets were linked to miraculous deeds which belonged to the religious language of the day. Hence, miracles were more about "meaning" and less about "causality." Since few Christians today know about the first-century context, *the church's sixth deadly secret* is that Jesus' miracles are prologue, not proof. This chapter exposes this cover-up in four steps. First, the challenges of the Enlightenment are examined. Second, the Greco-Roman and Jewish contexts are described. Third, the Second

Testament portraits of Jesus the miracle-worker are presented. And fourth, some implications for the religious life are posited.

The Challenges of the Enlightenment

As the watershed event in Western civilization, the Enlightenment principles of the seventeenth and eighteenth centuries gradually undermined the orthodox Christian theological portrait of Jesus in general and the traditional image of Jesus the miracle-worker in particular. This section briefly examines the development of the scientific, philosophical, and historical challenges to the possibility of miracles and concludes with an assessment of current approaches.[12]

Prior to the Enlightenment, the conventional argument for the reliability of Jesus' miracles was twofold: "the historical credibility of the miracles stories was based on the theological doctrine of the divine nature of Jesus, which was in turn validated by the presumed scientific and philosophical possibilities of miracles."[13] This circular reasoning worked as long as the separate elements were accepted. But the Enlightenment principles of the scientific worldview and the rise of historical consciousness disputed these individual claims and irreparably broke the circle.[14]

Although Isaac Newton (1643–1727) unequivocally advanced the new scientific paradigm, he also tried to preserve the role of the divine in the natural world. According to Jaroslav Pelikan, "There was, [Newton] asserted . . . 'nothing of contradiction' in acknowledging that as the First Cause, God could 'vary the laws of Nature' (thus apparently allowing for the miraculous) and yet at the same time in assuming that the world 'once formed . . . may continue by those laws for many ages' (thus apparently precluding the miraculous)."[15]

Newton's ambiguous endorsement of the possibility of miracles was short-lived. As the emerging scientific paradigm provided answers to more and more questions about the nature of the world, the appeal to divine purpose and intervention became less and less necessary. People invoked the name of the deity *only* when science was unable to provide an adequate explanation. Yet the appeal to God to fill-in the "gaps" in scientific knowledge was vulnerable to the relentless and rapid advancement of empiricism.[16] Eventually God and Jesus' miracles would be retired at best or debunked at worst.

For many, David Hume (1711–1776), Scottish philosopher and author of "Of Miracles,"[17] supplied the lid for God's coffin. Because Christianity was "founded on *Faith*, not on reason," faith was the first and only miracle. Therefore, Hume answered the philosophical question of the possibility of miracles with a resounding "no,"[18] when he wrote:

> So that, upon the whole, we may conclude, that the *Christian Religion* not only was at first attended with miracles, but even at this day cannot be believed by any reasonable person without one. Mere reason is insufficient to convince us of its veracity: And whoever is moved by *Faith* to assent to it, is conscious of a continued miracle in his own person, which subverts all the principles of his understanding, and gives him a determination to believe what is most contrary to custom and experience.[19]

Although the ability of miracles to validate the uniqueness of Jesus was severely compromised by both scientific theories and philosophical arguments, the rise of historical consciousness supplied for many the nails for God's coffin. At the same time that Edward Gibbon (1737–1794), the English historian and author of *The History of the Decline and Fall of the Roman Empire*, cited miracles as one of the five historical causes for the victory of Christianity in the Roman Empire,[20] some of his contemporaries eagerly applied Enlightenment historical principles to the life of Jesus. Beginning with Hermann Samuel Reimarus (1694–1768), who claimed in his book *On the Intention of Jesus* that Jesus' purpose was to establish a political kingdom to rival Roman rule in contrast to his disciples' post-Easter plan to establish a new religion, scholars tried to separate the Jesus of history from the Jesus of the Gospels.[21] German theologian and historian David Friedrich Strauss (1808–1874) was unquestionably the pioneer of historical Jesus research. In his revolutionary book *The Life of Jesus Critically Examined,* he posited a third approach to Jesus study that dismissed, on the one hand, the "supernaturalists," who defended the historical accuracy of the biblical narratives and therefore divine intervention, and, on the other hand, the "rationalists," who claimed that violations of the laws of nature were impossible and therefore natural explanations were necessary. Applying a "mythical approach," Strauss argued that the Gospel texts used the "imagery of the early church's inherited religious and literary tradition" to portray the "spiritual significance of Jesus." Although his conclusions are now obsolete, his methodology changed forever the landscape of biblical criticism.

The rise of historical consciousness not only spawned a new approach for interpreting the books of the Bible but also imposed limits on the historian.[22] Because the modern definition of a miracle assumes at most a "supernatural violation of natural laws"[23] and at least a contradiction in the "normal workings of nature in such a way as to be virtually beyond belief and to require an acknowledgment that supernatural forces have been at work,"[24] the historian cannot make a judgment, since there is no public access to supernatural agency. Moreover, history is unrepeatable and predicated on probability. The further back in history one investigates, the more difficult it is to establish what really happened. Furthermore, miracles are exceedingly rare since the chances of them happening by definition are infinitesimal. Thus, the concept of miracle not only lies outside the realm of historical inquiry, but it is also a "least probable occurrence." In short, historians cannot determine the historical reliability of Jesus' miracles; they can only affirm that according to ancient narratives, he performed them.

The challenges of the Enlightenment to the possibility of miracles have generated a range of approaches.[25] At one end of the spectrum is the absolute denial of their possibility. Invoking the philosophy of Hume and other skeptics, this position asserts the impossibility of miracles by definition: (1) miracles are a violation of natural law; (2) natural laws are uniform and unchangeable; and (3) therefore, they do not occur.[26] This approach, however, is unacceptable since it assumes a modern definition of miracle that completely ignores the first-century worldview. At the other end of the spectrum is the absolute belief in the possibility of biblical miracles. Presuming the historical reliability of the Gospel narratives and therefore a literal reading of scripture, this position endorses the factuality of the biblical miracles as the foundation of faith.[27] Currently there are two variations of this approach. The first affirms that miracles happened then and happen now. The second views the biblical period as a "special revelatory period," and, as such, miracles happened then but not now. This approach is also unacceptable since it rejects the critical reading of scripture endorsed in chapter 5 of this book.

Between these untenable end positions there exist three moderate approaches: the rationalistic explanation, the mythological explanation, and the contextual-kerygmatic (preaching) explanation.[28] Although the rationalistic explanation acknowledges that these marvelous events actually happened, this position claims that such events were misidentified as miracles. Most important, rationalists hold that amazing occurrences can be explained naturally. For example, exorcisms and healings recount psychosomatic cures by Jesus.[29] The feeding of the multitudes presents a lesson in sharing. Walking on water was either an optical illusion, or Jesus stepped on submerged rocks. Regardless of the explanation's plausibility, this approach fails on at least two levels. First, it disregards the historical context of the time and, second, it explains away the religious or theological significance of Jesus' miracles.

The mythological explanation is not interested in natural rationalizations or supernatural interventions. Following the trajectory of David Friedrich Strauss, this approach understands miracle stories as "imaginative forms that expressed the faith of early Christians." Contrary to popular perception, "myth" for scholars of religion is not a negative term that is synonymous with fairy tales or fictional accounts. More important, myth names a literary genre that conveys religious truth.[30] As an indispensable cultural element, myth tells a sacred story about the purpose of human life and the world. Although this approach is a vast improvement over the previous alternatives, it, too, ignores the historical context when it extracts the story from its original setting to discern universal meaning.

This study prefers the contextual-kerygmatic explanation, since it incorporates and implements the thesis of chapter 1 that there is no meaning without context. Consequently, the next section situates the stories of the miracles of Jesus within two concurrent contexts: the larger Greco-Roman context of his day and the specific Jewish context of his time. In addition, this approach acknowledges the kerygmatic, or preaching, function of the Gospel narratives. Because the miracle stories disclose the theological meaning of Jesus, or a Christology, their purpose is not to prove that he is the Christ. As our contextual study reveals, other people in the first century CE performed miracles, so Jesus' deeds did not necessarily distinguish him to the original readers. Written for insiders to express and clarify faith, Jesus' miracles inaugurated the Kingdom of God on earth.

The Greco-Roman and Jewish Contexts

Two reasons compel an investigation into both the Greco-Roman and Jewish contexts to understand the meaning of

Jesus' miracles. One, we must favor the worldview "assumed by both the performer of the miracle and the reporter of the event."[31] Because the meaning of an act in its original context cannot be separated from the larger interpretive framework of the narrative's actor, author, and audience; the cultural presuppositions inherent within that context are essential. Traditionally Jesus scholars have focused almost exclusively on the Jewish setting of the Gospel texts since the actors, authors, and audiences were mostly Jews. Although this attention is warranted (as argued in chapter 4), Jews and early Jesus followers (both Jewish and Gentile) also participated in the Mediterranean Greco-Roman world. Therefore, a thorough examination of Jesus' miracles must address two elements: the "power" at work in these stories (the next section) and the particular contexts of the stories (this section).[32]

Two, we must restrain our own cultural biases by employing critical methods. John Dominic Crossan makes a convincing argument when he writes: "The case is not that [ancient writers] told silly stories and that we got smart enough after the Enlightenment to understand them. The case is that they told profound parables and that we got dumb enough after the Enlightenment to misunderstand them."[33] Thus, a contextual analysis is an important first step both to minimize the imposition of our modern predispositions onto the text and to maximize our knowledge of Jesus' world.

The Greco-Roman Context

At the time of Jesus, the Greco-Roman world was replete with stories of miracles performed by gods, demigods, and specially endowed humans. Contrary to our modern inclination, these miracles were less about their "extraordinariness" and more about their role in experiencing the divine.[34] Contemporary Americans usually emphasize the exceptionality of events and therefore call them miraculous (as the introduction to this chapter illustrates), whereas ancients were more interested in the "revelatory power" of signs than in their remarkable character. This fundamental difference reflects two divergent worldviews.

Radically distinct from our scientific worldview, which interprets the universe as a closed system of matter and energy that operates according to uniform and consistent natural laws, ancients inhabited a world where good and evil spirits interfered in daily events. For them, the world was divided into three levels: the upper world, the underworld, and the earth in the middle. Like a giant domed athletic stadium, the massive firmament arched over the earth, and the "pillars of heaven" were anchored at the extreme ends of the earth. The upper world was the place of the gods and other heavenly beings. The intermediate space between heaven and earth was inhabited by good spirits, while the underworld was the realm of death and chaos, as well as nefarious powers. Because traffic between these various levels of the world was constant, the normal course of events was often attributed to the activity of these forces. Hence, miracles were axiomatic to the ancient world.[35] Following the typology of Wendy Cotter in *The Miracles in Greco-Roman Antiquity*, this section describes a representative figure from her three categories: the gods (Asclepius); human heroes (Apollonius); and Roman rulers (Vespasian).

The most popular and most famous healer in the Greco-Roman world was Asclepius, the god of healing. Born at Epidaurus, Greece (which was the Lourdes of the ancient world), he was the son of the god Apollo and the mortal Coronis. According to the myth, his powers were so great that he returned people from the dead and thereby upset Fate and Hades, brother of Zeus and god of the underworld. Although Zeus had Asclepius killed, he continued to serve humanity "as the compassionate god of healing."

The more than three hundred sanctuaries dedicated to Asclepius functioned like present-day outpatient clinics. While people came to the centers to receive holistic treatment for the

body, mind, and spirit; they ultimately sought a healing encounter with Asclepius as they slept and dreamed. Testimonies
preserved at Epidaurus, which had 160 guest rooms, included
cures for broken limbs, kidney and gall stones, stomach and
throat maladies, extended pregnancies, speech disorders, bald-
ness, tumors, lice, worms, headaches, infertility, tuberculosis,
and blindness. These healing centers permeated the first-century world of the early church.

Apollonius of Tyana in Cappadocia (eastern Turkey today)
is portrayed in two separate biographies as a first-century CE
miracle-worker who, among other miracles, exorcised a youth
of a demon, healed the lame and the blind, and raised a bride
from the dead. However, historians debate the reliability of
both books since Philostratus' *Life of Apollonius* was commis-
sioned by empress Domna Julia early in the third century to re-
fute charges that he was a magician and a fraud, and Hierocles'
biography at the end of the third century deliberately portrayed
Apollonius as a "great sage, miracle-worker, and exorcist" like
Jesus. Nonetheless, the purpose of his miracles was to testify to
his superior wisdom, not his magical powers, thereby confirm-
ing his god-given abilities that even nature honored.[36]

According to Roman historians Tacitus and Suetonius,
Vespasian in 69 CE healed two men, one blind and one lame, in
Alexandria, Egypt, on his way to Rome to assume the imperial
throne after the suicide of Nero. As the first Roman emperor
not from the founding dynasty, these miracles legitimated
his credentials as well as confirmed his authority to govern.
Significant for our study, in the healing of the blind person
Vespasian used spittle, considered a healing agent in the ancient
world. Jesus also employed spittle in healings (Mark 7:31–37
and 8:22–26).[37]

For Wendy Cotter, the myriad testimonies of miracles in
antiquity demonstrate not only the various functions that they
served in first century CE but also the fact that these different

purposes would have been known to the early followers of Jesus.[38]

The Jewish Context

Because Judaism was the primary cultural cradle for early Christian thought on miracles, we must explore the salient roles that the First Testament and rabbinic stories played in the Christian portrait of Jesus the miracle-worker. Two preliminary notes, however, are essential. First, biblical Hebrew has no equivalent word to the English word "miracle." Although the Hebrew words *pele'* and *nifla'ot* are often translated as "wonders" (Exod 3:20 and Josh 3:5) and "miracles" (Ps 78:11), respectively, the two key Hebrew words are *'otot* and *mofetim*, which are usually rendered as "signs" (Exod 4:8 and 1 Kgs 13:3). These providential acts signal God's sovereignty in history. Second, the First Testament "makes no distinction between signs proper and miraculous divine intervention in human history" since the modern concepts of "nature" and "natural law" are unknown in Judaism. Therefore, the world is not a closed system that God occasionally interrupts but the realm of God's continuous and astonishing activity.[39]

Considering both the time span of the Jewish story and the length of the Jewish scriptures, few miracle stories are reported. They appear in two forms: extraordinary acts performed by God on behalf of the people Israel and acts performed by divinely endowed individuals who serve as agents of God.[40] The first category includes events such as the creation (the foundational sign of God's sovereignty), the exodus (Exod 12:51 and Josh 24:5), the conquest of Canaan (Josh 11:20 and 24:13), and the heroics in the book of Daniel (3:17 and 6:26–27). The second category includes but is not limited to biblical prophets like Moses, Elijah, and Elisha. Moses, for example, brought forth water from a rock (Exod 17:6) and carried out most of the plagues against Pharaoh and the Egyptians (Exod 7–11).

Both the prophet Elijah (1 Kgs 17:17–24) and his successor, Elisha (2 Kgs 4:32–37), raised children from the dead. Elisha also fed a multitude (2 Kgs 4:42–44), cured a leper (2 Kgs 5:1–14), and made an ax head float on water (2 Kgs 6:1–7).

Rabbinic literature also contains stories of miraculous deeds. Rabbi Gamaliel calmed a storm, and other rabbis healed the sick and cast out demons.[41] Yet the most famous first-century CE Jewish Palestinian miracle-worker was Rabbi Hanina ben Dosa. According to the Mishnah and the Babylonian Talmud, he healed the sons of Rabbi Gamaliel and Rabbi Johanan ben Zakkai from a distance by prayer, and miraculously provided bread for his wife.[42] Thus, Judaism at the time of Jesus knew miracle-workers both past and present.

Jesus the Miracle-Worker

According to ancient narratives, Jesus was a miracle-worker. In the only non-Christian, first-century source that mentioned Jesus, the Jewish historian Josephus described him in book 18 of *The Antiquities of the Jews* as "the achiever of extraordinary deeds."[43] All of the other first-century sources that reference Jesus were Christian. Therefore, this section briefly examines Jesus the miracle-worker in Christian canonical sources by first providing an overview of the Second Testament's treatment of miracles in general and Jesus' miracles in particular; by investigating the role of Jesus' miracles in the canonical Gospels; by describing the three forms of Jesus' miracles; and then by positing four themes related to Jesus the miracle-worker.

The Second Testament's Treatment of Miracles and Jesus' Miracles

Although Jesus' miracles certainly attracted special attention in the books of the Second Testament, the Gospel writers used the Greek word for "amazing" or "marvel" (*thaumata*) only once (Matt 21:15). The preferred Second Testament terms were "act/deed of power" or "mighty work" (*dunameis*),[44] "signs" (*sēmeia*),[45] "wonders" (*terata*, always used with *sēmeia*),[46] and "works" (*erga*).[47] The cumulative effect of these different terms should cause the modern reader to shift attention away from the "marvelous" or "amazing" dimension of Jesus' miracles to the theological or kerygmatic meaning of these "mighty works" and "signs."[48]

As we discovered in the previous section, there were various miracle-workers in both Greco-Roman and Jewish literature. The same was true for the Second Testament. In addition to Jesus, miracles were performed by God directly;[49] by God through an angel;[50] by apostles;[51] by good disciples, missionaries (such as Paul), and ordinary Christians;[52] by bad, false, and unbelieving disciples;[53] and by Jews and pagans.[54] Because many people in the ancient world performed miracles, Jesus' miracles by themselves did *not* prove his uniqueness.

Surprisingly, the Gospels are the only canonical books that refer directly to Jesus' miracles. Paul, the first canonical author, who wrote his letters in the decade of the 50s, never mentioned Jesus' miracles, although he did affirm the reality of miracles. The book of Acts cites Jesus' miracles indirectly in two passages: Acts 2:22 ("a man attested to you by God with deeds of power, wonders, and signs") and 10:38 ("he went about doing good and healing all who were oppressed by the devil"). Consequently, the remainder of this section concentrates on the miracles of Jesus as recorded in the four Gospels.

The Miracles of Jesus in the Canonical Gospels

For the Gospel writers, Jesus the miracle-worker is neither incidental nor marginal. There are thirty-two different miracle stories of Jesus (not counting summaries) that occur a total of sixty-four times in the four narratives. With the exception of the cursing of the "fig tree" in Matt 21:18–19 and Mark 11:12–14, all of the Gospel miracles benefit people. Unlike some of the Greco-Roman literature, the canonical Gospels do not contain stories in which miraculous power is used vindictively or punitively.[55]

In Mark, the earliest Gospel and the one on which both Matthew and Luke literarily depend, Jesus is an exceptionally powerful miracle-worker. According to Alan Richardson's count, "some 209 verses of a total of 666 (counting up through Mark 16:8) deal directly or indirectly with miracles."[56] Approximately one-third of the Gospel material relates the eighteen miracles and their summaries. Since all of the miracles occur before Jesus begins his journey to Jerusalem except one (Mark 9:14–29), the identity of Mark's pre-passion Jesus is directly linked to miracles. Yet for Mark, Jesus' miracles are less important than his passion and death on the cross, which reveals the true identity of Jesus as the crucified and suffering Son of God (Mark 15:39).

Although the Gospel of Matthew includes more miracles (20) than any other Gospel,[57] Jesus' first miracle story does not occur until the cleansing of the leper in chapter 8.[58] More significant for Matthew, Jesus delivers the Sermon on the Mount in the three previous chapters. Like a literary diptych, or double panel, the ministry of Jesus is one of word and deed.[59] However, unlike Mark, Matthew gives prominence to Jesus the "teacher-preacher" (the new Moses[60]) over Jesus the miracle-worker.

In Luke, Jesus is the eschatological prophet[61] whose nineteen miracles disclose his source of power as well as the arrival of the Kingdom of God. After Jesus' temptation and the devil's departure in 4:1–13, Jesus in verse 14 is "filled with the power of the Spirit" and in verse 21 is confirmed as a prophet. Luke's version of the Beelzebul controversy story emphatically makes both points,[62] when Jesus claims in 11:20, "But if it is by the finger of God that I cast out the demons, then the kingdom of God has come to you." Not only does Luke add the phrase "the finger of God" to underscore Jesus' true source of power, but the coming of the Kingdom is already manifest in Jesus' mighty deeds.[63]

In contrast to the Synoptic Gospels (Matthew, Mark, and Luke), the Gospel of John not only has far fewer "signs" at seven,[64] but they point beyond themselves to the true identity of Jesus and not to the coming of the Kingdom. Although John 20:30 and 21:24–25 mention "many other signs" that Jesus did, the seven "are written so that you may come to believe that Jesus is the Messiah, the Son of God, and that through believing you may have life in his name" (20:31). For John, these seven deeds serve as "signs of the greater sign." That is, the seven signs progress in magnitude until they reach "a crescendo in the raising of Lazarus." The final sign then "prefigures the great sign of the death and resurrection" of Jesus. Thus, the seven signs in "the first half of the Gospel reveal the *identity* of Jesus,"[65] as well as the new reality of eternal life now available (John 5:24–25).[66]

The Three Forms of Jesus' Miracles

Most scholars divide the miracle stories of Jesus into three different forms: nature miracles, exorcisms, and healings. According to Robert Funk's count, there are seven nature miracles, six exorcisms, and nineteen healings.[67]

Nature miracles, which only the disciples witness, can be subdivided into those that demonstrate power over nature—like the stilling of the storm[68]—and those that involve feedings—like the multiplication of loaves and fishes for 5,000.[69] Because ancients viewed the world in three levels, the waters of the sea often represented the powers of chaos which threatened God's cosmos.[70] To first-century readers or hearers, Jesus' rebuke of the wind and command of the sea to "be still" (Mark 4:39) would have reminded them of God's initial act of creation as recounted in Ps 104:6b–7: "The waters stood above the mountains. At your rebuke they flee; at the sound of your thunder they take to flight." Hence, the answer to the disciples' question, "Who then is this, that even the wind and the sea obey him?" (Mark 4:41b), was Jesus, the Lord of creation.

Jesus' feeding miracles were equally evocative since they looked forward to the Last Supper as well as looked backward to the exodus. Paralleling the fourfold verb action that Jesus used at the Last Supper—take, bless, break, and give (Mark 14:22–25)—Jesus fed the multitudes using the same sequence of words (Mark 6:41–44).[71] Imitating God, who fed the Hebrews in the wilderness (Exod 16), Jesus fed the people and thereby prefigured the "messianic banquet" in the future kingdom (Mark 14:25). The nature miracles of Jesus intentionally identified Jesus with God by replicating divine acts of creation and sustenance and by invoking images of the future Kingdom of God.

Both the stories of Jesus' exorcisms and healings followed a set pattern: (1) the illness or situation was described; (2) the technique or process was told; and (3) the cure was demonstrated to the satisfaction of the spectators.[72] Because exorcisms are a subset of healing stories, they are treated together. Two themes were common to these stories. First, readers learned that the time of the evil powers was at an end and the time of the Kingdom of God was at hand. When the Gerasene demons saw Jesus, they shouted, "What have you to do with us, Son of God? Have you come here to torment us before the time?" They not only recognized the power of Jesus but also acknowledged the timeline. In Luke 10:17–18, the disciples exclaimed, "Lord, in your name even the demons submit to us!" And Jesus replied, "I watched Satan fall from heaven like a flash of lightning." Jesus' healings and exorcisms announced the end of Satan's rule and the beginning of God's reign on earth.[73]

Second, healing miracles and exorcisms revealed Jesus' identity. When John the Baptist in Matt 11:2–6, via his followers, asked Jesus, "Are you the one who is to come, or are we to wait for another?" Jesus answered with a litany of his healing miracles. Then he concluded with these poignant words, "And blessed is anyone who takes no offense at me." To understand the miracles of Jesus, one must first understand Jesus himself. Miracles by themselves do not validate Jesus as the Son of God. The key is the alleged source. For Jesus' enemies, it was Beelzebul, the ruler of the demons (Matt 12:24), but to his followers it was "the Spirit of God" (12:28).[74]

Four Themes

Our examination of Jesus the miracle-worker has yielded four important and interrelated themes. One, Jesus' miracles produced controversy and conflict. The controversy, however, did not focus on his ability to perform miracles. That was given. Even false prophets and messianic pretenders could work miracles (Matt 7:15–23; 24:24). According to the Gospels, Jesus just did them better than anyone else.[75] The real controversy was the source of his power: Was it from the devil or from God? For these stories, the ultimate conflict was between the Kingdom of Satan and the Kingdom of God. Each of Jesus' miracles can be interpreted, therefore, as a single episode in the ongoing life-and-death power struggle between the forces of evil and the forces of good. And God, the creator and source of all that is good (Gen 1:4, 10, 12, 18, 25, 31), empowered Jesus.

Two, Jesus' miracles raised the question of his identity. In the very first miracle story in the Gospel of Mark, the "unclean spirit" recognized Jesus and cried out, "What have you to do with us, Jesus of Nazareth? Have you come to destroy us? I know who you are, the Holy One of God" (Mark 1:24). Jesus' first miracle in Mark introduces the two themes of conflict and identity since they are inevitable and inseparable—two sides of the same coin. There is conflict because Jesus is of God, and

God opposes evil in the form of illness and disease, hunger and demonic possession.

Three, Jesus' miracles were prophetic acts which symbolized the arrival of the Kingdom of God on earth. Immediately after Jesus' baptism, which identified him as God's "Son, the Beloved" (Mark 1:11), and after Jesus' temptation, which identified Satan as his adversary (Mark 1:13), Jesus began his Galilean ministry with these words, "The time is fulfilled, and the kingdom of God has come near" (Mark 1:15). "In the kingdom there will be no demons, and so Jesus casts out demons; in the kingdom there will be no disease, and so Jesus heals the sick; in the kingdom there will be no more death, and so Jesus raises the dead."[76] As signs of God's transformative powers at work in the world, Jesus' miracles signified the presence and power of divine love. Miracles for Jesus were inextricably and inescapably linked to the message of the Kingdom of God: "Cure the sick . . . and say to them, 'The kingdom of God has come near to you'" (Luke 10:9).

Four, Jesus' miracles were prologue, not proof. Because the accomplishments of other miracle-workers stippled the pages of ancient literature, the performance of miracles by Jesus did not make him unique or divine. When this interpretive context is ignored, the tendency for moderns is to fixate on the "extraordinariness" of the action and not on its kerygmatic meaning. That is, the "sign function" of miracles—their ability to point beyond themselves to something more—is lost. To limit the miracle to the stupendous stilling of the water, or to the phenomenal healing of the sick, or to the fantastic feeding of the multitude, is to see only an awesome act conducted by yet another miracle-worker. Jesus is reduced to "see what he can *do*." The more important discernment is to "see *who Jesus is*."

Although wondrous deeds are notable, their theological import is more significant since they link the tangible to the transcendent. Like the incarnation, which paradoxically holds together the human and the divine, miracles as signs hold together the physical and the metaphysical. To the eyes of faith, miracles are less about the performance and more about the performer. As doors to the sacred, the remarkable sign-acts of Jesus point beyond themselves to the transformative and redemptive love of God in him available in the ordinariness of daily life.[77] Because faith as trust includes "those who have not seen and yet have come to believe" (John 20:29), Jesus in all four Gospels refused to confirm his identity by doing miracles on demand.[78] His miracles functioned as prologue to the reign of God on earth, and not as proof of his divinity.

Implications for the Religious Life

Now that *the church's sixth deadly secret* is exposed—Jesus' miracles are prologue, not proof—at least three implications follow for the religious life.

First, the church must distinguish between fact and faith. Many Christians equate faith in Jesus with belief in the historical credibility of Jesus' miracles. Faith for them means at most "believing the unbelievable" and at least making the leap more reasonable. Yet people in scripture believed that Jesus was a miracle-worker and did not confess him as Lord and Savior. The truth of the Gospel, therefore, is not tethered to a cosmology that endorses spirits and demons. Today we are not forced to choose between two competing paradigms—an ancient one that believed in miracles regardless of one's religion and a modern one that believes miracles are violations of the natural law. We must not only recognize the differences between these two worldviews but also must respect the language of miracles.[79] For first-century Christians, miracles were a familiar literary vehicle to communicate an experience of the holy in Jesus. Today this unfamiliar language perplexes us, since it sounds irrational and irresponsible. The result is that skeptics mock cynically and believers retort defensively. Both reactions misinterpret the nature and purpose of kerygmatic, or preaching, language.[80] When faith fixates on the factuality of Jesus' miracles, the intellectual offense of the miracle replaces the theological offense of the cross.[81]

Second, the church must integrate the tangible and the transcendent.[82] When we mistakenly impose the modern definition of "miracle" (a violation of natural law by a supernatural agent) onto Jesus' actions, we restrict God's presence and power to the extraordinary, as well as promote ethical dilemmas. That is, if God primarily resides outside of the natural world and is invoked only to explain what science cannot, "God of the gaps" theology[83] reduces divine activity to an ever shrinking domain. Moreover, this way of thinking assumes that God is present only on rare occasions. God is "not here" more than God is "here." Thus, the objectification of miracles perpetuates ethical questions: Why does God intervene so rarely? Why does God heal only a few? What kind of love stays inactive more than active? When "miracles" are only seen as exceptional events, their sign-function is lost and God's intentions are misunderstood. The church must reimagine the relationship of the tangible and the transcendent.

Third, the church must never forget that Jesus' miracles are prologue, not proof. The good news of the Gospel is that God in Christ is reconciling the world. This theological truth is not subject to empirical verification or historical investigation. As kerygmatic sign-acts, Jesus' miracles witness to the Gospel when they invite us to see beyond the ordinary and to have faith—to trust—in the extraordinary one in our midst. In the words of William Sloane Coffin, "Miracles do not a messiah make. But a messiah can do miracles."[84]

7

The Church's Seventh Deadly Secret

My Religion and God Are Violent

This chapter reveals *the church's seventh deadly secret*: "My religion and God are violent." Although churchgoers pray for peace on earth as it is in heaven, Christianity has contributed to the world's carnage. Because the church can no longer remain silent about its role in perpetuating violence, this chapter investigates this topic in four steps: first, it presents an explanation of the relationship of violence and human identity; second, it explores violence against the neighbor; third, it examines violence by God; and fourth, it posits implications for the Christian life.

From the pulpit to the pew, Christians affirm that God is love (1 John 4:8b). From Sunday School to church camp, Christians praise Jesus as the "Prince of Peace" (Isa 9:6). Even football fans know that "God so loved the world that he gave his only Son" (John 3:16). Although faith, hope, and love are the core characteristics of Christianity, the "greatest of these is love" (1 Cor 13:13).

Love and peace are twin traits of the Christian life. Made in the image of God, humanity is created to love God (Deut 6:5) and your neighbor as yourself (Lev 19:18b).[1] And peace on earth as it is in heaven (Rev 21:1–4) is our polar star.

Yet war is common and constant. James Hillman in *A Terrible Love of War* estimates that there have been 14,600 wars in the 5,600 years of recorded history, or two to three wars per year.[2] Chris Hedges in *What Every Person Should Know about*

War calculates that over the past 3,400 years humans have been entirely at peace only 268 years, or 8 percent of human history. Moreover, between 1900 and 1990, 43 million soldiers have died in wars, while in the same period 62 million civilians have been killed. However, from 1990 to 2000, civilian deaths accounted for 75–90 percent of all war deaths.[3] The chaplain in Bertolt Brecht's play *Mother Courage and Her Children* observes, "I say, you can't be sure the war will *ever* end. Of course it may have to pause occasionally—for breath. . . . [War] has really nothing to worry about, it can look forward to a prosperous future. . . . I'd say there's peace even in war, war has its islands of peace. . . . War is like love, it always finds a way. Why *should* it end?"[4]

Religions have ravaged the globe in the name of their deity. Blaise Pascal (1623–1662), the French mathematician and devout Catholic, was correct when he remarked that "Men never do evil so completely and cheerfully, as when they do it from religious conviction."[5]

Regrettably, Christianity in the name of God and Jesus has contributed to the world's carnage. Under the banner of the cross and with the battle cry of *Deus Vult* (God wills it), Christian Europe crusaded for two hundred years against the Muslim infidels in Palestine. Saint Bernard of Clairvaux (1090–1153) exalted the soldiers by preaching, "He serves Christ when he kills. He serves himself when he is killed."[6] During the Protestant Reformation of the sixteenth century, Christian zeal promoted Roman Catholic and Protestant wars, as well as Protestant-on-Protestant wars.[7] Martin Luther (1483–1546), the founder of Protestantism, defended violence when he wrote: "The very fact that the sword has been instituted by God to punish the evil, protect the good, and preserve peace [Rom 13:1–4; 1 Pet. 2:13] is powerful and sufficient proof that war and killing . . . have been instituted by God."[8] During World War I, German soldiers marched into battle with the assurance that *Gott mit uns* (God is with us), while at the same time the bishop of London urged his countrymen to "Kill them . . . to kill the good as well as the bad, to kill the young men as well as the old."[9]

Yet even more disturbing than the brutality and butchery either sponsored or endorsed by institutional religion is the linkage between violence and the God of the Bible. In Exod 15:3, "The Lord is a warrior." In Deut 20:16, the rules of warfare are clear: "But as for the towns of these people that the Lord your God is giving you as an inheritance, you must not let anything that breathes remain alive." This unvarnished and unapologetic affirmation of violence in the name of God[10] is also found in the Second Testament.

> Then I saw an angel standing in the sun, and with a loud voice he called to all the birds that fly in midheaven, "Come, gather for the great supper of God, to eat the flesh of kings, the flesh of captains, the flesh of the mighty, the flesh of horses and their riders—flesh of all, both free and slave, both small and great" . . . And the rest were killed by the sword of the rider on the horse, the sword that came from his mouth; and all the birds were gorged with their flesh. (Rev 19:17–21)

Because of 9/11, few people now dispute the assertion that religion is the most powerful and the most pervasive force on earth—for both good and evil. President Barack Obama in his Nobel Peace Prize acceptance speech on December 10, 2009, in Oslo, Norway, acknowledged this ambivalence when he stated:

> Most dangerously, we see [this ambivalence] in the way that religion is used to justify the murder of innocents by those who have distorted and defiled the great religion of Islam. . . . These extremists are not the first to kill in the name of God; the cruelties of the Crusaders are amply recorded . . . Such a warped view of religion is not just

incompatible with the concept of peace, but the purpose of faith—for the one rule that lies at the heart of every major religion is that we do unto others as we would have them do unto us.[11]

Christians should not be surprised, therefore, by the pronouncement of the "new atheists"[12] that "religion poisons everything."[13] According to Christopher Hitchens in *God Is Not Great*, the Bible not only contains "a warrant for trafficking in humans, for ethnic cleansing, for slavery, for bride-price, and for indiscriminate massacre,"[14] but the history of the Abrahamic religions (Judaism, Christianity, and Islam) is an untold story of misery and death.

Critical of Hitchens' one-sided critique, Christians seldom indict religion for crimes against humanity. Yet we should at least listen to his conclusion.

> If I cannot definitely prove that the usefulness of religion is in the past, and that its foundational books are transparent fables, and that it is a man-made imposition, and that it has been an enemy of science and inquiry, and that it has subsisted largely on lies and fears, and been the accomplice of ignorance and guilt as well as of slavery, genocide, racism, and tyranny, I can most certainly claim that *religion is now fully aware of these criticisms.*[15]

But are we? Jon Stewart of the *Daily Show* joked that religion was "a powerful healing force in a world torn apart—by religion."[16] Christians easily affirm the former, but do we admit the latter? T.S. Eliot quipped that "Human kind cannot bear too much reality."[17] If true, the Christian drug of choice is either fantasy that imagines the romantic instead of the real, or hypocrisy that preaches what it will not practice, or both.

It is time, however, for intellectual and moral honesty. Christians must confess *the church's seventh deadly secret* that my religion and God are violent. Because the church can no longer remain silent about its complicit and culpable role in perpetuating violence, this chapter investigates this topic in four steps: first, it presents an explanation of our format and the relationship of violence and human identity; second, it explores violence against the neighbor; third, it examines violence by God; and fourth, it posits implications for the Christian life.

Violence and Human Identity

Before we begin our examination of religious violence against the neighbor and violence by God, a brief explanation of our format is necessary. Two reasons justify bifurcating our treatment of violence. First, both testaments command dual loyalties from humanity—love of God and love of neighbor. In the Hebrew Bible, the Ten Commandments specify proper conduct toward the divine (the first four commandments, Exod 20:4–11) and toward the neighbor (the last six commandments, Exod 20:12–17). According to the Synoptic Gospels (Matt 22:34–40, Mark 12:28–31, and Luke 10:25–27), Jesus concurs when he recites from the First Testament that "love the Lord your God" (Deut 6:5) and "love your neighbor as yourself" (Lev 19:18b) are the two greatest commandments. Important for our format, a person's attitudes and actions are directed toward two specific others—the transcendent God and the earthly neighbor.

Second, the formation of human identity involves the self and others. Human beings are constituted by subjectivity (awareness of the self in the world) and intersubjectivity (awareness of the reciprocal interactions of the self and others in the world). Consciousness of one's self and one's relationship to others is, therefore, prerequisite for human identity.

Regina Schwartz in *The Curse of Cain*[18] incorporates these ideas into her thesis that the origins of violence are located in the act of identity formation, which includes one's relationship to others. Because the creation of the self (either individual or collective identity) requires distinguishing and separating oneself from the other (boundary making), it lays the foundation for violence to occur. Yet more basic than the violence that we either project or inflict on the other is the potential for violence inherent in the sheer acknowledgment of the other. Since the act of identity formation is a negative for the very reason that the other is labeled as not one of us, the outsider is regarded as a threat to the insider. The awareness of the other produces insecurity because the other by definition resides on the wrong side of the boundary line. Perceived as wanting to get in, the outsider creates fear for the insider. The delicate balance between defense and danger usually tips in favor of violence toward the other due to the historical factors of ethnicity, nationalism, race, gender, and religion.[19]

Accepting the above insights about the formation of human identity, this chapter presumes that Christian identity is shaped by an adherent's reciprocal interactions with both the neighbor and God.

Violence against the Neighbor

Violence against one's neighbor happens very early in the Genesis narrative. Soon after Adam and Eve are expelled from the garden, their son Cain, a farmer, kills his brother Abel, a shepherd. The Bible recognizes that civilization starts with fratricide and that we, the descendants of Cain, continue to murder our brothers and sisters.

This section on violence against the neighbor addresses three concerns: one, a theological explanation for the possibility of sin[20] in a perfect world; two, an interpretation of the story of Cain and Abel; and three, a brief description of the three classic Christian responses to war.

The Possibility of Sin

Before we can offer an interpretation of the story of Cain and Abel, we must address two basic questions that arise from the creation and fall narratives as told in the first three chapters of the Book of Genesis: How did Adam and Eve sin in the perfect world of the Garden of Eden? And why did God permit it? Traditional Christian responses avoid two extremes—the tragic view of the world which locates evil in God and thereby denies the essential goodness of God, and the dualistic view of the world which posits a good god and an evil god and thereby denies monotheism. Instead, Christianity affirms a single, loving God *and* the Adamic myth[21] (a "truthful" story about the interior life of humanity), which describes the creation of humanity as finite, free beings, as well as the inclusion of a tragic element in the world.

As the model story of both the creation and the fall of humanity, the Adamic myth is foundational for Christian theology. Created in the image of God (Gen 1:26–27), humans possess freedom, like God, but are limited, unlike God. There exists then a qualitative distinction between the divine creator and the human creature. According to twentieth-century theologian Paul Tillich, humans are characterized by "self-transcending finitude" or "finite freedom."[22]

The story of the fall of Adam and Eve can be interpreted as God drawing an ethical line on the ground and forbidding humans to cross it: "You shall not eat of the fruit of the tree that is in the middle of the garden, nor shall you touch it, or you shall die" (Gen 3:3). Regrettably, the first humans disobey God's command and their punishment is expulsion from the garden: "So when the woman saw that the tree was good for food, and that it was a delight to the eyes, and that the tree was to be desired to make one wise, she took of its fruit and ate; and she also gave some to her husband, who was with her, and he ate. . . . [Therefore] the Lord God sent him forth from the garden of Eden" (Gen 3:6 and 23a).

Paramount for theology, the story narrates both the rise of human consciousness and the fall of humanity from perfection.

In seven succinct verses (Gen 3:1–7), humanity transitions from "dreaming innocence," or a state of pre-reflective naivete, to self-consciousness: "For God knows that when you eat of it [fruit from the tree] your eyes will be opened, and you will be like God, knowing good and evil. . . . Then the eyes of both were opened, and they knew that they were naked" (Gen 3:5 and 7a).

A careful reading of the story discloses, however, that God does not tell the whole truth. God prohibits eating of the fruit from the tree of the knowledge of good and evil because to eat it is to die that day (Gen 2:17). Yet death is not immediate. Unlike the other animals, humans are now aware of their eventual demise. On behalf of all people, Adam and Eve select moral knowledge (morality) over eternal life (eternity). Humans cannot have both. That belongs to God alone. Therefore, the banishment from the garden is less about divine punishment and more about human preference. Eternal life is rejected in favor of self-determination (volition) and self-conscious awareness of our human condition ("they were naked").[23]

The possibility of sin, which concurrently links human disobedience of God's command and the rise of human consciousness, results from the fragility and vulnerability of the interior structure of finite free beings. For humanity, anxiety locates the tension between freedom and finitude, and therefore the likelihood of defiance. Although anxiety is not sin, it functions as one of the two preconditions of sin. Temptation is the other prerequisite. The serpent both symbolizes and functions as the external element of the narrative by which the story builds into the world a structural bias toward sin. This inclusion not only balances the individual component (anxiety) with a social component (the serpent), but it also introduces the tragic element into the story.[24] The possibility of sin is present but not enacted. The serpent's enticement that "you will be like God, knowing good and evil" (Gen 3:5) activates within Eve the desire to be infinite and thereby overreach her finitude. Although all animals have limits, only humans are both conscious of their finite capabilities and yet try to transcend them.

Theologically the possibility of sin is endemic to all humans. The decision of Adam and Eve to eat the fruit, which activates human consciousness, is the same decision that each and every individual makes. Hence, sin is universal. Anxiety locates the interior feature of possibility, while temptation pinpoints the exterior feature of activation. On the one hand, sin is inevitable, since all humans choose self-consciousness, but, on the other hand, sin is not necessary, since God neither creates nor commands it. What is significant for Christian theology is that God is not responsible for sin in the world. However, authentic relationships with God and with neighbor require genuinely free decisions. Like faith and love, sin emanates from freedom.

As the story of the fall reports, a prohibition stimulates the human desire to transgress our limitations as finite free creatures. The balance between finitude and freedom is precarious. Refusal to acknowledge our finitude produces idolatry (elevating a finite object to infinite value) and refusal to exercise our freedom of responsibility produces sloth (spiritual or emotional laziness). The former (idol making) explains the sins of racism and sexism in the world (the false elevation of one human trait over all the others), while the latter (forfeiture of obligation) explains the passivity and apathy of ordinary people who either indifferently ignore violence in their midst or silently participate in the structures of oppression.[25] After Adam and Eve select morality over eternity, humanity must continually decide whether to obey God's commandment not to murder (Exod 20:13 and Deut 5:17).

The Cain and Abel Story

> Now Abel was a keeper of sheep, and Cain a tiller of the ground. In the course of time Cain brought to the Lord

an offering of the fruit of the ground, and Abel for his part
brought of the firstlings of his flock, their fat portions. And
the Lord had regard for Abel and his offering, but for Cain
and his offering he had no regard. So Cain was very angry,
and his countenance fell. The Lord said to Cain, "Why are
you angry, and why has your countenance fallen? If you do
well, will you not be accepted? And if you do not do well,
sin is lurking at the door." . . . Cain said to his brother Abel,
"Let us go out to the field." And when they were in the field,
Cain rose up against his brother Abel, and killed him. (Gen
4:2b–8)

For whatever reason,[26] God rejects Cain's offering and then
inquires why he is angry. Because Cain suffers God's judgment
before he kills his brother, many people want to know what
kind of God arbitrarily privileges one offering over another. For
Regina Schwartz in *The Curse of Cain*, the answer is a mono-
theistic God who demands loyalty to only one deity,[27] but who
favors only one brother. In this story, she claims, there are no
multiple allegiances either directed toward God or initiated by
God. "Cain kills in the rage of his exclusion. And the circle is
vicious: because Cain is outcast, Abel is murdered and Cain is
cast out."[28] As heirs of Cain, we, too, live in a world of insiders
and outsiders, boundary makers and trespassers.

For Schwartz, the tragic principle of scarcity is Cain's legacy
to his progeny. That is, scarcity is encoded in the Bible in the
form of "Oneness" (one land, one people, one nation, one
baptism, one faith) and, most important, in the concept of
monotheism (one God). Exclusivity spawns violence.[29]

Narrated through the classic stories of sibling rivalries (Cain
and Abel, Jacob and Esau[30]), "not enough to go around"
produces destruction and death. And one of the most lethal
forms of collective identity is nationalism. Because God favors
ancient Israel ("you shall be my treasured possession out of all
the peoples"[31]), violence against the other is sanctioned ("You

shall annihilate them"[32]). Although extermination is a persistent subtext of the First Testament, conversion is its counterpart in the Second Testament. Both reactions to the other are grounded in and justified by the principle of scarcity which characterizes the one God of the Bible.[33]

The Three Classic Christian Responses to War

According to the biblical story, the first act of violence occurred when brother killed brother. Nothing has changed. Evils perpetrated against the brother-neighbor in the name of religion in general and Christianity in particular are etched in the pages of human history. Under the sign of the cross, crusades were fought against Muslim infidels in Palestine, and pogroms[34] were waged against Jews at home. With theological justification, Africans and Native Americans were enslaved and eliminated. By church decree, women were excluded from ecclesial leadership and even burned at the stake. Because of humanity's broken relationship with God and the subsequent hate and hurt inflicted upon the neighbor, three responses to war have emerged in Christendom: pacifism, just war, and crusade.[35]

For the first three centuries of the church, Christians were primarily a counter-culture, antiwar sect. Obeying Jesus' Sermon on the Mount to "love your enemies and pray for those who persecute you" (Matt 5:44) and imitating his "way of the cross," most Jesus followers were pacifists. For example, Christian writers emphasized the incompatibility of warfare with (most) biblical teachings. Origen of Alexandria (185–254) admonished, "We Christians do not become fellow soldiers with the Emperor, even if he presses for this."[36] Tertullian (160–220), the first great Latin theologian, was unambiguous when he stated that "Christ [in the garden] in disarming Peter ungirt every soldier."[37] Furthermore, Tertullian inquired, "If we are enjoined to love our enemies, whom have we to hate? If injured we are forbidden to retaliate. Who then can suffer injury at our hands?"[38] Clement of Alexandria (150–215) concurred when he explained to the non-Christian, "If you enroll as one of God's people, heaven is your country and God your lawgiver. And what are his laws? . . . Thou shalt not kill. . . . Thou shalt love thy neighbor as thyself. To him that strikes thee on the one cheek, turn also the other."[39] However, with the conversion of Constantine and the eventual Christianization of the empire in the fourth century, the pacifist tradition was suppressed but not eliminated.

With the victory of Constantine in 312 at Rome's Milvian Bridge after his vision in which Christ appeared and commanded him to carry the sign of the cross into battle, the church became a steward of the state. Nonviolence was no longer a viable political or theological option. Not only was Christ's cross converted into Constantine's sword, but the church was also reduced to a sanctuary for souls. From then on, the emperor claimed the physical bodies of the citizens, while the church managed their spiritual salvation.

Lamenting the necessity of war, Augustine of Hippo (354–430) formulated what is now called the doctrine of "just war." Refined by Thomas Aquinas (1225–1274) and endorsed by mainstream Protestant Reformation theologians, the purpose of a "just war" was to wage war only out of necessity and with the intention to restore peace. Traditionally four criteria must be met in order to conduct a "just war": "(i) it must be proclaimed by lawful authority; (ii) the cause must be just; (iii) the belligerents should have a rightful intention, to advance good or avoid evil; (iv) the war must be fought by proper means."[40] Additional measures, which have been added over the years, include: "(v) action should be against the guilty; (vi) the innocent should not suffer; (vii) war must be undertaken as a last resort; (viii) there must be a reasonable chance of success."[41] Because these criteria are not grounded in specific Christian teachings and are not easy to apply in particular situations to determine if a war is actually just, they have served in practice to solidify the power of church and state against any perceived "unjust" threat. In short, the "just war" doctrine allows church leaders to preach nonaggression while concurrently supporting violence. If your goals are just (as you define them), then violence is sanctioned.

Although renounced today as barbaric and a betrayal of Christ, the doctrine of a "crusade" or "holy war" to recover the Holy Land from Muslim occupation was ratified by the church of the Middle Ages. The ecclesial authorities not only approved violence against God's enemies but also rewarded participants. In a sermon preached by Pope Urban II at the Council of Clermont on November 27, 1095, he promised remission of sins and indulgences to those who went on crusades.[42] After two hundred years of carnage and cruelty,[43] the war machinery of feudal Europe was finally exhausted and the possibility of liberating the Holy Land was decisively thwarted.

It is probably fair to say that the overwhelming majority of contemporary Christians support the position that war is regrettable but necessary, and therefore some version of a "just war" theory is desirable.[44] Pacifism, the practice of the early church until Constantine became emperor, was preserved in monastic communities. It reappeared most prominently in the person of Francis of Assisi (1181/2–1226) and in the Reformation historic peace churches of the Quakers (The Religious Society of Friends), the Church of the Brethren, the Mennonites, and the Amish. The concept of a crusade, or holy war, is no longer found in Christianity.

Violence by God

Because human identity is shaped and sustained by the reciprocal interactions of the self and others, Christian identity is, too. Not only are Christians formed by their interactions with other Christians, but they are especially determined by their

interactions with God. Thus, the church's fundamental theological inquiry for the issue of religion and violence concerns
the nature of God: "What is God like?"[45]

For most people in the pew, God is the Supreme Being who
loves and cherishes the world. In the First Testament, God creates the world, rescues the Hebrew people from bondage, and
sends the prophets to preach peace and justice. In the Second
Testament, God in Jesus heals the sick, feeds the hungry, forgives sin, and reconciles the world. In the words of Ps 27:1, the
person of faith rejoices, "The Lord is my light and my salvation;
whom shall I fear? The Lord is the stronghold of my life; of
whom shall I be afraid?" Yet the Christian recites every Sunday
the "Lord's Prayer" that includes this line, "and lead us not
into temptation, but deliver us from evil" (Matt 6:13, KJV).
The God who creates and cares for the world also possesses the
power to tempt us and even destroy us—and comes perilously
close in the flood story (Gen 7)!

If human beings are made in the image of God (Gen 1:26–
27) and human beings maim and murder one another, does
that mean that God is violent and that we are just imitating
God? Although the traditional Christian answer is that humans
are sinful and violent because of their fall from perfection (see
the section above, "The Possibility of Sin"), we must explore
more thoroughly the God who is portrayed in the Bible. Do
Christians worship the God who loves the peacemaker and the
enemy, or the God who loves vengeance and violence? This
section investigates the relationship of religion and violence by
briefly examining both the violent God of the First Testament
and the violent God of the Second Testament, and then concludes by positing two Christian responses.

The Violent God of the First Testament

The biblical God of the patriarchs and the prophets is frequently
characterized as irenic—a promoter of peace. According to Isa

2:3–4, God is the professor of peace: "'Come, let us go up to the mountain of the Lord, to the house of the God of Jacob; that he may teach us his ways and that we may walk in his paths.' . . . [They] shall beat their swords into plowshares, and their spears into pruning hooks; nation shall not lift up sword against nation, neither shall they learn war any more."

Although this passage was quoted at the signing of the Camp David Peace Accords on September 17, 1978, two traits more commonly associated with the God of the First Testament are belligerence and bloodthirstiness. God drowns almost all of creation and humanity in a flood (Gen 6:13; 7:19–23), demands human sacrifice but recants (Gen 22:2, 9b–12), commands people to execute children who curse their parents (Lev 20:1–2a, 9), orders the murder of all men, women, and children after battle (Deut 20:16–17a), and sends imperial armies to slaughter sinful people (Isa 13:3–17). According to Raymund Schwager, "there are six hundred passages of explicit violence in the Hebrew Bible, one thousand verses where God's own violent actions of punishment are described, a hundred passages where Yahweh expressly commands others to kill people, and several stories where God irrationally kills or tries to kill for no apparent reason (for example, Exod 4:24–26)."[46]

The most gruesome example of violence by God in the First Testament is the practice of the "ban" (in Hebrew *ḥerem*) at the conclusion of a "holy war." The phrase "utterly destroy" is found in Num 21:1–3; Deut 2:30–35; 3:3–7; and 7:1–2; and Josh 6:17–21; 10:28; and 11:10–11 to describe the consecration of war booty that belongs to God. Because the purpose was not revenge but sacrificial ritual, the defeated peoples and their animals, as well as their possessions, were regarded as gifts for God. Etymologically, *ḥerem* "belongs in the semantic field of the holy, hallowed, which in fact justifies the translation 'consecration to destruction.'"[47] Thus, the "ban" is the negative side of the "holy," where the captured peoples, animals, and objects were ritually sanctified and dedicated to God. Although the practice of the "ban" was not unique to the Hebrew people,[48] war to capture the Promised Land was holy business for Israel, which means in Hebrew, "El [God] fights."[49]

As narrated in 1 Sam 15:2–3, ethnic cleansing was ordered by God: "Thus says the Lord of hosts, . . . 'Now go and attack Amalek, and utterly destroy all that they have; do not spare them, but kill both man and woman, child and infant, ox and sheep, camel and donkey.'" Not only does God command violence but God also seems to appreciate human sacrifice. According to Deut 7:1–6, two factors justify this type of violence: (1) Israel must worship only one god (monotheism) and (2) the land is given to Israel by divine decree. God's chosen people and covenant partner are given the command to slaughter the Canaanites in order to conquer the land. One god, one people, and one land are the prerequisites for divine violence.

Whether we accept these texts as historically factual or ideological fiction, the ethical implication is the same—God authorizes genocide. The collective identity of the Hebrew people is defined negatively vis-à-vis the indigenous people of the land and positively vis-à-vis a belligerent and bloodthirsty God.[50]

The Violent God of the Second Testament

For many churchgoers, the bellicose God of the First Testament is the Jewish God, while the irenic God of the Second Testament is the Christian God. They are quick to declare the God of Jesus as peaceful and merciful. According to the Gospel of Matthew, Jesus blessed the peacemakers (5:9), instructed followers to turn the other cheek if someone strikes you (5:39), and told his followers to "love your enemies and pray for those who persecute you" (5:44).

Yet the early church renounced Marcion,[51] who believed in two different gods—a wrathful, legalistic god of the Jewish scriptures and a loving, gracious god of the Gospels. According to Christian tradition, there is no violent god for the Jews and no nonviolent god for Christians. The two sides of the one God exist side by side. Although the Christian canon contains two testaments, it witnesses to one and the same God. The God of Abraham and Sarah is also the God of Mary and Jesus.

Unknown to most Christians, the redemptive drama of the Second Testament starts and ends with violence, and a heinous act of brutality locates its central act. On the very first pages of the Second Testament after the infant Jesus is born, Herod slaughters the innocent children of Bethlehem under the age of two (Matt 2:16–18). On the very last pages of the Second Testament, a great war occurs where the enemies of God are thrown into the fiery lake or killed by the sword (Rev 19:20–21). And the crucifixion of Jesus—a bloody human sacrifice—atones for the sin of humanity (Heb 10:12–14). Violence, either sponsored by God or subsequent to God's action, frames and defines the salvation history of the Second Testament.

The most graphic illustration of these dueling images of God (nonviolent and violent) in the Second Testament is the twin portraits of Jesus—the incarnational First Coming of Jesus (Jesus of the Gospels)[52] and the apocalyptic Second Coming of Jesus (Jesus of Revelation).[53] On Palm Sunday, the incarnational Jesus rides into Jerusalem on a donkey to inaugurate a nonviolent demonstration,[54] while at the end of history the apocalyptic Jesus leads a violent attack on a war horse.[55] Even more dramatic, the nonviolent, slaughtered Lamb of God Jesus on the cross[56] morphs into the violent, slaughterer Lamb-Lion Jesus at the Second Coming who executes wrath and wages war.[57] Moreover, the apocalyptic divine warrior Jesus opens the scrolls and unleashes on earth the infamous Four Horsemen of the Apocalypse (conquest, war, famine, and death).[58] Finally, the caring Jesus, who feeds the hungry, heals the sick, and hosts the Last Supper,[59] is transformed at the end of the Second

Testament into a conquering Christ who prepares a gruesome banquet of God.

> Then I saw an angel standing in the sun, and with a loud voice he called to all the birds that fly in midheaven, "Come, gather for the great supper of God, to eat the flesh of kings, the flesh of captains, the flesh of the mighty, the flesh of horses and their riders—flesh of all, both free and slave, both small and great." . . . And the rest were killed by the sword of the rider on the horse, the sword that came from his mouth; and all the birds were gorged with their flesh. (Rev 19:17–21)

Two Christian Responses

How do Christians respond to these horrid and horrific images of God contained in both testaments? We can neither ignore nor deny them. Selective memory and convenient amnesia will not work. Both fidelity to the Bible and intellectual honesty demand better. Two prominent Christian scholars have proposed two very different solutions. In this section we briefly explore the responses of Miroslav Volf in his book *Exclusion and Embrace* and John Dominic Crossan in his book *God and Empire*, and then conclude with a supplementary statement on the doctrine of the Trinity.

For Volf, the contrast between the nonviolent Jesus of the Gospels and the violent Jesus of the Book of Revelation is reconcilable since they are "two sides of the same coin."[60] A "nice" God, writes Volf, "is a figment of liberal imagination."[61] God "will judge, not because God gives people what they deserve, but because some people refuse to receive what no one deserves; if evildoers experience God's terror, it will not be because they have done evil, but because they have resisted to the end the powerful lure of the open arms of the crucified Messiah."[62]

According to Volf, some people are "irredeemable." Both the "patient love of God" and the "fury of God's wrath" are therefore necessary, since some individuals and groups interpret the suffering of Christ on the cross as divine weakness. Thus, the divine anger and violence which are narrated in Revelation are the *"symbolic portrayal of the final exclusion of everything that refuses to be redeemed by God's suffering love."*[63] Underscoring the foundational difference between creator and creature, Volf concludes that God alone can use violence. Without the certainty of God's final judgment at the end of history, Christianity cannot denounce human violence in the midst of history. In a world of irrepressible and irredeemable violence, the inescapable option, for Volf, is "either God's violence or human violence." He condones the former and condemns the latter. Yet Volf's solution raises at least two salient questions: (1) Are anger and violence intrinsic to God's nature? and (2) Does the certainty of God's judgment and justice at the end of time undermine our confidence in God's caring and embracing in the present time?

For Crossan, the contrast between the peace-loving Jesus and the vicious slaughtering Jesus is irreconcilable since the latter "seems to be *the* crime against divinity, *the* sin against the Holy Spirit."[64] If Christianity affirms the Second Coming apocalyptic Jesus and rejects the First Coming incarnational Jesus, then the church "finds itself waiting for God to act violently while God is waiting for us to act nonviolently."[65] Furthermore, the Jesus of the Gospels who rides to his demise on a docile donkey trumps the divine warrior Jesus of Revelation. To the credit of both testaments, they pose for Crossan the inevitable question: "How do we reconcile the ambiguity of our Bible's violent and/or nonviolent God?" His response is that *"the Christian Bible presents the radicality of a just and nonviolent God repeatedly and relentlessly confronting the normalcy of an unjust and violent civilization."*[66]

When the faith community reads scripture, it cannot avoid the ongoing struggle between the world's perennial program of "peace through victory" and God's alternative program of "peace through justice." This tension, for Crossan, anchors both the integrity and authority of the Bible. He concludes, "If the Bible were only about peace through victory, we would not need it. If it were only about peace through justice, we would not believe it."[67]

To complement and support Crossan's solution, a supplementary statement on the doctrine of the Trinity warrants our consideration. If the church's fundamental theological inquiry for the issue of religion and violence concerns the nature of God ("What is God like?"), then the church's foundational pronouncement on the nature of God is the doctrine of the Trinity—the Christian claim that both God's interior life and God's exterior relationship to the world are triadic. Not only does the Trinity confirm self-giving love as the essence of God's inner life, but it also affirms love as the guiding principle of the divine's interaction with the world. Thus, the Trinity, which models for Christians how they should embrace, and not exclude, the other, both strengthens Crossan's proposal and rebuts Schwartz's thesis that the origins of violence are located in the negative act of identity formation and monotheism.

Like all the Abrahamic traditions, the theological bedrock of Christianity is the inexhaustible mystery of God. Yet Christian language about God is specific, not abstract, since it is grounded in the historical actions of God as attested in scripture. Based on select acts of revelation, Christianity praises God as the sovereign creator of the cosmos who redeems the world through the work of Jesus the Christ and who continues to act in the world through the power of the Holy Spirit. By the fourth century, this confession of God's triune identity became known as the Trinity—God is the Father, the Son, and the Holy Spirit.[68]

Most significant for our inquiry, the doctrine of the Trinity professes that both the interior and the exterior interactions of God are triadic. Early Christian thinkers, therefore, espoused

two interrelated forms of the Trinity. First, there was the economic[69] Trinity, or how God relates to the world and orches-
trates salvation through the threefold agency of the Father, the
Son, and the Holy Spirit. This formulation is what most people
today mean by the Trinity. Second, early theologians reasoned
that if we experience God in the world in a triadic way, then
God's interior life, or immanent Trinity, must also be triune.
This claim is exceedingly important since it reveals two salient
truths about the nature of God: God is self-conscious and God
is love. Because identity formation requires awareness of the
reciprocal interaction of the self and others, God's internal
life evidences consciousness when the Father knows the Son
through the agency of the Holy Spirit. God is then a subject
to God's own self. That is, God possesses self-consciousness.
Moreover, God as love also requires a triadic structure: The
lover (God the Father), the loved (the Son), and the love between them (the Holy Spirit). Succinctly, the triadic structure
of God's interior life is manifested as God creates and cares
for the external world. The author of the First Letter of John
echoes this structure when he proclaims:

> Beloved, let us love one another, because love is from God;
> everyone who loves is born of God and knows God. Whoever
> does not love does not know God, for God is love. God's
> love was revealed among us in this way: God sent his only
> Son into the world so that we might live through him. In this
> is love, not that we loved God but that he loved us and sent
> his Son to be the atoning sacrifice for our sins. Beloved, since
> God loved us so much, we also ought to love one another.
> No one has ever seen God; if we love one another, God lives
> in us, and his love is perfected in us. (1 John 4:7–12)

To summarize, the Christian doctrine of the Trinity affirms
at least three principles about the nature of God. First, the internal life of God is relational.[70] The immanent Trinity asserts
the communal nature of God in God's self. Hence, God's love

for the world emanates from God's own giving and receiving in love (the Spirit is the binding love that unites the Father as self and the Son as other). As a community of persons in love, the immanent Trinity grounds the economic Trinity, or the distinct way in which Christians talk about God's presence in the world as Father, Son, and Holy Spirit. Because the interior life of God includes otherness (a presupposition of love), God's love for the world is rooted in God's triune life of love. Second, God exists in community. Because the divine life is social (immanent Trinity), God establishes and maintains relationships. Thus, the creation and redemption of the world are the outward expressions of God's internal communal nature. Third, self-giving love characterizes God's life. The good news of the gospel is that God's love for the world is stronger than sin and death. Grounded in the Second Testament's story of the life, death, and resurrection of Jesus the Christ, the doctrine of the Trinity proclaims that the hope of all creation resides in the God who is decisively revealed in Jesus and empowered by the Holy Spirit.

In conclusion, the doctrine of the Trinity strengthens Crossan's response by refuting both the charge that God is innately violent and Schwartz's thesis that the origin of violence is in the negative act of identity formation and monotheism. Human beings, made in the image of God, are created for a communal life distinguished by love. Because this affirmation defines the nature of both God and humans, the act of identity formation for both creator and creature is inherently positive— respect and honor, love and embrace the other.[71] Although humans fall from perfection by sin, Christian hope resides in a God who does not. Consequently, Christians must make a decision. God cannot be both a God of steadfast love and a God of systematic violence. The violent and nonviolent biblical portraits of God are simply incompatible. We must choose the God in which to place our faith, trust, and love.[72]

Implications for the Christian Life

According to the Teacher in the book of Ecclesiastes, "For everything there is a season, and a time for every matter under heaven . . . a time to kill, and a time to heal . . . a time for war, and a time for peace" (3:1, 3a, 8b). Although the recognition of this historic truth and the exposure of *the church's seventh deadly secret* that my religion and God are violent are neither pleasant to hear nor easy to accept, it is imperative for responsible adherents of religion. If taken seriously, there are at least three implications for the Christian life.

First, people of faith must put away their childish thoughts and awake from their sanctimonious slumbers. Christians cannot afford to mouth pious platitudes about love and peace, while ignoring the lethal deeds of our tradition and the toxic texts in our canon. Like the Apostle Paul, we must claim the ambiguity of our actions: "For I do not do what I want, but I do the very thing I hate" (Rom 7:15b). Religion, because it is lived by human beings, is necessarily flawed and capable of fomenting violence. It is preposterous to think otherwise and perilous to deny. When Adam and Eve ate of the fruit from the tree of the knowledge of good and evil, they were empowered to rise as high as the angels or to sink as low as the beasts. Hence, religion reflects in life and in scripture both the holiness and the horror of humanity. It is time for people of faith to answer the query of Matthew's Jesus, "Why do you see the speck in your neighbor's eye, but do not notice the log in your own eye?" (7:3).

Second, people of faith must not be afraid to critique the character of Christianity. Because violence is perpetrated in the name of God and by God in both tradition and text, there are some tenets of historic Christianity that are simply not worthy of human imitation. Denial of our religion's ambiguity leads not only to delusionary God-like certainty but also to cocksure arrogance and an increased likelihood for violence. Regrettably, Christianity in general and the Bible in particular are not infallible guides to Christ-like behavior.[73] While acknowledging the worst side of religion, we must also identify and practice its best side. And a good place to begin is with Alexis de Tocqueville's observation that "As long as man has religion, he will not believe in his own perfectibility."[74]

Third, people of faith must utilize our religious resources for repentance and reconciliation. Every time a Christian prays, "Thy kingdom come, thy will be done on earth as it is in heaven," we remind ourselves of the gap between the ideal and the real in our individual and corporate lives. In the presence of the holy, our false loyalties and our ubiquitous need for confession are confirmed. Christ's death on the cross not only reveals and condemns our world of violence but also extends the healing love of God that beckons a new future of reconciliation and respect. Although Christians claim the crucified Christ for our inner worlds of sin and shame, few of us want him in our outer worlds of politics and public policy. Constantine not only co-opted the cross for "peace through victory," but he also spiritualized the gospel message by claiming the physical bodies of the citizens and leaving the disembodied souls for the church. Caesar runs our lives, while Jesus rules our hearts. Christians must reclaim God's question to Cain, "Where is your brother?" (Gen 4:9).

After the murder of around five thousand people in a small Rwandan village in 1994, the local Roman Catholic church was converted into a memorial to the dead and a witness for the living. Hanging from the rafters and the walls are the bloodstained clothing of the victims. Displayed on shelves are rows of human skulls. Above them, a sign reads: "If you knew me, and you knew yourself, you would not kill me."[75]

Postscript

Identity Formation from Within

Because Christians are made, not born, identity theft is a perennial problem for the church. This realization compels the church to reclaim its identity-conferring authority through corporate worship. As the primary delivery system by which the church teaches its mission and meaning, congregational worship must incorporate the church's seven deadly secrets, now exposed, into the content of the worship service. The postscript develops the theme of Christian identity formation from within the church in three moves: first, it offers a brief analysis of the contemporary situation; second, it posits the theological resources in corporate worship by which the church sustains and transmits its distinct identity; and third, it presents a matrix of Christian identity formation.

C hristians are made, not born. Because sanctification—growing or maturing in the faith—is an ongoing process, identity theft is a perennial problem. The preceding chapters have focused on the vulnerability of the church to identity theft from within and temptations from without when the community of faith neglects its history and heritage. The church's seven deadly secrets spring from this neglect, and, if left unchecked, they inevitably undermine Christian identity formation.

In the first documented use of the phrase "going to church," Clement of Alexandria (ca. 200 CE) laments the appeal of secular temptations to churched followers of Jesus:

Women and men should go to church decently attired, with natural step, clinging to silence, possessing genuine love, being pure in body and pure in heart, and fit to offer prayers to God . . .. Those dedicated to Christ ought to present

169

and shape themselves throughout life in the same manner as they fashion themselves with propriety in the churches. They ought thus to be—and not just seem to be—gentle, pious, and loving. And yet I know how they change their dress and manners with their location, just like an octopus . . .. Indeed after their departure thence [from the church], laying aside the inspiration of the assembly, these people become just like the masses with whom they associate.[1]

The temptation to conform to one's surroundings is constant. Carl Jung (1875–1961), the Swiss psychiatrist, once remarked that "the world will ask who you are, and if you cannot answer, the world will tell you."[2] That is, the prevailing and predominant forces of the culture will shape our identity and determine our thoughts and values unless we intentionally immerse ourselves in an alternative process of identity formation.

Because the individual choice to become a Christian is made in the midst of other cultural options, an examination of the dynamics of Christian identity formation is less about a person's private decision and more about social conditioning. The church must deliberately present and promote its faith and practice so that an individual may have a real opportunity to hear and respond to the Gospel message. A concise explanation follows.

Although learning about the church's seven deadly secrets is important for the overall process of identity formation, there is a fundamental difference between "knowing the Gospel" intellectually and "living the Gospel" experientially. If theology, which is derived from the two Greek words *theos* (God) and *logos* (word), is the human attempt to make sense of the word "God," then our thoughts about the divine must originate from our encounters with God and be anchored to the community of faith. Corporate worship is the principal vehicle by which the Christian community proclaims the Good News of the Gospel, hears the story of God's activities in history, celebrates God's transformative work in the world, praises the living God in Christ, and encounters the presence of the holy.

Christian worship is not only the lifeblood of theology but also the primary locus of Christian identity formation. Therefore, the church must continually reclaim its identity-conferring authority if it wants to make and mold Christians for life in-but-not-of the world. This postscript develops the theme of Christian identity formation from within the church in three moves. First, a brief analysis of the contemporary situation and a short statement on the mission of the church is offered. Second, the theological resources in corporate worship by which the church sustains and transmits its distinct identity are posited. Third, a matrix of Christian identity formation is presented.[3]

An Analysis of the Situation and the Mission of the Church

The contemporary American church is experiencing identity theft for at least two reasons: (1) the church is heavily enculturated by the dominant societal ethos;[4] and (2) the church suffers from ecclesial amnesia.[5] As the body of Christ in the world, the church inescapably lives in and is influenced by the pervasive cultural milieu. Moreover, the educational mission of the church, which identifies and interprets the meaning of the Gospel for the present time, seeks intellectual and ethical faithfulness. When the ecclesia[6] neglects its teaching role, it simultaneously weakens its abilities to define the nature and purpose of the church, and to defend itself against worldly temptations.

According to the late novelist David Foster Wallace, there is no such thing as atheism, since there is no such thing as not worshiping.[7] Everybody worships something. One of the advantages of selecting a traditional religion, he notes, is that many alternatives "will eat you alive." For example, if you worship money and things, you will never have enough.

Venerate your body and beauty, and aging will inevitably reveal the ravages of time. Bow at the altar of power and you will feel weak and afraid such that fear will never subside. Prostrate yourself before the prowess of your intellect and you will end up feeling stupid and always on the verge of being discovered. Because contemporary culture encourages such distortions, the church must be especially vigilant in shaping Christians capable of withstanding such temptations.

In a "What's in it for me?" society, only personal (and often immediate) gratification validates our choices. Consequently, the cultural perceptions of time are aligned against history and hope. Memories of the past and promises for the future are abandoned in favor of the "urgent now." But when social institutions forsake their collective memory—their tap root to the wisdom and resources of their heritage—they become anemic and susceptible to cultural infections.

These observations about Christian identity formation in the twenty-first century underscore two interrelated concerns. First, they highlight the interconnection between identity and memory. When the church ignores at best and abdicates at worst its teaching tradition, the distinct Christian way of perceiving and living in the world is eventually supplanted by the dominant cultural assumptions. Ellen T. Charry advances a persuasive rationale when she asserts:

> Yet while youngsters think they are creating themselves, they are in reality being formed by television; by the sports, entertainment and advertising industries; by the shopping malls and by the streets. The market forces behind these institutions are not interested in children's moral, social and intellectual development.
>
> Intentional Christian nurture is necessary because our culture shapes children for a world shorn of God. Christians see power in the crucified Jesus; popular culture defines power as winning in athletic or commercial combat. A Christian learns

about hope from the resurrection; our culture sees hope in a new-car showroom. The church is again called upon to rescue people out of paganism.[8]

Second, these observations highlight the interconnection between memory and authority. Amnesia, the loss of memory, undermines every form of authority because our thoughts go unchallenged and our actions go uncensored. This realization grounds Stanley Hauerwas' audacious proposal that we should take "the Bible away from North American Christians" since the egalitarian principles of democracy have corrupted the church. The people in the pews, he declares, "believe that they are capable of reading the Bible without spiritual and moral transformation." In essence, they "feel no need to stand under the authority of a truthful community to be told how to read."[9]

Although the erosion of ecclesiastical authority and the threat of enculturation are not new to the life of the church, our current situation seems especially ominous. The societal challenges of the early twenty-first century are both resolute and relentless. More significant, the present crisis of identity theft threatens the very nature of the church. At one time the church taught that the chief purpose of humanity was to glorify God. Now the culture advocates the reverse—the chief purpose of God is to glorify humanity.

In light of these insidious cultural threats, the church must unashamedly reclaim and proclaim its central mission, which remains the same from age to age. Christians are called to declare and embody the Good News of what God has done and is doing for us in Jesus of Nazareth. In addition, we are called to provide an alternative vision of life that is defined more by our understanding of God's self-disclosure in Jesus as attested in the tradition and scripture, and less by the predominant assumptions of the culture or the individual believer. Furthermore, we are called to sustain a separate identity that is discerned only when we enter into a different history, embrace a different memory, and live with different promises.[10] For this separate identity to emerge, Christians need to be socialized into a particular world of meaning. Consequently, the perennial task of the church is to transmit its identity to the next generation. The church must, therefore, reclaim its identity-conferring authority and rededicate itself to this vocation.

Corporate Worship as Identity Formation

In our contemporary culture, the omnipresent attitudes presume that the autonomous individual is the measure of all things and that social institutions can exist without recourse to memory and authority. Hence, one of the church's primary responsibilities is to identify and implement the theological resources in corporate worship by which the church sustains and transmits its distinct identity. Before we can address, however, the formation of Christian identity in particular, we need to understand how individuals acquire social identities in general.

As discussed in chapter 7, human beings in the world are constituted by both subjectivity (awareness of the self in the world) and intersubjectivity (awareness of the reciprocal interactions of the self and others in the world). As individuals, we are conscious of our existence in the world of time and space, as well as conscious that these elements of life are shared with and dependent upon other individuals. Cognizance of one's self and one's relationships to others is, therefore, prerequisite for social existence.

Because human identity is shaped by both personal decisions and communal associations, every social world the individual inhabits plays a role in identity formation. Whether it is a college sorority or fraternity, a civic club or professional auxiliary, the dynamics are the same. Christianity, understood as a constructed world of meaning and therefore a particular way of living in the world, is no different. Thus, Christian identity formation requires participation in the communal life of the church. John Calvin (1509–1564), the first Protestant systematic theologian, makes a compelling argument for the church as the "mother" of all believers in his seminal work the *Institutes of the Christian Religion*:

> But because it is now our intention to discuss the visible church, let us learn even from the simple title "mother" how useful, indeed how necessary it is that we should know her. For there is no other way to enter into life unless this mother conceive us in her womb, give us birth, nourish us at her breast, and lastly, unless she keep us under her care and guidance until, putting off mortal flesh, we become like the angels. Our weakness does not allow us to be dismissed from her school until we have been pupils all our lives.[11]

In theological terms, the church or ecclesial existence is a distinct way of living with others in the world, or a specific intersubjectivity. That is, Christians relate to one another and to God according to patterns of behavior which are informed by tradition and scripture. Membership in the church, therefore, means sharing this common world of meaning, where corporate memories and hopes, as well as celebrations of the inaugural and normative events of the community, bridge the generations of ecclesial life. Hence, ritual acts of identity formation connect the present with both the founding events in the past (Jesus's death and resurrection) and the anticipated events in the future (Jesus's second coming and the fulfillment of the Kingdom of God on earth). Corporate worship functions, then, as the primary vehicle by which the Christian faith community determines, sustains, and transmits its particular way of living in the world before God and neighbor. Specifically, proclamation of the Word and participation in the sacramental rites comprise the core of Christian worship.

To summarize, individuals acquire their social identities by sharing in communal worlds of meaning. Only by encountering people who profess and practice the specific ways in which a particular group relates to one another can a person be shaped and formed by that distinct social world of meaning. Thus, identity formation never occurs in isolation. It is always communal. And every distinct community originates from a normative event in history. Consequently, the founding events are re-presented by the community's ritual activities and its peculiar ways of organizing time and space. By participating in these communal rites, the individual is incorporated into this specific way of living in the world.

For Christianity, corporate worship is the centering activity by which the community of faith determines, sustains, and transmits its unique way of being in the world before God and others. Although individuals encounter God in solitude as well as in the world, Christian faith-consciousness is mediated only by interacting with other Christians. A person who has encountered neither a Christian nor a Christian ritual has never participated in—let alone internalized—the distinctive Christian social world of meaning.[12] To read about a tradition is not the same as living a tradition. Without participating in corporate or congregational worship, the individual can neither encounter nor be changed by the God who is proclaimed and praised via the matrix of Christian identity formation.

A Matrix of Christian Identity Formation

Congregational worship communicates the Christian vision of life in three ways: (1) by re-telling the Christian story, primarily through the reading of scripture and the preaching of the homily/sermon; (2) by re-presenting the distinct Christian way of relating to God and neighbor, primarily through the rituals of baptism and eucharist/Lord's Supper; and (3) by re-enforcing the particular Christian meanings of time and space, primarily through the observance of the Christian calendar (the liturgical year) and through the arrangements of the liturgical spaces.

Together, these constitutive features of Christian corporate worship—story, rituals, time and space—establish a matrix of Christian identity formation.

Highly significant, this matrix describes the primary and perennial delivery system by which the church teaches its mission and meaning. Also important, the church's seven deadly secrets, now exposed, must be incorporated into this matrix via the content of the worship service, especially by the preaching of the clergy.

Story

The church is a story-formed community that is rooted in the crucifixion and resurrection of Jesus the Christ.[13] This dual yet inseparable event functions for Christians as both the normative self-disclosure of God in history and the means of redemptive transformation.

In order for the community of faith to endure through time and to withstand the threats of enculturation, the story of what God has accomplished for the Hebrew people and the Christian community must be continually re-told in corporate worship. This narrative is taught primarily through the service of the Word. Traditionally, the Word refers to that portion of the Christian service where the scriptures are professed and the sermon or homily is preached. On the one hand, the scriptures recite the story of God's saving acts in history from the creation in Genesis to the second coming of the Christ in Revelation. On the other hand, preaching announces the definitive revelations of God in the past so that the present community may be included in the unfolding story of God's transformative activity in the world.

Because stories both convey and constitute reality, the Christian story structures our understanding of contemporary faith in the world. Through the hearing of the scriptures and the sermon, the decisive past events of the church are incorporated into the present existence of both the community of faith and the individual members. Thus, the redemptive power of the original Jesus event is made available for Christians today. In this way, contemporary followers can "know" Jesus and his transformative presence.

Rituals

Although scripture and sermon tell the story of God's saving acts in history, rituals are needed to both embody a community's story and define a community's boundaries. As repetitive and performative acts that integrate symbols and beliefs, rituals allow participants to find their place in the world and thereby secure an identity. And because there is no community without cultic activity, corporate worship locates the center of the church's life.

When Christians refer to the liturgy (the work of the people), they generally mean the ritual actions of the worshiping community that re-present the Christ event. In particular, the sacraments (the traditional name that refers to an outward and visible sign of God's inward and invisible grace entrusted to the church and instituted by Christ) are those designated ritual activities which the Christian community performs so that the meaning it proclaims can become efficacious in the lives of its worshipers.[14] Neither the liturgy nor the sacraments invoke, however, God's presence or secure redemption. Rather, and most important, God's grace is already present in the world, and it is precisely this truth that worship in general and the sacraments in particular announce and celebrate. Hence, the specific rituals of baptism and eucharist (Lord's Supper or Holy Communion) are designed to incorporate their participants into the Christian story—the particular Christian way of meaning and relating to God and neighbor that distinguishes the life and practice of the church from other social institutions.

Baptism, as the sacrament of initiation into the community of faith, is the public rite by which the individual's positive response to the hearing of the Word is received and the death and resurrection of Jesus are reenacted. Most significant, the waters of baptism occasion the deconstructive phase of secular society's claim on the individual (death of the old self) and the constructive phase of the individual's new life in Christ (resurrection).[15] In baptism, a person's identity (one's history and loyalties, memories and hopes) is transferred from one social world of meaning to another. This interpretation explains why baptism is traditionally identified with renunciation of the devil, the forgiveness of sin, the gift of the Holy Spirit, union with Christ, incorporation into the body of Christ, and new birth. All of these images are associated with the change of the individual's primary identity from one shaped by the dominant culture to one formed by the church. In baptism, the spiritual formation or sanctification of the Christian begins.[16]

Unlike baptism, the eucharist, or Lord's Supper,[17] is the repeated central rite of the church that Christians observe from baptism until death. At Holy Communion, participants experience God's self-giving through receiving the material elements of bread and wine.[18] This dramatic re-enactment of Jesus' last supper not only communicates the specific interactions that structure Christian life but it also conveys "an ethical ideal that Christians are in turn expected to embody in their lives."[19]

Seven interrelated images, located in both scripture and tradition, attend the meaning of the eucharist.[20] First, the image of "joyful thanksgiving" appears in the earliest narrative: "...the Lord Jesus on the night when he was betrayed took a loaf of bread, and when he had given thanks..." (1 Cor 11:23–24). In the Second Testament, the Greek word *eucharistia* (thanksgiving) usually refers to giving thanks to God and explains the derivation of the English word "eucharist."

Second, in the Pauline account Jesus says, "Do this in remembrance of me" (1 Cor 11:24). Thus, an image of commemoration or remembrance is tied to the Greek word *anamnesis*. Although this term is difficult to render in English, when Christians "do this," they recall Christ's redemptive work in the past.

Third, Paul also understands the eucharist as a communion meal, or a moment of genuine fellowship: "The cup of blessing that we bless, is it not a sharing in the blood of Christ? The bread that we break, is it not a sharing in the body of Christ? Because there is one bread, we who are many are one body, for we all partake of the one bread" (1 Cor 10:16–17). The Greek term *koinonia* (communion) expresses the unity which results from table fellowship with Christ and Christ's church.

Fourth, the image of sacrifice pervades all four Second Testament accounts.[21] To take one example, Jesus says in Luke 22:20: "This cup that is poured out for you is the new covenant in my blood." In an effort to expand the interpretative context of sacrifice, contemporary theologians understand Christ's sacrifice to include his whole ministry and not just his death. "Thus, the eucharist is a memorial of all of Christ's work (sacrifice) on earth."[22]

Fifth, the church affirms Christ's presence at the Lord's Table.[23] Yet Christ's eucharistic presence is not an immediate presence. Rather, it is a "presence-in-absence." Christ's presence is linked to the incarnation of Jesus of Nazareth, which belongs to the past, and to the eschatological[24] presence of Christ at the *parousia,* or second coming, which belongs to the future. Therefore, the celebration of Christ's presence at the eucharist includes a backward referent to the crucified Jesus now absent, as well as a forward referent to the coming Christ now anticipated.[25]

Sixth, from the congregation's gathering to its dismissal, the action of the Holy Spirit infuses and informs corporate worship. Although the Spirit was at one time identified only with the single moment of eucharistic consecration, when the bread becomes Christ's body and the wine becomes Christ's blood, the operation of the Spirit makes Christ present to the worshiping community as well as to the individual communicants.

Seventh, the eucharist is an eschatological event that serves as a foretaste of the final consummation of the world. Although Christ's presence (the fifth image) alludes to the anticipatory nature of the Lord's Supper, the future expectation of the messianic banquet is vividly portrayed in the eucharistic texts. Jesus looked forward to eating the Passover again when "the kingdom of God comes" (Luke 22:18) and to drinking "it new [with you] in the Kingdom of God" (Mark 14:25; parallel in Matt 26:29). And Paul maintained that the eating and the drinking "proclaim the Lord's death until he comes" (1 Cor 11:26).

In summary, as the church's dramatic re-enactments of God's self-giving, the sacraments in general, and baptism and eucharist in particular, communicate the distinctive Christian way of living in the world. In turn, participation in these ritual activities restructures individual and collective consciousness by incorporating the celebrants into the Christian story. The sacraments are, then, the formative communal rites in which the Christian community's distinctive ways of relating to God and neighbor are expressed and by which the individual is drawn into the church's specific intersubjectivity.

Time and Space

Members of a story-formed community also share common perceptions of social time and social space. That is, temporal and spatial meanings are included in the network of reciprocal interactions that constitutes specific ways in which people relate to one another.

With respect to time, the past persists in the collective memory of a community, while the future is anticipated. What persists in memory, however, is neither the total events of all time past nor even the total past events of a specific people. Rather, in the present, the past is remembered and the future is anticipated in particular ways. The past is governed by the normative events of the community, while the horizon of the future is established by the selective memory of the past. How the community remembers its past directly determines, then, what the community envisions for its future. Thus, specific peoples limit the range of their memories and their hopes, thereby creating common perceptions of social time and social space via their foundational story.

For example, the Christian community limits its memories and its hopes through the creation of the biblical canon,[26] which in turn designates the readings and informs the preaching in worship services. Some early church writings were included (what we now call the canonical books), while other writings were excluded (extracanonical books[27]). The authoritative manuscripts that made the cut narrate specific stories that share common time and place references. In particular, the Jesus story assumes familiarity with the story of the Jewish people, as well as knowledge of messianic expectations. Christian identity necessarily and appropriately restricts the range of its memories and hopes.

In Christian corporate worship, all three temporal meanings converge. The risen Christ is available to the worshiping community through the abiding presence of the Holy Spirit. Yet participants also remember the decisive events of Christ's life, death, and resurrection, as well as anticipate his eschatological presence at the *parousia*. Succinctly, Christian corporate worship remembers the historical Jesus of Nazareth from the past, celebrates the presence of the living Lord in the present, and anticipates the second coming of the Christ in the future.

Because the decisive historical actions of God occurred at definite times and places, time necessarily structures Christian corporate worship. Using the recurring rhythms of the day, the week, and the year as set forth in the Christian calendar or liturgical year, the faith community intentionally re-presents and re-experiences the saving actions of God in history—especially the life, death, and resurrection of Jesus. Since the Easter story (as the inaugural and normative event) forms and re-forms the church, every Sunday is a little Easter. Moreover, the simplest, and most effective, visible reminders of the passage of time in worship are the changing colors of the vestments[28] and banners. Each change of color signals the changing days and seasons in the Christian year.

Succinctly, there are two major seasons in the Christian calendar: The season of Jesus's birth and the manifestation of God in Christ to the world (Advent-Christmas-Epiphany), and the season of Jesus's death and resurrection (Lent-Easter-Pentecost). Advent is the four-week time of preparation (starting with the fourth Sunday before Christmas which is the first day of the Christian year) for both the birth of Christ (Christmas) and his second coming (the *parousia*). Epiphany, which means manifestation, refers to the incarnation of God in Jesus of Nazareth. The feast of Epiphany on January the sixth celebrates the birth of Christ (in some traditions), the coming of the Magi (in the Western church), the baptism of Jesus, and Jesus' first miracle at the wedding in Cana of Galilee.

The forty days of Lent (not including Sundays) is the time of preparation for Easter (the day of Christ's resurrection). Lent is subdivided into Ash Wednesday (the first day of Lent when ashes are imposed on the forehead) and Holy Week. The latter begins with Palm Sunday (Jesus's entrance into Jerusalem) and includes Maundy Thursday (the day that Jesus celebrated his Last Supper and washed his disciples' feet) and Good Friday (the day of Christ's crucifixion). The ascension of Jesus into heaven is celebrated forty days after Easter, and Pentecost, which commemorates the birthday of the church (Acts 2), is celebrated fifty days after Easter. Ordinary Time designates the periods of the liturgical year, which occur after the seasons of Epiphany and Pentecost.[29]

When the church remembers the historical events in the life of Jesus, those recollections are neither abstract nor generic. Rather, they occur within an orientation established by our historical embodiment in time and space. Thus, remembrances of the past and expectations for the future include not only a time referent but also a place referent.

In corporate worship, the backward referent to the events in the life of the Jewish people, as well as to the life, death, and resurrection of Jesus, is mostly linked to spatial meanings associated with Palestine (Israel) in general and Jerusalem in particular. The forward referent to the second coming of Christ is traditionally associated with images of heaven and hell,[30] as well as to the Kingdom or reign of God on earth. Furthermore, the actual configuration of worship space, where the congregation gathers, communicates meaning. Everything from the windows (plain or stained glass) to the seating arrangements (forward facing pews or chairs in the round) tells the participants the purpose of the space. Corporate worship usually consists of six different liturgical spaces: (1) gathering space or the narthex; (2) movement space; (3) congregational space, or nave; (4) choir space; (5) baptismal space; and (6) sanctuary space, or apse. The four primary liturgical centers are the baptismal font or pool, the pulpit, the altar or table, and the presider's chair.[31]

The precise arrangement of these spaces and centers provides practical and theological clues to the respective community's interpretation of the Christian story. For example, the architectural focal point of the gathering area (pulpit/lectern or altar/table) tells the participants whether this congregation privileges Word or sacrament. Church architecture, in turn, influences liturgical music, art, and dance. Thus, a matrix of Christian identity formation for corporate worship necessarily includes the common meanings of social time and social space that attend the Christian life.

Conclusion

Corporate worship is the church's primary and perennial defense against ecclesial amnesia from within and enculturation from without. The societal elevation of the self, the secular reduction of the individual to an economic entity, and the cultural repudiation of mystery are all confronted by the Christian vision of life presented and promoted in Sunday worship. Therefore, challenges to the future of Christianity in general and to Christian identity in particular should not be perceived as irrefutable or insurmountable. On the contrary, they compel the church to reclaim its identity-conferring authority through corporate worship. And the more comprehensively the features of the matrix of Christian identity formation are actualized and the church's seven deadly secrets are incorporated, the more effectively congregational worship can serve as the church's active immunization against ecclesial amnesia and enculturation. In conclusion, Christian corporate worship functions as the church's principal vehicle for identity formation from within.

Notes

Introduction

1. Founded in 1780, Transylvania University is the sixteenth oldest college in the country, affiliated with the Christian Church (Disciples of Christ), and located in Lexington, Kentucky.

2. *USA Today*, July 6, 2009, 8C, and September 22, 2011, 12A.

3. They are pride, envy, gluttony or avarice, lust, anger or wrath, greed, and sloth.

4. *Ecclesia* is the Greek word that is usually translated as "church."

5. Grossman, "Most Americans Believe in God but Don't Know Religious Tenets," *USA Today*, September 28, 2010.

6. According to the 2011 *Newsweek* U.S. Citizenship Test, 38 percent of the 1,000 American respondents failed. Both civic illiteracy and religious illiteracy are rampant. See Romano, "How Dumb Are We?" *Newsweek*, 56–60.

7. See Williamson and Allen, *The Teaching Minister*.

8. Prothero, *Biblical Literacy*, 23.

9. Prothero, *Biblical Literacy*, 24.

10. Prothero, *Biblical Literacy*, 30.

11. Biblical illiteracy is assumed by most churches: worship bulletins usually list the page number(s) for the scriptural text(s) so members can locate the day's reading(s).

12. See Brueggemann, *Finally Comes the Poet*, 1–3.

13. Potok, *In the Beginning*, 404.

14. Migliore, *Faith Seeking Understanding*, 6.

15. Tillich, *The Protestant Era*, trans. Adams, 185.

16. This is my paraphrase of Migliore, 9: "If theory without practice is empty, practice without theory is blind."

17. Williamson and Allen, 75. Italics appear in the original.

Chapter 1

1. Steinhauser, "Poll: Did Obama's Reaction to Gates Arrest Hurt Him?,"

2. This book uses the neutral designations BCE (Before the Common Era) and CE (Common Era) as alternatives to the traditional designations of bc (Before Christ) and ad (*anno Domini* = "in the year of the/our Lord"). The numerical values remain the same.

3. Armstrong, *The Great Transformation*, 221.

4. Carroll, *Constantine's Sword*, 314.

5. Barrett, Kurian and Johnson, eds., *World Christian Encyclopedia*.

6. The Age of the Enlightenment refers to the eighteenth-century Western philosophical and cultural life in which reason was employed as the primary source of authority and knowledge.

7. The following comments on the meaning and function of paradigms are indebted to Covey, *The 7 Habits of Highly Effective People*, 29–31.

8. Placher, *A History of Christian Theology*, 163–67.

9. Covey, 30–31.

10. Schaefer, "Its Sense of Awe of God" in the *Lexington Herald-Leader*, May 4, 1996. Micklethwait and Wooldridge in *God Is Back*, 35, make a similar point when they write, "replacing the worship of God with the worship of man." Barna writes in *Futurecast: What Today's Trends Mean for Tomorrow's World*, "We are a designer society. We want everything customized to our personal needs . . . . Now it's our religion."

11. David Brooks, the *New York Times* columnist, writes: "In most times and places, the group was the essential moral unit. A shared religion defined rules and practices. Cultures imposed moral disciplines. But now more people are led to assume that the free-floating individual is the essential moral unit. Morality was once revealed, inherited and shared, but now it's thought of as something that emerges in the privacy of your own heart." *Lexington Herald-Leader*, Sunday, September 18, 2011, E2.

12. Grossman, "Redrawing the Map of American Religion," 1A.

13. Carter, *The Culture of Disbelief*, 22. Barry Kosmin, co-author of the 2009 American Religious Identification Survey, agrees: "...religion has become more like a fashion statement, not a deep personal commitment for many." See footnote 12 above: Grossman, 6A.

14. Mark 3:25, with parallels in Matt 12:25 and Luke 11:17.

15. Having to do with the nature and authority of the church.

16. The following comments are indebted to Johnson, *The Real Jesus*, 59–60.

17. Johnson, *The Real Jesus*, 59.

18. Johnson, *The Real Jesus*, 60.

19. According to the Apostles Creed, the major doctrines are God, Christ, Holy Spirit, and church.

20. I refer to the major pronouncements of the church both past and present on public policy issues like slavery, women, homosexuality, marriage, stem cell research, abortion, ecology, human rights, poverty, economic distribution of wealth, genocide, pacifism, and war.

21. Tiner, *Isaac Newton*.

22. Ayers, *Judaism and Christianity*, 298.

23. Carroll, 593.

24. Einstein, *The World As I See It*.

25. McCullough, *The Trivialization of God*, 16.

26. Epistemology is the branch of philosophy that studies the nature and theory of knowledge. It addresses the following questions, among others: What is knowledge? How is knowledge acquired? What do people know? How do we know what we know? Why do we know what we know?

27. Although Kant's concept of the active mind was *a priori* or independent of experience, thinkers after Kant early on reinterpreted the activity of the mind to include cultural and historical influences.

28. This principle was evident during the July 2009 Senate Judiciary Committee's confirmation hearing for Supreme Court nominee Sonia Sotomayor when senators responded differently to her earlier statement, "I hope that a wise Latina woman, with the richness of her experiences, would more often than not reach a better conclusion than a white male who hasn't lived that life."

29. Story taken from "Gaining Consciousness" in *Context: Martin E. Marty on Religion and Culture*, 7.

30. Gen 3:24.

31. See the first paragraph of the earlier section on "The Scientific Worldview."

32. See Steiner, *After Babel.*

33. According to Mark 12:30, Jesus said that "you shall love the Lord your God with all your heart, and with all your soul, and with all your *mind*, and with all your strength" (italics added). See parallels in Matt 22:37 and Luke 10:27.

34. Grossman, "Redrawing the Map of American Religion," 1A and 6A.

35. Quoted in Armstrong, *The Battle for God*, 144.

36. Pelikan, *The Vindication of Tradition*, 55.

37. Nels F.S. Ferré in his book *The Sun And the Umbrella* treats this theme via a parable of a people who call themselves Sunworshipers.

38. Carroll, 555.

39. Ayers, 357–62. The "Decree of Ecumenism" also affirms that "Christ summons the Church, as she goes her pilgrim way, to that continual reformation of which she always has need, insofar as she is an institution of men here on earth" in Abbott, ed., *The Documents of Vatican II*, 350.

40. Tracy, *The Analogical Imagination*, 363. Subsequent comments on the church's conversation are indebted to Carroll, 594–98.

41. Because God is greater than any one religious expression, the Christian conversation about the holy begins with its own voices as narrated in tradition and scripture but it also includes voices from other religious and nonreligious expressions.

42. Any introductory textbook on the Second Testament will describe these various portraits. See Ehrman, *The New Testament.*

43. 1 Cor 1:10–17.

44. This assertion does not preclude the claim that the texts and their writers were inspired. See chapter 3.

45. Rom 13:9–10; 1 Corinthians 13; and 1 John 4:7–21. The popular Christian hymn "They'll Know We Are Christians by Our Love" makes the point.

46. See chapter 2, "Faith and Doubt," for my interpretation of their interrelationship.

Chapter 2

1. Chopra, *The Third Jesus*, 61.

2. Ritschl, "Faith: Overview" in *The Encyclopedia of Christianity*, ed. Fahlbusch et al., 2:261.

3. Borg, *The Heart of Christianity*, 25–26.

4. Smith, *Faith and Belief*, 7.

5. See the classic by Tillich, *Dynamics of Faith*, 4–5.

6. Quoted in Wolpe, *Why Faith Matters*, 195.

7. This section is indebted to Smith, 128–42. The quotation appears on p. 140.

8. The Paleolithic or Old Stone Age is traditionally dated from 2.5 million years ago to around 10,000 BCE, and covers approximately 99 percent of human history. Most important for the study of religion, evidence for belief in the afterlife associated with burial rituals begins in the Middle or Upper Paleolithic period.

9. For a comprehensive study of the religious development in India, China, Israel, and Greece during the Axial Age, see Karen Armstrong, *The Great Transformation*.

10. Smith, 142.

11. Tillich, 14.

12. Tillich, 15, and Otto, *The Idea of the Holy*, trans. Harvey, 12–24, 31–40, 52.

13. Heschel, *Man Is Not Alone*, 91.

14. See chapter 1, especially "The Copernican Revolution in Thinking."

15. Both quotations are taken from Inbody, *The Faith of the Christian Church*, 72.

16. Migliore, *Faith Seeking Understanding*, 160.

17. See Mark 8:27–30; Matt 16:13–20; Luke 9:18–20; John 1:1–18; Rom 3:21–31; and Heb 12:1–2.

18. Ebeling, *The Nature of Faith*, trans. Smith, 44–45.

19. "Faith," in *The Oxford Dictionary of the Jewish Religion*, ed. Werblowsky and Wigoder, 249.

20. Translated and explained by my colleague, Rabbi William J. Leffler of Kennebunkport, Maine, in a personal conversation on June 1, 2009.

21. In Judaism these verses are known as the "Shema," which is taken from the first word in the Hebrew text: *shema* (hear).

22. Although Judaism does not espouse a creed, "The Thirteen Principles" by Maimonides is the closest statement that Judaism has to a creed and is included in many prayer books.

23. As translated by Rabbi William Leffler in a personal conversation on June 1, 2009.

24. "Faith," in *The Oxford Dictionary of the Jewish Religion*, 249.

25. Inbody, 71.

26. For example, Paul writes in Rom 5:1 that "we are justified by faith" and in Gal 2:16 that "a person is justified . . . through faith in Jesus Christ."

27. Laughlin, *Remedial Christianity*, 180.

28. The following section on the four Latin words for faith is indebted to Borg, 28–36.

29. Although the literal translation of the Greek *orthodoxos* is "straight belief," it is usually translated as "right" or "correct" belief.

30. This paragraph is influenced by Smith, 76–78.

31. Also see Armstrong, *The Case for God*, 98.

32. This paragraph is indebted to Borg, *Jesus: Uncovering the Life, Teachings, and Relevance of a Religious Revolutionary*, 20–21, and Armstrong, 87.

33. Pelikan, "Faith," in *The Encyclopedia of Religion*, ed. Jones, 5:2958.

34. The best illustration is the eucharistic debates of the sixteenth century between Martin Luther, Ulrich Zwingli, John Calvin, and the Roman Catholic Council of Trent. See Jones, *Christ's Eucharistic Presence*, 117–67.

35. Armstrong, 173.

36. Smith, 123.

37. The belief element in Christianity is the emotionally laden component and registers the level of investment. See Leffler and Jones, *The Structure of Religion: Judaism and Christianity*, 18–20, 58–59.

38. Smith, 125.

39. Heschel, 166.

40. Carse, *The Religious Case against Belief*, 14–15.

41. McCullough, *The Trivialization of God*, 71.

42. See chapter 1, "The Copernican Revolution in Thinking," where the consequences of the Kantian bifurcation in epistemology are stated: "As heirs of Kant, contemporary Christians frequently identify science as a hard discipline that is based in fact and open to public investigation, while religion is a soft discipline that is based in feeling and open to only private faith."

43. See Mark 12:30; Matt 22:37; and Luke 10:27.

44. Derived from the Greek *apologia* ("speaking in defense"), Christian apologetics is that branch of Christianity that defends the "truth" of the tradition by answering those who oppose or question the basic tenets of the church.

45. Migliore, 2.

46. These traditional Christian terms attempt to capture the transcendent, or "more," dimension of Jesus.

47. Because all the stories of Jesus' words and deeds are redacted (edited by the Gospel writers), I use phrases like "Matthew's Jesus" or "according to Mark's Jesus."

48. MacGregor, "Doubt and Faith," in *The Encyclopedia of Religion*, 5:2424.

49. Tillich, 116.

50. Tillich, 18.

51. Carse, quoted on the page prior to the Table of Contents.

52. Quoted in Palmer, *The Promise of Paradox*, 52.

53. Palmer, xxix.

54. Augustine wrote, "I have been made a question to myself." Quoted in Caputo, *Philosophy and Theology*, 73.

Chapter 3

1. Emmons, "His Word is Truth," 13.

2. Nearly two-thirds of Americans (63 percent) believe that their religion's sacred book is the Word of God. However, 33 percent think it should be interpreted literally, while 27 percent say it should not be taken literally. These statistics are from the Pew Forum on Religion and Public Life, "U.S. Religious Landscape Survey," 5.

3. Peters, *The Children of Abraham*, 3.

4. In Judaism the Hebrew word *Adonai* (translated "Lord") was substituted for Yahweh (YHWH, the Tetragrammaton), the biblical name for God, to avoid taking the name of the Lord in vain.

5. Smith, "word" in *HarperCollins Bible Dictionary*, ed. Achtemeier, 1221.

6. The Roman Catholic response to the challenges of the Enlightenment was different. At the First Vatican Council in 1870, the doctrine of papal infallibility was affirmed by a vote of 533 to 2.

7. Canon is the English translation of the Greek word *kanon*, which means "ruler," or "straight edge."

8. Diaspora in Greek means "scattered."

9. Gnuse, *The Authority of the Bible*, 106.

10. The term Pentateuch (literally the "five scrolls" in Greek) designates the first five books of the Bible, also called the Torah or the Law of Moses (Genesis, Exodus, Leviticus, Numbers, and Deuteronomy).

11. For an excellent summary of the canonization process for the First Testament, see Frick, *A Journey Through the Hebrew Scriptures*, 5–11.

12. Judaism was the first "religion of the book" in Western Civilization, according to Ehrman, *Misquoting Jesus*, 17.

13. Gnuse, 106–7. According to Jewish tradition, but questioned by recent scholarship that finds little evidence to substantiate the meeting, the (hypothetical) Council of Jamnia (Yavneh) strengthened post-Temple Judaism by completing the canonization of the scriptures, giving a precise form to the daily prayers, and transferring to the synagogue and Sanhedrin some of the observances once associated with the Jerusalem Temple.

14. Spieckermann, "Word of God, OT," in *The Encyclopedia of Christianity*, ed. Fahlbusch et al., 750.

15. Although there was no formal action taken by a church council until the Council of Trent in the sixteenth century, most scholars consider the Easter Festival Letter of Bishop Athanasius of Alexandria in 367, which names for the first time the exact number of books (27) in their current order, as the time period when consensus began to emerge. For a brief summary of the canonization process for the Second Testament, see Ehrman, *Misquoting Jesus*, 29–36, and Ehrman, *Jesus, Interrupted*, 189–223. For the standard academic treatment, see Metzger, *The Canon of the New Testament*.

16. Bird, "The Authority of the Bible," in *The New Interpreter's Bible*, 1:45–49.

17. Wolter, "Word of God, NT," in *The Encyclopedia of Christianity*, 751–52.

18. Malcolm, "Word of God, Systematic Theology" in *The Encyclopedia of Christianity*, ed. Fahlbusch et al., 753.

19. The Reformation section is indebted to Bird, 51–52.

20. From its origins, writings played a prominent role in the development of Christianity. See Erhman, *Misquoting Jesus*, 20–29. Although books were central to the life of the early church, the presence of the living Lord and the emphasis on sacraments precluded Christianity from becoming a "Bible-centered religion."

21. Bird, 52.

22. The Apocrypha (from the Greek *apokrypha*, which means "things which are hidden or secret") refers to the collection of Jewish books that are included in the canons of Roman Catholic and Eastern Orthodox Christianity but not in the Protestant Christian canon. However, the number of texts varies. The "deuterocanonical" (literally "second canon," or those writings added later) books of the Roman Catholic Church, the Greek Orthodox Church, and the Russian Orthodox Church are not the same.

23. Bird, 53.

24. Malcolm, 755.

25. For a more detailed description and analysis see chapter 1, "The Scientific Worldview."

26. Bird, 58.

27. For a more detailed description and analysis see chapter 1, "The Rise of Historical Consciousness."

28. The following section is indebted to Bird, 54–56, and Hodgson, "Scripture and Tradition" in *Christian Theology*, ed. Hodgson and King, 72–77.

29. Many typologies have been suggested. See Gnuse, 3–4; Migliore, *Faith Seeking Understanding*, 47–50; and Farley and Hodgson, 76–81.

30. The descriptions of these two positions are informed by Farley and Hodgson, 76–78.

31. Farley and Hodgsen, 76.

32. Kelsey, *The Uses of Scripture in Recent Theology*.

33. This description is heavily dependent on Cottrell, "The Nature of Biblical Authority: A Conservative Perspective," in *Conservative, Moderate, Liberal*, ed. Blaisdell, 21–40.

34. Cottrell, xi.

35. Cottrell, 27.

36. Cottrell, 28.

37. Both of these points are informed by Achtemeier, *The Inspiration of Scripture*, 107–8.

38. For an extensive list of discrepancies and inconsistencies, see Achtemeier, 60–69, as well as Ehrman, *Jesus, Interrupted*.

39. Gen 1:1–2:4a and 2:4b–25.

40. In the Gospel of Mark, Jesus dies during the festival of Passover (15:6), while in the Gospel of John Jesus dies on the day of preparation *before* the Passover (19:31).

41. Docetic comes from the Greek *dokeo* that means "to seem" or "to appear." The biblical text seems or appears to be a historical document but in reality it is supernatural and not subject to historical conditioning or criticism. Docetism was a heresy in the early church that denied the humanity of Jesus.

42. This point is indebted to Achtemeier, 52–53, 70–73.

43. This claim begs the question of whether it is permissible or desirable to translate our oldest manuscripts. If a person cannot study the Bible in its original languages (Hebrew and Greek), does the individual who reads a translation, let alone a paraphrase, still have access to God's meaning ?

44. Achtemeier, 104.

45. For example, Deut 20:16–17; Josh 11:20; Matt 2:16–18; and Rev 19:11–21. This topic is addressed in chapter 7.

46. For example, the flat-earth claims found in Isa 11:12; Ezek 7:2; and Rev 20:8, or the claim that the sun and the moon stood still for Israel (Josh 10:12–13). The miracles of Jesus are addressed in chapter 5.

47. For a developed argument, see Blaisdell, "A Liberal Response," in *Conservative, Moderate, Liberal,* 41–48.

48. This section is indebted to Kelsey, 32, 39–55.

49. Kelsey, 39–40.

50. Placher, "The Nature of Biblical Authority," in *Conservative, Moderate, Liberal,* 12.

51. These comments are indebted to Migliore, 40, 275.

52. This section relies heavily on Kelsey, 90–97.

53. Kelsey, 91. The italics are Kelsey's. The topic of Christian identity formation will be discussed in the postscript.

54. Kelsey, 91. The italics are Kelsey's.

55. Kelsey, 213.

56. Farley and Hodgson, 85–86.

Chapter 4

1. Quoted in "Gaining Consciousness," in *Context: Martin E. Marty on Religion and Culture,* 6.

2. A large color photograph of a blond, blue-eyed, Caucasian Jesus, as a life-size wax figure that will be displayed in the Fort Worth, Texas, Christian Arts Museum, appeared in the "Faith/Values" section of the *Lexington Herald-Leader,* November 8, 2008, C8. Even more astonishing, the centerpiece stained glass window in the chapel of the Bethlehem (West Bank) Lutheran Center depicts an Aryan Jesus.

3. Fleishner, "The Shoah and Jewish-Christian Relations," in *Seeing Judaism Anew,* ed. Boys, 8.

4. Carroll, *Constantine's Sword,* 635 n3.

5. See Heschel, *The Aryan Jesus.*

6. Isaac, *The Teaching of Contempt.*

7. The increasing focus on Jesus' divinity did not, however, separate him from his maleness. This observation is indebted to Professor Amy-Jill Levine.

8. Peters, *The Children of Abraham*, 22.

9. Pelikan, *Jesus through the Centuries*, 20.

10. This chapter will use the term "Shoah" (from the Hebrew word for catastrophe or calamity) instead of the more traditional term "Holocaust" (which refers to an offering made by fire to God). Although the word "Holocaust" is generally employed to describe the genocide of six million European Jews perpetrated by Nazi Germany during the Second World War, such an atrocity should not be associated with the God of the Jewish people. On the contrary, the Final Solution is at minimum an insult to God and at maximum an assault on God.

11. A succinct definition of anti-Semitism is "opposition to Jews as Jews." The use of the hyphenated word (anti-Semitism) has been criticized since it both assumes "the existence of something called 'Semitism'" to which one is opposed and "reflects the bipolarity that is at the heart of the problem of antisemitism" (see Carroll, *Constantine's Sword*, 628–29 n17). Because the majority of authors cited use the hyphenated version of the word, this book will employ it to avoid confusion.

12. Gager, *The Origins of Anti-Semitism*, 13.

13. Flannery, *The Anguish of the Jews*, 266.

14. The earliest followers of Jesus were Galilean and Judean Jews, but with the missionary efforts of Paul and others more and more Gentiles entered the movement. Throughout the first century CE, however, many followers of Jesus participated in Jewish activities like synagogue worship (John 9:22; 12:42; 16:2).

15. Judaism is not a race, but a people. Historically, this confusion dates to the Spanish Inquisition. Although many Jews converted to Catholicism and were baptized, they were still perceived suspiciously. Therefore, an additional reason was invented to legitimize persecution after baptism. Spanish Inquisitors imposed the category of "blood" or race onto the "New Christians"—later called *Marranos*, often thought to mean "pigs." The new legal barriers excluded anyone from certain positions of power who did not have the requisite *limpieza de sangre* or "purity of blood." Although in 1879 Wilhelm Marr, a German journalist, was the first person to use the term "anti-Semitism," it was Adolf Hitler who solidified in the modern era the association of "race" and Jews when he justified the Final Solution on racial grounds.

16. See Fredriksen, "What 'Parting of the Ways'?" in *The Ways that Never Parted*, eds. Becker and Reed, 37, for an explication of the term "formal."

17. "Samuele Bacchiocchi Responds," 60.

18. Acts 15:1–35 and Gal 2:1–10.

19. Because Jesus followers refused to participate in the imperial cult, they in effect denied the ritual affirmation of the emperor as head of state. See Peters, 54.

20. Boring, *Revelation*, 11–13, and Ehrman, *The New Testament*, 410, 422.

21. Fredriksen and Reinhartz, "Introduction," in *Jesus, Judaism & Christian Anti-Judaism*, ed. Fredriksen and Reinhartz, 5.

22. Etymologically, supersessionism means "to sit upon" and thus the term means that the Jesus movement replaced the Jews as the chosen people of God. James Carroll in *Constantine's Sword* cites theologian Mary Boys' definition as summarized by O'Hare in *Enduring Covenant*. The eight tenets that define supersessionism are: "(1) revelation in Jesus Christ supersedes the revelation to Israel; (2) the New Testament fulfills the Old Testament; (3) the church replaces the Jews as God's people; (4) Judaism is obsolete, its covenant abrogated; (5) post-exilic Judaism was legalistic; (6) the Jews did not heed the warning of the prophets; (7) the Jews did not understand the prophecies about Jesus; (8) the Jews were Christ killers" (633n1).

23. See Vermes, "Introduction: Parallel History Preview," in Shanks, *Christianity and Rabbinic Judaism*, xvii, and Boccaccini, "Multiple Judaisms," 38–41, 46.

24. The Talmud is a record of rabbinic discussions about Jewish law, customs, and history and is a central text of Rabbinic Judaism. The Jerusalem Talmud, separate from the Babylonian Talmud, was completed around 400 CE.

25. JT *Sanhedrin* 10.6.29c, as cited in Feldman, "Palestinian and Diaspora Judaism in the First Century," in Shanks, *Christianity and Rabbinic Judaism*, 12n65.

26. *Jewish Antiquities*, XVIII, 1, and *The Jewish War*, II, 117. See *Josephus: The Essential Writings*, trans. Maier, 260–62.

27. Although the destruction of the Second Temple was a key moment in Jewish history, it would be a mistake to interpret the rise of Rabbinic Judaism as a new religion without ties to the Judaism that preceded it. Rather, the founders of Rabbinic Judaism were Jewish and the movement remained exclusively Jewish. Historically speaking, it was a reform movement rather than the revolutionary creation of a new religion. (These insights were gleaned from correspondence with Professor Laurence Kant, former associate professor of religious studies at Lexington Theological Seminary, Lexington, Kentucky.)

28. The Pharisees, punctilious observers and skillful interpreters of the laws, were one of four known Jewish groups at the time of Jesus mentioned by Josephus, the Jewish historian, but, most important, the only group to survive the first Jewish war with Rome.

29. Peters, 45.

30. Neusner's quotation is found in Boccaccini, "Multiple Judaisms," 40.

31. Christianity's canon includes two testaments: the First Testament (Hebrew Scriptures) and the Second Testament.

32. See Boccaccini, "Multiple Judaisms," 41; Levine, *The Misunderstood Jew*, 5; Madigan and Levenson, *Resurrection*, 235; and Ruether, *Faith and Fratricide*, 254–57.

33. Segal, *Rebecca's Children*, 1 and 179.

34. Although Pauline Christianity did not respond to the destruction (since Paul wrote in the 50s), the canonical Gospels do. See especially Mark 11:12–26 and John 2:13–22.

35. Ruiz, "Ancient Jewish-Christian Rivalries," in *Seeing Judaism Anew*, 62.

36. Fredriksen, "The Birth of Christianity," in *Jesus, Judaism, and Christian Anti-Judaism*, 15.

37. See Wylen, *The Jews in the Time of Jesus*, 190–92, for a more detailed description of the "historical causes of the split between Judaism and Christianity," and Nickelsburg, *Ancient Judaism and Christian Origins*, 194–95, for a nuanced interpretation of internal Jewish reasons for the separation.

38. The use of the term "salvation" is problematic since the original Jewish meaning has been overshadowed by a very different Christian understanding. For Judaism, salvation focuses on this world. The individual is "saved" from a meaningless existence by living a sanctified life in the here and now. For Christianity, salvation is usually associated with proper belief that in turn is related to a concern for life-after-death.

39. "Apocalyptic" refers to a worldview shared by many but not all ancient Jews and Christians that the present age is controlled by forces of evil and that God will soon intervene in history to destroy the old age and usher in a new age (called the "Kingdom" or "reign of God" by many Christians).

40. Levine, *The Misunderstood Jew*, 17.

41. Moltmann, "Israel's No: Jews and Jesus in an Unredeemed World," 1021–24.

42. Sanders, "Reflections on Anti-Judaism in the New Testament and in Christianity," in *Anti-Judaism and the Gospels*, ed. Farmer, 266.

43. Levine, "Anti-Judaism and the Gospel of Matthew," in *Anti-Judaism and the Gospels*, 14.

44. Sanders, "Reflections on Anti-Judaism in the New Testament and in Christianity," 267.

45. For example: Matt 27:25; John 8:42–44; Acts 2:23, 4:10. Because the canonical Gospels are the written record of the Christian communities' experiences of God as known in the person of Jesus of Nazareth, they are both embedded in and subject to the vicissitudes of history. Regardless of the sacredness of the texts, they are the record of human perceptions and not exempt from historical conditioning. If the Gospels are read only as sacred and therefore devoid of human particularity, these passages can become lethal. This recognition underscores the necessity of reading the Bible critically, a subject addressed in chapter 5.

46. Marcion, a second-century Christian scholar, was labeled a heretic for his docetic views of Jesus and his belief in two Gods—the harsh legalistic God of the Jews and the merciful and loving God of Jesus. He proposed a Christian Bible that only consisted of the Gospel of Luke and ten letters of Paul. Although his canon was rejected by the early church, it jump-started the process of canonization of the Christian Bible.

47. TaNaK is an acronym made up of the first letters from the Hebrew words designating the three major sections of the First Testament: Torah (Law), Nevi'îm (Prophets) and Ketuvîm (Writings).

48. The last section of the Hebrew Bible consists of the Writings. This is something of a catchall category, which includes historical books (Ezra, Nehemiah, Chronicles), poetic compositions (Psalms, Song of Songs, Lamentations), Wisdom books (Job, Proverbs, Ecclesiastes), short stories (Ruth, Esther), and one prophetic or apocalyptic composition (Daniel).

49. All three versions separate what we now call the Former Prophets (Joshua, Judges, Samuel, and Kings) from the Latter (Isaiah, Jeremiah, Ezekiel, and Book of the Twelve Minor Prophets).

50. See Matt 11:10–14; 17:10–13; Mark 1:2–4; 9:13; and Luke 1:17. John 1:21 denies the Elijah connection.

51. Crossan posits a compelling argument, that I endorse, against the idea of Jesus as "uniquely unique" in "Why Is Historical Jesus Research Necessary?" in *Jesus Two Thousand Years Later*, ed. Charlesworth and Weaver, 18–19.

52. This section is especially indebted to Levine, *The Misunderstood Jew*, 124–66.

53. There are 613 mitzvot, or commandments, in the Torah.

54. See especially Matt 5:21–48.

55. Approximately eight hundred manuscripts, dating from the third or second century BCE, were found beginning in 1947 in eleven caves at Qumran on the northwest shore of the Dead Sea.

56. Levine, *The Misunderstood Jew*, 127–28. Caligula was assassinated (unrelated) before the statue was erected in the Temple.

57. For example, Rev 14:20.

58. For example, Gen 1:1–31; Exod 3:7–8; Isa 40:1–11; Jer 31:31–4; and Hos 11:1–12.

59. See Levine, *The Misunderstood Jew*, 132–49, for multiple examples.

60. The Mishnah is the first major written redaction of the Jewish oral traditions called the "Oral Torah" and the first major work of Rabbinic Judaism. It was edited in approximately 200 CE.

61. See Malina, *The New Testament World*, 161–197; Klawans, "Moral and Ritual Purity" in *The Historical Jesus in Context*, ed. Levine et al., 266–84; and Sanders, "Jesus, Ancient Judaism, and Modern Christianity: The Quest Continues" in *Jesus, Judaism, and Christian Anti-Judaism*, 35–41.

62. The Christian sacraments of baptism and eucharist have Jewish antecedents in baptism and ritual cleansing (mikvah), and in the feast of the unleavened bread (Passover) and table fellowship.

63. As a child Jesus is presented by his parents in the Temple (Luke

2:22–40) and as a twelve-year-old boy Jesus' parents find him learning in the Temple (Luke 2:41–52).

64. Carroll, *Constantine's Sword*, 104.

65. See Crossan and Reed, *In Search of Paul*, 38–40, for a discussion of the Greek term *Theosebeis*, often translated "God-fearers" or "God-worshipers."

66. Levine, *The Misunderstood Jew*, 159. This rabbinic statement is even broader in scope than Paul's inclusive pronouncement in Gal 3:28.

67. Reinhartz, "The Gospel of John: How the 'Jews' Became Part of the Plot" in *Jesus, Judaism & Christian Anti-Judaism*, 112–15.

68. Levine, *The Misunderstood Jew*, 125.

69. Levine, 23–51, and Levine, "Misusing Jesus," 20–25.

70. Sanders, "Jesus, Ancient Judaism, and Modern Christianity," in *Jesus, Judaism & Christian Anti-Judaism*, 54–55. Also see Sanders, *Jesus and Judaism*, chap. 9.

71. This section is informed by Levine, *The Misunderstood Jew*, 7–16.

72. For example, plots to kill Jesus (Mark 11:18 and 12:12, and John 11:45–54); the "cleansing of the Temple" (Mark 11:12–25 and parallels); and the denigrating words of Jesus (John 8:39–47).

73. Judaism has its own interpretive traditions. See Neusner, *A Short History of Judaism*, 8 and 132.

74. Belief in the second coming does not require a physical return of Jesus. My point is that both Jews and Christians live in a posture of waiting, and it is precisely that anticipation of "more" which makes space for mutual respect.

75. Rosemary Ruether proposes six specific reforms in theological curricula in *Faith and Fratricide*, 259–61.

76. A Hebrew phrase that means "to repair the world" or "perfecting the world" through acts of social justice. Although connected to both classical rabbinic literature and Lurianic Kabbalah, the term currently means "human responsibility for fixing the world."

Chapter 5

1. http://www.gallup.com/poll/1690/religion.aspx.

2. Although the early church also read the scriptures allegorically, it assumed an initial literal or historical layer of interpretation. See Origen, *On First Principles*, bk. 4, chap. 1–3, trans. Butterworth. Traditionally there were two schools of interpretation: the Alexandrian (allegorical) and the Antiochene (literal). Origen is a representative of the former, while Theodore of Mopsuestia is a representative of the latter.

3. Borg, *Reading the Bible Again for the First Time*, 8.

4. Hermeneutics is the study of the theory and practice of interpretation.

5. See Smart, *The Strange Silence of the Bible in the Church*.

6. These comments are dependent on Coogan, "The Great Gulf between Scholars and the Pew," 44–48, 55.

7. The anger and antagonism directed toward the Jesus Seminar (whose goal is to share the methods and the results of biblical scholarship with the general public) by the press, the church, and the academy confirm this point. See Miller, *The Jesus Seminar and Its Critics*.

8. Ehrman, *Jesus, Interrupted*, 282.

9. In Greek and Roman mythology, an oracle was a place or a person by which the gods were consulted.

10. These principles are taken from Holladay, "Contemporary Methods of Reading the Bible," vol. 1, 126–28, and Farley and Hodgson, "Scripture and Tradition" in Hodgson and King, *Christian Theology*, 38–41.

11. The Bible is understood as a divine medium or mouthpiece.

12. The subsequent comments are based on information from Ehrman, *Misquoting Jesus*, 88–89, 222–23 n13.

13. Ehrman, *Jesus, Interrupted*, 184.

14. The official version of the Bible for the Roman Catholic Church that was translated from the Hebrew and the Greek into Latin by Jerome at the end of the fourth century CE.

15. Ehrman, "Did Jesus Get Angry or Agonize?," 17. One way that scholars address this problem is to classify manuscripts into "text families" which provides a more reliable method of evaluating the internal integrity of the texts.

16. For example, "r" and "d" side-by-side could mean "red," "rod," or "road." Although the context of the sentence provides strong interpretive clues, it does not guarantee the correct word choice.

17. Although there are *hapaxes* in both testaments, many of the Greek words not found in scripture are found in other Greek texts of the time, which help scholars determine their meaning.

18. An Aramaic substratum is still present in the Second Testament. See for example Mark 5:41; 7:34; and 15:34.

19. The early Jesus movement also read from a Greek translation (the Septuagint) of the Hebrew Bible.

20. An appeal to the Holy Spirit or God's inspiration to authenticate a particular interpretation of a text is also unacceptable since an alternative reading can make the same appeal.

21. Discrepancies, inconsistencies, and contradictions stipple the pages of both testaments.

22. The term Synoptics, which means "a common perspective," refers to the first three canonical Gospels: Matthew, Mark, and Luke. Matthew and Luke share the storyline of Mark.

23. Matt 2:1–12 and Luke 2:8–20.

24. Although the order may vary, the texts are: Luke 23:34; 23:43; John 19:26–27; Matt 27:46 and Mark 15:34; John 19:28; 19:30; and Luke 23:46.

25. Oliver "Buzz" Thomas, in *10 Things Your Minister Wants to Tell You*, provides an entertaining list on pp. 70–71.

26. Carse, *The Religious Case against Belief*, 198–99.

27. Trible, *God and the Rhetoric of Sexuality*, 16.

28. This statement is not meant to exclude God, Christ, and the Holy Spirit, or the larger tradition.

29. I am indebted for these two rules to James O. Duke, my esteemed teacher and current Professor of History of Christianity and History of Christian Thought at Brite Divinity School, Texas Christian University.

30. See "The Rise of Historical Consciousness" and "The Copernican Revolution in Thinking" in chapter 1.

31. The term "historical criticism" is a sub-discipline of the broader term "biblical criticism." Biblical criticism in the broadest sense refers to any approach to the study of the Bible that employs scientific and nonsectarian methodologies. Before the middle of the twentieth century, biblical criticism was virtually synonymous with historical criticism. Now biblical criticism includes non-historical approaches. The terms "historical criticism" and "the historical-critical method" are equivalent.

32. This claim is not the same as declaring that all the people mentioned in the Bible are historical persons.

33. The following comments are taken from Holladay, "Contemporary Methods," 128–36.

34. Introductory books on the various methods include Hayes and Holladay, *Biblical Exegesis: A Beginner's Handbook*, 3rd ed.; McKenzie and Haynes, eds., *To Each Its Own Meaning*; Soulen and Soulen, *Handbook of Biblical Criticism*; and the general essays in Keck, ed., *The New Interpreter's Bible*, vol. 1. For a historical overview of biblical interpretation see Grant with Tracy, *A Short History of the Interpretation of the Bible*, 2nd ed., and Armstrong, *The Bible: A Biography*.

35. *Sitz im Leben* is a German phrase that roughly translates as "setting in life." In form criticism it refers to the social context of the text and the various occasions for which the text was originally designed to be used.

36. The redaction of Mark's Gospel by the authors of Matthew and Luke further undermines the principles of the divine oracle model.

37. Although canonical criticism does not aim at the original meaning and therefore is not, technically speaking, a part of historical criticism, it does acknowledge the later interpretive context of the canonical writings. See Holladay, "Contemporary Methods," 134, and Holladay, "Canonical Criticism," in *The HarperCollins Bible Dictionary*, ed. Achtemeier, 145.

38. The description of these two limits is indebted to Johnson, *The Writings of the New Testament*, 10.

39. The following comments are dependent on Holladay, "Contemporary Methods," 136–40.

40. These descriptions are indebted to Holladay, "Contemporary Methods," 140–44, as well as two entries in the *HarperCollins Bible Dictionary*, ed. Achtemeier: Kingsbury, "Narrative Criticism," 739–40, and McKnight, "Reader-Response Criticism," 915–18.

41. See Powell, *What Is Narrative Criticism?*

42. McKnight, "Reader-Response Criticism" in McKenzie and Haynes, eds., *To Each Its Own Meaning*, 230.

43. See McKnight, *Postmodern Use of the Bible.*

44. See Russell, ed., *Feminist Interpretation of the Bible*; Newsom and Ringe, eds. *The Women's Bible Commentary*, and Clifford, *Introducing Feminist Theology.*

45. See Cone, *A Black Theology of Liberation* and *God of the Oppressed.*

46. Especially see Gutiérrez, *A Theology of Liberation*, and Luis Segundo, *Doing Theology in a Revolutionary Situation.*

47. For example, Achtemeier, ed., *HarperCollins Bible Dictionary*, Freedman, ed., *Eerdmans Dictionary of the Bible*; and Sakenfeld, ed., *The New Interpreter's Dictionary of the Bible.*

48. There are many one-volume commentaries, such as Mays, ed., *HarperCollins Bible Commentary*, and multiple-volume commentaries such as Keck, ed., *The New Interpreter's Bible: A Commentary in Twelve Volumes.*

49. Ehrman, *Misquoting Jesus*, 29.

50. Obviously the First Testament, or Hebrew Bible, belonged to Judaism before Christianity appropriated it. The statement that "the Bible is the church's book" does not vitiate that prior claim.

51. See Brueggemann, *The Bible Makes Sense*, rev. ed., esp. 119–25.

52. Marcus Borg makes this point exceedingly well in *The Heart of Christianity*, 50–51, when he talks about "metaphorical truths."

53. These comments are indebted to Brueggemann, *The Bible Makes Sense*, 27–31.

54. See chapter 1, "Implications for Religious Life Today."

55. This qualification ("principal partner" as opposed to "only partner"), which undermines the Protestant affirmation of *sola scriptura* (scripture alone), acknowledges the paramount role of the community in the formation of the Bible and the tradition's ongoing conversation about biblical interpretation and meaning.

Chapter 6

1. *USA Today*, Thursday, March 5, 2009, 1C, and Tuesday, March 10, 2009, 1A.

2. Lewis, *God in the Dock*, 80.

3. Blanton, "More Believe in God than Heaven."

4. *U.S. Religious Landscape Survey*, 11.

5. Remus, "Miracle (NT)" in *The Anchor Bible Dictionary*, ed. Freedman, vol. 4, 868.

6. Quoted in Copan, ed., *Will the Real Jesus Please Stand Up?*, 24.

7. Armstrong, *The Case for God*, 88, and Peters, *The Children of Abraham*, 23.

8. GotQuestions.org, "Are the Miracles in the Bible to Be Taken Literally?"

9. Bultmann, "New Testament and Mythology" in *Kerygma and Myth*, ed. Bartsch, trans. Fuller, 5. Meier in *The Marginal Jew*, vol. 2, 520, translates the final phrase as "miracles."

10. According to the contemporary philosopher Richard Swinburne, the word "miracle" is defined as a "violation of a law of nature by a god." See Swinburne, *The Concept of Miracle*, 11.

11. Although this question is legitimate, it cannot be answered, since it was not an issue for people of antiquity in general and the Gospel writers in particular. Moreover, the historian cannot investigate supernatural agency. Both of these concerns are addressed in this chapter.

12. This section does not address the theological and ethical challenges to the possibility of miracles, such as the infrequency of intervention, which raises the issue of God permitting suffering (theodicy); the immorality of inaction, which raises the question of God's integrity; and the arbitrariness of action, which raises the issue of God's selectivity.

13. Pelikan, *Jesus through the Centuries*, 183.

14. See "The Scientific Worldview" and "The Rise of Historical Consciousness" in chapter 1.

15. Pelikan, 183.

16. Empiricism is a branch of epistemology (the theory of knowledge, or how humans know things) which asserts that knowledge arises from sense experience. Hence, experience and evidence (gleaned from experiments) are paramount in the acquisition of knowledge.

17. The title of section X of Hume's *Enquiries Concerning Human Understanding and Concerning the Principles of Morals*, 109–31.

18. Students of Hume acknowledge two ways to read him—a "hard" and a "soft" interpretation. The former declares miracles as impossible since (1) miracles are a violation of natural law; (2) natural laws are uniform and unchangeable; and (3) therefore, they do not occur. The latter judges miracles as incredulous since (1) a miracle by definition is rare; (2) natural law by definition describes a regular occurrence; (3) evidence for the regular is greater than for rarity; (4) a rational person grounds belief on greater evidence; and (5) therefore, a rational person should not believe in miracles. See Geisler, "Miracles and the Modern Mind" in *In Defense of Miracles*, ed. Geivett and Habermas, 75. For an opposing view to Hume, see Twelftree, *Jesus the Miracle Worker*, 38–53.

19. Hume, 131.

20. Pelikan, 184.

21. The following comments are indebted to Borg, "The Search Begins," 17–19.

22. The following comments are based on Ehrman, *The New Testament*, 3rd ed., 225–29. For an opposing view, see Beckwith, "History and Miracles" in Geivett and Habermas, 86–98.

23. Both David Hume and C.S. Lewis agree. See Hume, 114, and Lewis, *Miracles: A Preliminary Study*, 15.

24. John Meier, 512, agrees when he writes: "A miracle is . . . an event that finds no reasonable explanation in human abilities or in other known forces that operate in our world of time and space, and . . . [is] an event that is the result of a special act of God, doing what no human power can

do." Manabu Waida concurs when he defines miracles in the *Encyclopedia of Religion* as "events, actions, and states taken to be so unusual, extraordinary, and supernatural that the normal level of human consciousness finds them hard to accept rationally. These miracles are usually taken as manifestations of the supernatural power of the divine being fulfilling his purpose in history...." See Waida, "Miracles" in *Encyclopedia of Religion*, ed. Jones, 2nd ed., vol. 9, 6049. For a catalog of definitions, see Twelftree, 24–27.

25. This typology of approaches is partially based on Boring, "The Gospel of Matthew," in *The New Interpreter's Bible*, ed. Keck, vol. 8, 248–49.

26. See footnote 18 in this chapter.

27. In 1910, the Presbyterians of Princeton University "issued a list of five dogmas which they deemed essential: (1) the inerrancy of Scripture, (2) the Virgin birth of Christ, (3) Christ's atonement for our sins on the cross, (4) his bodily resurrection, and (5) the objective reality of his miracles." This statement is found in Armstrong, *The Battle for God*, 171.

28. *Kerygma* is the Greek word for proclamation or preaching. The term "contextual-kerygmatic explanation" is the author's phrase.

29. A recent example is Capps, *Jesus the Village Psychiatrist*.

30. For a brief explanation of the meaning of "religious myth," see Livingston, *Anatomy of the Sacred*, 3rd ed., 81–88.

31. Kee, *Miracle in the Early Christian World*, 2.

32. See Cotter, "Miracle Stories" in *The Historical Jesus in Context*, ed. Levine et al., 166–67.

33. Crossan, "Why Is Historical Jesus Research Necessary?" in *Jesus Two Thousand Years Later*, ed. Charlesworth and Weaver, 19.

34. The following comments are indebted to Hendrickx, *The Miracle Stories*, 3–5.

35. For the primary texts that narrate both Greco-Roman and Jewish miracle-workers at the time of Jesus, see Cartlidge and Dungan, *Documents for the Study of the Gospels*, 151–65.

36. See Meier, 576–81; Cotter, 169; and Kee, 256–65.

37. Meier, 594–95.

38. Cotter, 170.

39. See Zakovitch, "Miracle (OT)," in *The Anchor Bible Dictionary*, ed. Freedman, vol. 4, 845–46, and Licht, "Miracle," in *Encyclopaedia Judaica*, ed. Berenbaum and Skolnik, vol. 14, 305.

40. Kee, 147.

41. See Boring, 247, for the Babylonian Talmud references.

42. For the text of the stories, see Cartlidge and Dungan, 158–59.

43. Maier, trans. and ed., *Josephus: The Essential Writings*, 265 excursus.

44. See Matt 7:22; 11:20, 21, 23; 13:54, 58; Mark 5:30; 6:2, 5, 14; 9:39; Luke 1:17; 10:13; 19:37; and Acts 2:22; 8:13; 10:38.

45. In the Gospel of John all miracles are called "signs" (John 2:11, 18, 23; 3:2; 4:48, 54; 6:2, 14, 26, 30; 7:31; 9:16; 10:41; 11:47; 12:18, 37; 20:30). Other Second Testament texts that use this term are Matt 12:38,

39; 16:1, 3, 4; 24:3, 24, 30; Mark 8:11, 12; 13:4, 22; Luke 11:16, 29, 30; 21:7, 11, 25; 23:8; and Acts 2:19, 22, 43; 4:30; 6:8; 7:36; 14:3; 15:12.

46. See Matt 24:24; Mark 13:22; John 4:48; Acts 2:19, 22, 43; 4:30; 5:12; 6:8; 7:36; 14:3; 15:12; Rom 15:19; 2 Cor 12:12; 2 Thess 2:9; and Heb 2:4.

47. See Matt 11:2; Luke 24:19; and John 7:3, 21; 9:3, 4; 10:25, 32, 37, 38; 14:10, 11, 12; 15:24.

48. The above discussion is based on Hendrickx, 10, and Cotter, "Miracle" in *The New Interpreter's Dictionary of the Bible*, ed. Sakenfeld, vol. 4, 104.

49. Matt 27:51–53 and Acts 2:1–4; 2:17.

50. Matt 1:18–25; 2:1–12; and Acts 12:6–11; 12:20–23.

51. Matt 10:1, 8, 20; Mark 6:7, 13; 13:11; Luke 9:1–2; 12:12 (exorcisms, healings, raising the dead); Acts 3:1–10; 5:1–11, 12–16; 9:32–35, 36–43; Rom 15:19; and 2 Cor 12:12.

52. Acts 6:8; 8:6, 13; 14:3, 8–12; 15:12; 16:16–18; 19:11; 1 Cor 12:10, 29; Gal 3:5; Heb 2:4.

53. Matt 7:22; 24:24; and Mark 13:22.

54. Matt 12:27; Luke 11:19; Acts 19:13–16; 2 Thess 2:9; and Rev 13:13–14; 16:14; 19:20. The above lists are taken from Boring, 246.

55. Boring, 244. This page also contains a chart of the number of different types of miracles in each Gospel. Funk, *Acts of Jesus*, 13–15, lists all thirty-two miracles and their respective Gospel passages, as does Boring, 242–43.

56. Meier, 619.

57. Boring, 241.

58. Ten of the twenty miracles occur in chapters 8 and 9.

59. Twelftree, 104 and 140.

60. Ehrman, 97–98.

61. Kee, 158, and Twelftree, 187. See Jesus' commissioning scene in Luke 4:14–30. Note that Luke's Jesus compares himself with Elijah and Elisha in vv. 25–27.

62. The parallel stories are Matt 12:22–30 and Mark 3:22–27.

63. Kee, 205.

64. They are: (1) turning water into wine at the wedding at Cana (2:1–12); (2) healing of an official's son (4:46–54); (3) healing of an invalid at the Pool of Bethzatha (5:1–18); (4) feeding of the 5,000 (6:1–14); (5) walking on the water (6:16–21); (6) healing of a man born blind (9:1–17); and (7) raising of Lazarus (11:1–44). Although some people count the appearance of Jesus to the disciples in Galilee after the resurrection as the eighth sign (21:4–14), most scholars judge John 21 as an appendix or epilogue and not part of the original text. In addition, there are no exorcisms in this Gospel. See Twelftree, 222–23, for elaboration.

65. Twelftree, 340.

66. Scholars call the present experience of eternal life in John "realized eschatology." See Twelftree, 228.

67. Funk, 13–15. As stated earlier, there are thirty-two distinct Jesus miracle stories.

68. Mark 4:35–41; Matt 8:23–27; and Luke 8:22–25.

69. Mark 6:35–44; Matt 14:15–21; Luke 9:12–17; and John 6:1–14.

70. The following comments on nature miracles are indebted to Fossum, "Understanding Jesus' Miracles," 17–23, 50.

71. Although the Gospel stories unfold chronologically, they were obviously written after the crucifixion and resurrection of Jesus. Therefore, the feeding narratives prefigured the Last Supper in terms of the storyline, but the fourfold verb action of the Lord's Supper was read back into the story.

72. See, for example, Mark 1:29–31, 40–45.

73. Fossum, 23.

74. Fossum, 23.

75. Elijah worked hard to raise a child from the dead (1 Kgs 17:17–24) but Jesus used only a word (Mark 5:35–43). Elisha fed a hundred people with twenty barley loaves (2 Kgs 4:42–44) but Jesus fed five thousand with just five loaves (Mark 6:30–44). Elisha made an ax head float on the water (2 Kgs 6:1–7), but Jesus himself walked on water (Matt 14:22–33; Mark 6:45–52; and John 6:16–21).

76. Ehrman, *Jesus, Interrupted*, 78.

77. Hendrickx, 16–18, and O'Day, "The Gospel of John" in *The New Interpreter's Bible*, vol. 9, 576.

78. See Matt 12:38–42; Mark 8:11–13; Luke 11:29–32; and John 2:13–22.

79. Boring, 250.

80. Spong, *Jesus for the Non-Religious*, 95.

81. Boring, 251.

82. See chapter 2, "The Universal Experience of Faith," where the "transcendent" is defined as "a reality that exceeds the mundane; a depth dimension that beckons beyond the ordinary; a horizon of meaning that locates both the end of human vision and the beginning of more; an acknowledgement that what people observe and know about this world does not exhaust its wonder and mystery."

83. For an explanation, see chapter 1, "The Scientific Worldview."

84. Coffin, *Credo*, 10.

Chapter 7

1. The parallel Gospel passages are: Matt 22:34–40; Mark 12:28–31; and Luke 10:25–27.

2. Hillman, *A Terrible Love of War*, 17.

3. Hedges, *What Every Person Should Know about War*, 1 and 7.

4. Brecht, *Mother Courage and Her Children*, trans. Bentley, 75–76.

5. Barash, ed., *Approaches to Peace*, 2nd ed., 221.

6. Barash, 221.

7. Bainton, *Christian Attitudes toward War and Peace*, 136–51.

8. Quoted in Hillman, 195.

9. Barash, 221. Mark Twain's "The War Prayer" and Bob Dylan's "With God on Our Side" are excellent examples of parodies.

10. The classic Christian hymns "Onward Christian Soldiers" and "Battle Hymn of the Republic" illustrate how our corporate worship can contribute to the endorsement of violence.

11. MSNBC.com, "Full text of Obama's Noble Peace Prize speech."

12. The "new atheists" and their respective books are Dawkins' *The God Delusion*, Harris' *The End of Faith* and *Letter to a Christian Nation*, and Hitchens' *God Is Not Great*.

13. Hitchens, 13.

14. Hitchens, 102.

15. Hitchens, 229. Italics added.

16. Krattenmaker, "Religion Can Help End Wars, Too," 15A.

17. Eliot, "Four Quartets," 118.

18. Schwartz, *The Curse of Cain.*

19. Schwartz, 5. As discussed in chapter 4, anti-Jewish writings of the early Jesus movement were produced to affirm the insider identity of the church over against the mainstream Jewish outsider. For an illustration see Jones, "From Intra-Jewish Polemics to Persecution," 161–97.

20. In this context, sin, as the denial of our relatedness to the divine, disrupts our essential relatedness to both God as transcendent other and neighbor as earthly other.

21. Myth does not mean fairy tale or fictional story. More important, myth for scholars of religion represents humanity's attempt to express the inner meaning or the depth dimension of life that eludes rational explanations. Thus, the Adamic myth (Gen 2:4b–3:24, but it can also include the creation story in Gen 1) narrates truths about the interior life of humanity.

22. Tillich, *Systematic Theology*, vol. 2, 31.

23. Crossan, *God and Empire*, 57–58.

24. Niebuhr, *The Nature and Destiny of Man*, vol. 1, 179–86, and Ricoeur, *The Symbolism of Evil*, trans. Buchanan, 256–60.

25. See Browning, *Ordinary Men.*

26. As an etiology (a story that explains the origins of the way things are in the world), Abel, the shepherd, represents the fading past, while Cain, the farmer, represents the emerging future. Furthermore, the Hebrews were nomadic and therefore favored the pastoral shepherd life. Not surprisingly, the murderer Cain founded the first city.

27. See the first and second commandments of the Decalogue, Exod 20:2–5.

28. Schwartz, 3.

29. Schwartz, xi.

30. Gen 25:19–34.

31. Gen 19:5.

32. Deut 20:17.

33. Schwartz, 18–19.

34. *Pogrom* is a Russian word which means "to wreak havoc, to de-molish violently." Historically the term usually refers to violent attacks by Gentiles against Jews.

35. For a recent treatment of these three responses, see Allman, *Who Would Jesus Kill?*

36. Kurlansky, *Non-Violence: The History of a Dangerous Idea*, 22.

37. Bainton, 73.

38. Bainton, 77.

39. Bainton, 77.

40. Quoted in Kimball, *When Religion Becomes Evil*, 160.

41. Kimball, 160.

42. Pelikan, *Jesus through the Centuries*, 173.

43. According to Raymund of Aguiles, an eyewitness, the massacre after the First Crusaders captured Jerusalem in July 1099 was horrific: "Wonderful sights were to be seen. Some of our men (and this was more merciful) cut off the heads of their enemies; others shot them with arrows, so that they fell from the towers; others tortured them longer by casting them into the flames. Piles of heads, hands and feet were to be seen in the streets of the city. It was necessary to pick one's way over the bodies of men and horses. But these were small matters compared to what happened at the Temple of Solomon, a place where religious services are normally chanted. What happened there? If I tell the truth it will exceed your powers of belief. So let it suffice to say this much, at least, that in the Temple and porch of Solomon, men rode in blood up to their knees and bridle reins. Indeed it was a just and splendid judgment of God that this place should be filled with the blood of the unbelievers since it had suffered so long from their blasphemies." Quoted in Armstrong, *Holy War*, 178–79.

44. Because advocates of a "just war" doctrine usually condone their own country's wars, religious institutions can be manipulated and used by political authorities to gain approval for violence. Recognizing the ease with which religious traditions can be distorted, Charles Kimball identifies five warning signs when religion becomes evil. They are: (1) religion makes "ab-solute truth claims," (2) religion encourages "blind obedience," (3) religion envisions an "ideal time" that can justify violence, (4) religion claims that "the end justifies the means," and (5) religion sanctions a "holy war." See Kimball, 41–185.

45. Volf, *Exclusion & Embrace*, 301.

46. Quoted in Wink, *The Powers That Be*, 84–85.

47. Lüdemann, *The Unholy in Holy Scripture*, trans. Bowden, 40.

48. The famous Moabite Stone, erected by the ninth-century BCE King Mesha to celebrate a victory over Israel, reads: "And Chemosh said to me, 'Go, take Nebo from Israel. So I went by night and fought against it from the break of dawn until noon, taking it and slaying all, seven thousand men, boys, women, girls, and maid-servants, for I had devoted them to destruc-tion for (the god) Ashtar-Chemosh.'" Quoted in Collins, *Does the Bible Justify Violence?*, 5.

49. Lüdemann, 43.

50. Lüdemann, 15.

51. Marcion, a second-century Christian scholar, was labeled a heretic for his belief in two Gods—the harsh legalistic God of the Jews and the merciful and loving God of Jesus.

52. A careful reading of the four canonical Gospels reveals a nuanced portrait of Jesus that occasionally endorses violence. See, for example, Jesus' saying in Matt 10:34 ("I have not come to bring peace, but a sword") and select parables (Matt 13:36–43; 47–50; and 18:23–35). In general, the Jesus of the Gospels is opposed to violence.

53. This section is indebted to Crossan, 217–31.

54. Matt 21:1–11; Mark 11:1–11a; and Luke 19:28–38. See Borg and Crossan, *The Last Week*, 1–30.

55. Rev 19:11–21.

56. John 1:29 and 19:31.

57. Rev 5:5–6, 12; 6:15–17; 17:14.

58. Rev 6:1–8.

59. The accounts of the Last Supper are found in 1 Cor 11:23–26; Matt 26:26–29; Mark 14:22–25; and Luke 22:14–20.

60. This description is based on Volf, 288–303.

61. Volf, 298.

62. Volf, 298.

63. Volf, 299. Italics in the original.

64. Crossan, 227. This paragraph is based on Crossan, 227–35.

65. Crossan, 230.

66. Crossan, 94. Italics in the original.

67. Crossan, 94.

68. This discussion of the doctrine of the Trinity is dependent on Migliore, *Faith Seeking Understanding*, 56–79. For a brief introduction to the historical development of the doctrine of the Trinity, see McGrath, *Christian Theology: An Introduction*, 247–69. For a detailed introduction, see Rusch, *The Trinitarian Controversy*.

69. The Greek word *oikonomia* means "economy" and refers to the way in which one's affairs are managed. For Christian theology, it refers to how God conducts the "economy" of salvation for the world.

70. These three principles are based on Migliore, 76–82.

71. Elaine Pagels makes a compelling case for the positive other in *The Origin of Satan*. See especially the "Conclusion," 179–84.

72. These concluding comments are indebted to an email exchange with Clark Williamson on April 5, 2010.

73. See Collins, 28–33, for a complete discussion.

74. Quoted in Wolpe, *Why Faith Matters*, 78.

75. "Church as Crypt," 8–9.

Postscript

1. Quoted in L. M. White, *From Jesus to Christianity*, 439.

2. Quoted in Roysden, "Will the Real Disciples Please Stand Up?," 20.

3. The following discussion is based on Jones, "We Are *How* We Worship: Corporate Worship as a Matrix for Christian Identity Formation," 346–60.

4. See Linn, *Christians Must Choose*, 80, and Westerhoff III, *Living the Faith Community*, 74.

5. The preceding seven chapters attest to this condition.

6. The Greek word *ecclesia* is usually translated as "church."

7. The following comments are based on "Gaining Consciousness" in Marty (ed.), *Context*, 6–7.

8. Charry, "Raising Christian Children in a Pagan Culture," 166.

9. These quotations are from Hauerwas, *Unleashing the Scripture*, 15–16.

10. Brueggemann, *The Bible Makes Sense*, 94–95 and 124.

11. Calvin, *Institutes of the Christian Religion*, ed. McNeill, trans. Battles, vol. xxi, bk. IV, chap. 1, sec. 4.

12. For a detailed statement, see Jones, "Worship as Identity Formation," 50–52.

13. The classic hymn, "Tell Me the Stories of Jesus," serves as an excellent example.

14. According to the Roman Catholic Church, there are seven sacraments: baptism, confirmation, eucharist, reconciliation (confession, or penance), anointing of the sick (extreme unction, or last rites), holy orders (ordination), and marriage. Some Protestant traditions avoid the word "sacrament" and use instead the word "ordinance." The former term places more emphasis on "what God does," while the latter term focuses more on "what the worshiper does." Protestant churches usually recognize only two sacraments or ordinances: baptism and Lord's Supper (eucharist).

15. See Rom 6:3–6; Eph 4:22–24; and Col 2:11–12 and 3:9–11.

16. For elaboration, see J. White, *Introduction to Christian Worship*, 3d ed., 217–25.

17. There are five traditional English names by which this event is identified: Holy Communion (1 Cor 10:16), Lord's Supper or Last Supper (1 Cor 11:20), the breaking of the bread (Acts 2:42), eucharist (1 Cor 10:16, 11:24), and Mass (employed almost exclusively by the Roman Catholic Church, this term is derived from the use of the Latin term *missio*, which refers to the dismissal of the nonmembers prior to the celebration of the ritual meal).

18. J. White, *Sacraments as God's Self Giving*, 52.

19. Power, *The Eucharistic Mystery*, 18. In addition, see Crossan's discussion of commensality—"the rules of tabling and eating as miniature models for the rules of association and socialization"—in *Jesus: A Revolutionary Biography*, 68–70.

20. The description of these images is indebted to J. White, *Sacraments*, 54–61.

21. 1 Cor 11:23–26; Matt 26:26–29; Mark 14:22–25; and Luke 22:15–20.

22. J. White, *Sacraments*, 57.

23. Transubstantiation is the traditional term by which the Roman Catholic Church affirms Christ's eucharistic presence. Never intended to assert his literal presence at the altar/table, it employs the philosophical constructs of the Middle Ages to proclaim the mystery of Christ's presence mediated by the material elements of bread and wine. Transignification, a term promoted by Edward Schillebeeckx, is an alternative Roman Catholic concept to understand the mystery of the "real presence" of Christ at the Mass. For a detailed discussion of the various interpretations of Christ's eucharistic presence, see Jones, *Christ's Eucharistic Presence*: on transubstantiation, 71–105; on Protestant positions, 118–46; and on Schillebeeckx and transignification, 220–31.

24. Derived from the Greek *eschaton*, which means "the end"; eschatology refers to the study of the last days or the end of time.

25. See Jones, *Christ's Eucharistic Presence*, 7–9.

26. See chapter 3, "The Word of God Theology."

27. See Ehrman, *Lost Scriptures*.

28. Vestments are the liturgical garments or clothing worn by the (clerical) leaders in corporate worship.

29. For more information, see J. White, *Introduction to Christian Worship*, 47–80.

30. These traditional Christian terms refer to the afterlife. Heaven suggests a blessed afterlife, while hell suggests a tormented afterlife. See Borg, *Speaking Christian*, 197–201.

31. See J. White, *Introduction*, 83–91, and J. White and S. White, *Church Architecture*, 18–37.

Bibliography

Abbott, Walter M., ed. *The Documents of Vatican II*. New York: Association Press, 1966.

Achtemeier, Paul J., gen. ed. *HarperCollins Bible Dictionary*. Rev. ed. New York: HarperCollins Publishers, 1996.

———. *The Inspiration of Scripture: Problems and Proposals*. Philadelphia: The Westminster Press, 1980.

Allman, Mark J. *Who Would Jesus Kill?: War, Peace, and the Christian Tradition*. Winona, MN: Anselm Academic, 2008.

Armstrong, Karen. *The Case for God*. New York: Alfred A. Knopf, 2009.

———. *The Bible: A Biography*. New York: Atlantic Monthly Press, 2007.

———. *The Great Transformation: The Beginning of Our Religious Traditions*. New York: Alfred A. Knopf, 2006.

———. *Holy War: The Crusades and Their Impact on Today's Word*. New York: Anchor Books, 2001.

———. *The Battle for God*. New York: Ballantine Books, 2000.

Ayers, Robert H. *Judaism and Christianity*. Lanham, MD: University Press of America, 1983.

Bacchiocchi, Samuele. "Samuele Bacchiocchi Responds." *Biblical Archaeology Review* 31 (July/August 2005): 60.

Bainton, Roland H. *Christian Attitudes toward War and Peace: A Historical Survey and Critical Re-evaluation*. Nashville: Abingdon Press, 1960.

Barash, David P., ed. *Approaches to Peace: A Reader in Peace*, 2d. ed. Oxford: Oxford University Press, 2010.

Barna, George. *Futurecast: What Today's Trends Mean for Tomorrow's World*. Carol Stream, IL: Tyndale House, 2011.

Barrett, David, George Kurian and Todd Johnson, eds. *World Christian Encyclopedia*. New York: Oxford University Press, 2001.

Beckwith, Francis J. "History and Miracles." Pp. 86–98 in *In Defense of Miracles: A Comprehensive Case for God's Action in History*. Edited by R. Douglas Geivett and Gary R. Habermas. Downers Grove, IL: InterVarsity Press, 1997.

Bird, Phyllis A. "The Authority of the Bible." Pp. 33–64 in vol.
    1 of *The New Interpreter's Bible*. Edited by Leander L. Keck.
    Nashville: Abingdon Press, 1994.

Blaisdell, Barbara S. "A Liberal Response." Pp. 41–48 in
    Conservative, Moderate, Liberal: The Biblical Authority Debate.
    Edited by Charles R. Blaisdell. St. Louis: CBP Press, 1990.

Blanton, Dana. "More Believe in God than Heaven," Friday,
    June 18, 2004. http://www.foxnews.com/printer_friendly_
    story/0,3566,99945,00.html.

Boccaccini, Gabriele. "Multiple Judaisms." *Bible Review* 11
    (February 1995): 38–41, 46.

Borg, Marcus. *Speaking Christian: Why Christian Words Have Lost
    Their Meaning and Power—And How They Can Be Restored*. New
    York: HarperCollins, 2011.

———. *Jesus: Uncovering the Life, Teachings, and Relevance of a
    Religious Revolutionary*. New York: HarperSanFrancisco, 2006.

———. "The Search Begins: The Fathers of Historical Jesus
    Scholarship." *Bible Review* (Summer 2005): 17–19.

———. *The Heart of Christianity: Rediscovering a Life of Faith*.
    New York: HarperSanFrancisco, 2003.

———. *Reading the Bible Again for the First Time*. New York:
    HarperSanFrancisco, 2001.

———, and John Dominic Crossan. *The Last Week: A Day-by-
    Day Account of Jesus's Final Week in Jerusalem*. New York:
    HarperSanFrancisco, 2006.

Boring, M. Eugene. "The Gospel of Matthew" Pp. 87–505 in vol.
    8 of *The New Interpreter's Bible*. Edited by Leander E. Keck.
    Nashville: Abingdon Press, 1995.

———. *Revelation*. Louisville: John Knox Press, 1989.

Brecht, Bertolt. *Mother Courage and Her Children*. Translated by
    Eric Bentley. New York: Grove Press, Inc., 1966.

Brooks, David. *Lexington Herald-Leader*. Sunday, September 18,
    2011, E2.

Browning, Christopher R. *Ordinary Men: Reserve Police
    Battalion 101 and the Final Solution in Poland*. New York:
    HarperPerennial, 1992.

Brueggemann, Walter. *The Bible Makes Sense*. Rev. ed. Cincinnati: St. Anthony Messenger Press, 2003.

———. *Finally Comes the Poet: Daring Speech for Proclamation*. Minneapolis: Fortress Press, 1989.

———. *The Bible Makes Sense*. Atlanta: John Knox Press, 1977.

Bultmann, Rudolf. "New Testament and Mythology." *Kerygma and Myth: A Theological Debate*. Edited by Hans Werner Bartsch. Translated by Reginald H. Fuller. London: SPCK, 1957.

Calvin, John. *Institutes of the Christian Religion*. Vol. 21 of The Library of Christian Classics. Edited by John T. McNeill. Translated by Ford Lewis Battles. Philadelphia: The Westminster Press, 1960.

Capps, Donald. *Jesus the Village Psychiatrist*. Louisville: Westminster John Knox Press, 2008.

Caputo, John D. *Philosophy and Theology*. Nashville: Abingdon Press, 2006.

Carroll, James. *Constantine's Sword*. New York: Houghton Mifflin Company, 2001.

Carse, James P. *The Religious Case against Belief*. New York: The Penguin Press, 2008.

Carter, Stephen. *The Culture of Disbelief*. New York: BasicBooks, 1993.

Cartlidge, David R. and David L. Dungan, *Documents for the Study of the Gospels*. Philadelphia: Fortress Press, 1980.

Charry, Ellen T. "Raising Christian Children in a Pagan Culture." *Christian Century* (February 16, 1994): 166–68.

Chopra, Deepak. *The Third Jesus*. New York: Three Rivers Press, 2008.

"Church as Crypt." *The Christian Century* (January 12, 2010): 8–9.

Clifford, Anne. *Introducing Feminist Theology*. Maryknoll, NY: Orbis, 2001.

Coffin, William Sloane. *Credo*. Louisville: Westminster John Knox Press, 2004.

Collins, John. *Does the Bible Justify Violence?* Minneapolis: Fortress Press, 2004.

Cone, James H. *God of the Oppressed*. New York: Seabury Press, 1975.

————. *A Black Theology of Liberation*. Philadelphia: Lippincott, 1970.

Coogan, Michael D. "The Great Gulf between Scholars and the Pew." *Bible Review* (April 1994): 44–48, 55.

Copan, Paul, ed. *Will the Real Jesus Please Stand Up?: A Debate between William Lane Craig and John Dominic Crossan*. Grand Rapids, MI: Baker Books, 1998.

Cotter, Wendy. "Miracle." P. 104 in vol. 4 of *The New Interpreter's Dictionary of the Bible*. Edited by Katharine Doob Sakenfeld. Nashville: Abingdon Press, 2009.

————. "Miracle Stories: The God Asclepius, the Pythagorean Philosophers, and the Roman Rulers." Pp. 166–78 in *The Historical Jesus in Context*. Edited by Amy-Jill Levine, Dale C. Allison Jr., and John Dominic Crossan. Princeton, NJ: Princeton University Press, 2006.

————. *The Miracles in Greco-Roman Antiquity*. London: Routledge, 1999.

Cottrell, Jack W. "The Nature of Biblical Authority: A Conservative Perspective." Pp. 21–40 in *Conservative, Moderate, Liberal: The Biblical Authority Debate*. Edited by Charles R. Blaisdell. St. Louis: CBP Press, 1990.

Covey, Stephen R. *The 7 Habits of Highly Effective People*. New York: Fireside, 1989.

Crossan, John Dominic. *God and Empire*. New York: HarperCollins, 2007.

————. "Why Is Historical Jesus Research Necessary?" Pp. 7–37 in *Jesus Two Thousand Years Later*. Edited by James H. Charlesworth and Walter P. Weaver. Harrisburg, PA: Trinity Press International, 2000.

————. *Jesus: A Revolutionary Biography*. New York: HarperSanFrancisco, 1994.

————, and Jonathan L. Reed. *In Search of Paul*. New York: HarperSanFrancisco, 2004.

Dawkins, Richard. *The God Delusion*. New York: Houghton Mifflin Company, 2006.

Ebeling, Gerhard. *The Nature of Faith*. Translated by Ronald Gregor Smith. Philadelphia: Fortress Press, 1967.

Ehrman, Bart D. *Jesus, Interrupted: Revealing the Hidden Contradictions in the Bible (and Why We Don't Know about Them)*. New York: HarperOne, 2009.

———. "Did Jesus Get Angry or Agonize?" *Bible Review* (Winter 2005): 16–26, 49–50.

———. *Misquoting Jesus: The Story Behind Who Changed the Bible and Why*. New York: HarperSanFrancisco, 2005.

———. *The New Testament: A Historical Introduction to the Early Christian Writings*. Third edition. New York: Oxford University Press, 2004.

———. *Lost Scriptures: Books that Did Not Make It into the New Testament*. New York: Oxford University Press, 2003.

Einstein, Albert. *The World As I See It*. New York: Philosophical Library, 1949. See http://www.aip.org/history/einstein/essay.htm.

Eliot, T.S. "Four Quartets." Pp. 115–45 in *The Complete Poems and Plays*. New York: Harcourt, Brace and Company, 1952.

Emmons, Richard D. "His Word is Truth." *Israel My Glory* (January/February 2009): 13.

"Faith." P. 249 in *The Oxford Dictionary of the Jewish Religion*. Edited by R.J. Zwi Werblowsky and Geoffrey Wigoder. New York: Oxford University Press, 1997.

Farley, Edward and Peter C. Hodgson. "Scripture and Tradition." Pp. 35–61 in *Christian Theology: An Introduction to Its Traditions and Tasks*. Edited by Peter C. Hodgson and Robert H. King. Philadelphia: Fortress Press, 1982.

———. "Scripture and Tradition." 2d ed. Pp. 61–87 in *Christian Theology: An Introduction to Its Traditions and Tasks*. Edited by Peter C. Hodgson and Robert H. King. Philadelphia: Fortress Press, 1985.

Feldman, Louis H. "Palestinian and Diaspora Judaism in the First Century." Pp. 1–39 in Shanks, *Christianity and Rabbinic Judaism*. Washington, DC: Biblical Archaeology Society, 1992.

Ferré, Nels F.S. *The Sun and the Umbrella: A Parable for Today*. New York: Harper & Brothers, 1953.

Flannery, Edward H. *The Anguish of the Jews*. Mahwah, NJ: Paulist Press, 1999.

Fleishner, Eva. "The Shoah and Jewish-Christian Relations." Pp. 3–14 in *Seeing Judaism Anew: Christianity's Sacred Obligation.* Edited by Mary C. Boys. Lanham, MD: Rowman & Littlefield Publishers, Inc., 2005.

Fossum, Jarl. "Understanding Jesus' Miracles." *Bible Review* (April 1994): 17–23, 50.

Fredriksen, Paula. "What 'Parting of the Ways'?" Pp. 35–63 in *The Ways that Never Parted: Jews and Christians in Late Antiquity and the Early Middle Ages.* Edited by Adam H. Becker and Annette Yoshiko Reed. Tübingen: Mohr Siebeck, 2003.

———. "The Birth of Christianity." Pp. 8–30 in *Jesus, Judaism, and Christian Anti-Judaism.* Edited by Paula Fredriksen and Adele Reinhartz. Louisville: Westminster John Knox Press, 2002.

———, and Adele Reinhartz. "Introduction." Pp. 1–7 in *Jesus, Judaism & Christian Anti-Judaism.* Edited by Paula Fredriksen and Adele Reinhartz. Louisville: Westminster John Knox Press, 2002.

Freedman, David Noel, editor-in-chief. *Eerdmans Dictionary of the Bible.* Grand Rapids, MI: William B. Eerdmans Publishing Company, 2000.

Frick, Frank S. *A Journey through the Hebrew Scriptures.* Belmont, CA: Thomson Wadsworth, 2003.

Funk, Robert. *Acts of Jesus: The Search for the Authentic Deeds of Jesus.* New York: HarperCollins Publishers, 1998.

Gager, John. *The Origins of Anti-Semitism: Attitudes toward Judaism in Pagan and Christian Antiquity.* New York: Oxford University Press, 1983.

Geisler, Norman L. "Miracles and the Modern Mind." Pp. 73–85 in *In Defense of Miracles: A Comprehensive Case for God's Action in History.* Edited by R. Douglas Geivett and Gary R. Habermas. Downers Grove, IL: InterVarsity Press, 1997.

Gnuse, Robert. *The Authority of the Bible.* Mahwah, NJ: Paulist Press, 1985.

Grant, Robert M. and David Tracy. *A Short History of the Interpretation of the Bible.* 2d ed. Minneapolis: Fortress, 1984.

Grossman, Cathy Lynn. "Most Americans Believe in God but Don't Know Religious Tenets." *USA Today* (September 28, 2010). See

http://www.usatoday.com/news/religion/2010-09-28-pew28_
ST_N.htm.

———. "Redrawing the Map of American Religion." *USA Today*
(Monday, March 9, 2009): 1A.

Gutiérrez, Gustavo. *A Theology of Liberation*. Maryknoll, NY: Orbis,
1973.

Harris, Sam. *Letter to a Christian Nation*. New York: Vintage
Books, 2006.

———. *The End of Faith*. New York: W. W. Norton & Company,
2004.

Hauerwas, Stanley. *Unleashing the Scripture: Freeing the Bible from
Captivity to America*. Nashville: Abingdon Press, 1993.

Hayes, John H. and Carl R. Holladay. *Biblical Exegesis: A Beginner's
Handbook*. 3d ed. Louisville: Westminster John Knox Press,
2007.

Hedges, Chris. *What Every Person Should Know About War*. New
York: Free Press, 2003.

Hendrickx, Herman. *The Miracle Stories: Studies in the Synoptic
Gospels*. San Francisco: Harper & Row Publishers, 1987.

Heschel, Abraham Joshua. *Man Is Not Alone*. New York: The
Noonday Press, 1979.

Heschel, Susannah. *The Aryan Jesus: Christian Theologians and the
Bible in Nazi Germany*. Princeton, NJ: Princeton University
Press, 2008.

Hillman, James. *A Terrible Love of War*. New York: Penguin Books,
2004.

Hitchens, Christopher. *God Is Not Great*. New York: Twelve,
Hachette Book Group USA, 2007.

Holladay, Carl R. "Canonical Criticism." P. 145 in *The
HarperCollins Bible Dictionary*. Edited by Paul J. Achtemeier.
New York: HarperSanFrancisco, 1996.

———. "Contemporary Methods of Reading the Bible." Pp. 125–
49 in vol. 1 of *The New Interpreter's Bible*. Edited by Leander L.
Keck. Nashville: Abingdon Press, 1994.

Hume, David. *Enquiries Concerning Human Understanding and
Concerning the Principles of Morals*. Oxford: The Clarendon
Press, 1963.

Inbody, Tyron. *The Faith of the Christian Church*. Grand Rapids, MI: William B. Eerdmans Publishing Company, 2005.

Isaac, Jules. *The Teaching of Contempt: Christian Roots of Anti-Semitism*. New York: Holt, Rinehart and Winston, 1964.

Johnson, Luke Timothy. *The Writings of the New Testament*. Minneapolis: Fortress Press, 1999.

———. *The Real Jesus*. New York: HarperSanFrancisco, 1996.

Jones, Paul H. "From Intra-Jewish Polemics to Persecution: The Christian Formation of the Jew as Religious Other." *Encounter* 67,2 (Spring 2006): 161–97.

———. "We Are *How* We Worship: Corporate Worship as a Matrix for Christian Identity Formation." *Worship* (July 1995): 346–60.

———. *Christ's Eucharistic Presence: A History of the Doctrine*. New York: Peter Lang Publishing, 1994.

———. "Worship as Identity Formation." *Lexington Theological Quarterly* (April 1991): 50–52.

Josephus: The Essential Writings. Edited and translated Paul L. Maier. Grand Rapids, MI: Kregel Publications, 1988.

Keck, Leander E., ed. *The New Interpreter's Bible: A Commentary in Twelve Volumes*. Nashville: Abingdon Press, 1994–1998.

Kee, Howard Clark. *Miracle in the Early Christian World: A Study in Sociohistorical Method*. New Haven: Yale University Press, 1983.

Kelsey, David H. *The Uses of Scripture in Recent Theology*. Philadelphia: Fortress Press, 1975.

Kimball, Charles. *When Religion Becomes Evil*. New York: HarperCollins, 2002.

Kingsbury, Jack Dean. "Narrative Criticism." Pp. 739–40 in the *HarperCollins Bible Dictionary*. Edited by Paul J. Achtemeier. New York: HarperCollins Publishers, 1996.

Klawans, Jonathan. "Moral and Ritual Purity." Pp. 266–84 in *The Historical Jesus in Context*. Edited by Amy-Jill Levine, Dale C. Allison, Jr., and John Dominic Crossan. Princeton: Princeton University Press, 2006.

Krattenmaker, Tom. "Religion Can Help End Wars, Too." *USA Today*, July 14, 2008: 15A.

Kurlansky, Mark. *Non-Violence: The History of a Dangerous Idea.* New York: Random House, 2006.

Laughlin, Paul Alan. *Remedial Christianity: What Every Believer Should Know About the Faith, but Probably Doesn't.* Santa Rosa, CA: Polebridge Press, 2000.

Leffler, William J. and Paul H. Jones. *The Structure of Religion: Judaism and Christianity.* Lanham, MD: University Press of America, 2005.

Levine, Amy-Jill. "Misusing Jesus." *The Christian Century* (December 26, 2006): 20–25.

———. *The Misunderstood Jew.* New York: HarperSanFrancisco, 2006.

———. "Anti-Judaism and the Gospel of Matthew." Pp. 9–36 in *Anti-Judaism and the Gospels.* Edited by William R. Farmer. Harrisburg, PA: Trinity Press International, 1999.

Lewis, C.S. *God in the Dock: Essays on Theology and Ethics.* Grand Rapids, MI: William B. Eerdmans Publishing Company, 1970.

———. *Miracles: A Preliminary Study.* New York: The MacMillan Company, 1947.

Licht, Jacob. "Miracle." P. 305 in vol. 14 of *Encyclopedia Judaica.* Edited by Michael Berenbaum and Fred Skolnik. Detroit: Macmillan Reference USA, 2007.

Linn, Jan G. *Christians Must Choose.* St. Louis: CBP Press, 1985.

Livingston, James C. *Anatomy of the Sacred: An Introduction to Religion.* 3d ed. Upper Saddle River, NJ: Prentice Hall, 1998.

Lüdemann, Gerd. *The Unholy in Holy Scripture: The Dark Side of the Bible.* Translated by John Bowden. Louisville: Westminster John Knox Press, 1997.

MacGregor, Geddes. "Doubt and Faith." P. 2424 in vol. 5 of *The Encyclopedia of Religion.* Edited by Lindsay Jones. Detroit, MI: Thomson Gale, 2005.

Madigan, Kevin J. and Jon D. Levenson. *Resurrection: The Power of God for Christians and Jews.* New Haven: Yale University Press, 2008.

Malcolm, Lois. "Word of God, Systematic Theology." P. 753 in *The Encyclopedia of Christianity.* Edited by Erwin Fahlbusch,

Jan Milic Lochman, John Mbiti, Jaroslav Pelikan, Lukas Vischer. Grand Rapids, MI: William B. Eerdmans Publishing Company, 2008.

Malina, Bruce. *The New Testament World.* Louisville: Westminster John Knox Press, 2001.

Marty, Martin, ed. "Gaining Consciousness." *Context: Martin E. Marty on Religion and Culture.* February 2009, part B, vol. 41, no. 2: 6–7.

Mays, James L., gen. ed. *HarperCollins Bible Commentary.* Rev. ed. New York: HarperCollins Publishers, 2000.

McCullough, Donald W. *The Trivialization of God.* Colorado Springs: Navpress, 1995.

McGrath, Alister E. *Christian Theology: An Introduction.* Oxford: Blackwell Publishers, 1994.

McKenzie, Steven L. and Stephen R. Haynes, eds. *To Each Its Own Meaning: An Introduction to Biblical Criticisms and Their Application.* Louisville: Westminster John Knox Press, 1999.

McKnight, Edgar V. "Reader-Response Criticism." Pp. 230–52 in *To Each Its Own Meaning: An Introduction to Biblical Criticisms and Their Application.* Edited by Steven L. McKenzie and Stephen R. Haynes. Louisville: Westminster John Knox Press, 1999.

———. *Postmodern Use of the Bible: The Emergence of Reader-Oriented Criticism.* Nashville: Abingdon Press, 1988.

———. "Reader-Response Criticism." Pp. 915–18 in the *HarperCollins Bible Dictionary,* Edited by Paul J. Achtemeier. New York: HarperCollins Publishers, 1996.

Meier, John P. *The Marginal Jew: Rethinking the Historical Jesus.* Vol. 2. New York: Doubleday, 1994.

Metzger, Bruce M. *The Canon of the New Testament: Its Origin, Development, and Significance.* Oxford: Clarendon Press, 1987.

Micklethwait, John and Adrian Wooldridge. *God Is Back: How the Global Revival of Faith Is Changing the World.* New York: The Penguin Press, 2009.

Migliore, Daniel. *Faith Seeking Understanding.* 2d ed. Grand Rapids MI: William B. Eerdmans Publishing Company, 2006.

———. *Faith Seeking Understanding.* Grand Rapids MI: William B. Eerdmans Publishing Company, 2004.

Miller, Robert J. *The Jesus Seminar and Its Critics.* Santa Rosa, CA: Polebridge Press, 1999.

Moltmann, Jürgen. "Israel's No: Jews and Jesus in an Unredeemed World." *The Christian Century* (November 7, 1990): 1021–24.

Neusner, Jacob. *A Short History of Judaism: Three Meals, Three Epochs.* Minneapolis, MN: Fortress Press, 1992.

Newsom, Carol A. and Sharon H. Ringe, eds. *The Women's Bible Commentary.* Louisville: Westminster/John Knox, 1992.

Nickelsburg, George W. E. *Ancient Judaism and Christian Origins.* Minneapolis: Fortress Press, 2003.

Niebuhr, Reinhold. *The Nature and Destiny of Man.* New York: Charles Scribner's Sons, 1964.

O'Day, Gail R. "The Gospel of John." Pp. 491–865 in vol. 9 of *The New Interpreter's Bible.* Edited by Leander L. Keck. Nashville: Abingdon Press, 1994

Origen. *On First Principles.* Bk. 4, chap. 1–3. Translated by G. W. Butterworth. London: SPCK, 1936; reprinted in Gloucester, MA: Peter Smith, 1973.

Otto, Rudolf. *The Idea of the Holy.* Translated by John W. Harvey. New York: Oxford University Press, 1970.

Pagels, Elaine. *The Origin of Satan.* New York: Random House, 1995.

Palmer, Parker J. *The Promise of Paradox: A Celebration of Contradictions in the Christian Life.* San Francisco: Jossey-Bass, 1980.

Pelikan, Jaroslav. "Faith." P. 2958 in vol. 5 of *The Encyclopedia of Religion.* Edited by Lindsay Jones. Detroit, MI: Thomson Gale, 2005.

———. *Jesus through the Centuries.* New Haven, Yale University Press, 1985.

———. *The Vindication of Tradition.* New Haven, CT: Yale University Press, 1984.

Peters, F.E. *The Children of Abraham: Judaism, Christianity, Islam.* Princeton: Princeton University Press, 2004.

Placher, William. "The Nature of Biblical Authority: Issues and
    Models from Recent Theology." Pp. 1–19 in *Conservative,*
    Moderate, Liberal: The Biblical Authority Debate. Edited by
    Charles R. Blaisdell. St. Louis: CBP Press, 1990.
————. *A History of Christian Theology.* Philadelphia: Westminster
    Press, 1983.
Potok, Chaim. *In the Beginning.* Greenwich CT: Fawcett Crest
    Book, 1975.
Powell, Mark Allen. *What Is Narrative Criticism?* Minneapolis,
    MN: Fortress Press, 1990.
Power, David N. *The Eucharistic Mystery.* New York: Crossroad,
    1992.
Prothero, Stephen. *Biblical Literacy: What Every American Needs to*
    Know—And Doesn't. New York: HarperSanFrancisco, 2007.
Reinhartz, Adele. "The Gospel of John: How the 'Jews' Became
    Part of the Plot." Pp. 99–116 in *Jesus, Judaism & Christian*
    Anti-Judaism. Edited by Paula Fredriksen and Adele Reinhartz.
    Louisville: Westminster John Knox Press, 2002.
Remus, Harold E. "Miracle (NT)." P. 868 in vol. 4 of *The Anchor*
    Bible Dictionary. Edited by David Noel Freedman. New York:
    Doubleday, 1992.
Ricoeur, Paul. *The Symbolism of Evil.* Translated by Emerson
    Buchanan. Boston: Beacon Press, 1967.
Ritschl, Dietrich. "Faith: Overview." P. 261 in vol. 2 of *The*
    Encyclopedia of Christianity. Edited by Erwin Fahlbusch, Jan
    Milic Lochman, John Mbiti, Jaroslav Pelikan, Lukas Vischer.
    Grand Rapids, MI: William B. Eerdmans Publishing Company,
    2001.
Romano, Andrew. "How Dumb Are We?" *Newsweek* 157,13 and 14
    (March 2, April 4, 2011): 56–60.
Roysden, Doug. "Will the Real Disciples Please Stand Up?"
    DisciplesWorld, September 2008: 20.
Ruether, Rosemary. *Faith and Fratricide.* Eugene, OR: Wipf &
    Stock Publishers, 1997.
Ruiz, Jean-Pierre. "Ancient Jewish-Christian Rivalries." Pp. 59–69
    in *Seeing Judaism Anew: Christianity's Sacred Obligation.*

Edited by Mary C. Boys. Lanham, MD: Rowman & Littlefield Publishers, Inc., 2005.

Rusch, William G. *The Trinitarian Controversy.* Philadelphia: Fortress Press, 1980.

Russell, Letty M., ed. *Feminist Interpretation of the Bible.* Philadelphia: Westminster Press, 1985.

Sakenfeld, Katharine Doob, gen. ed. *The New Interpreter's Dictionary of the Bible.* 5 vols. Nashville: Abingdon Press, 2006–2009.

Sanders, E.P. "Jesus, Ancient Judaism, and Modern Christianity: The Quest Continues." Pp. 31–55 in *Jesus, Judaism, and Christian Anti-Judaism.* Edited by Paula Fredriksen and Adele Reinhartz. Louisville: Westminster John Knox Press, 2002.

———. "Reflections on Anti-Judaism in the New Testament and in Christianity." Pp. 265–86 in *Anti-Judaism and the Gospels.* Edited by William R. Farmer. Harrisburg, PA: Trinity Press International, 1999.

———. *Jesus and Judaism.* London: SCM; Philadelphia: Fortress, 1985.

Schaefer, Tom. "Its Sense of Awe of God" in the *Lexington Herald-Leader,* May 4, 1996.

Schwartz, Regina M. *The Curse of Cain.* Chicago: The University of Chicago Press, 1997.

Segal, Alan F. *Rebecca's Children: Judaism and Christianity in the Roman World.* Cambridge, MA: Harvard University Press, 1986.

Segundo, Juan Luis. *Doing Theology in a Revolutionary Situation.* Philadelphia: Fortress Press, 1975.

Smart, James D. *The Strange Silence of the Bible in the Church: A Study in Hermeneutics.* Philadelphia: Westminster Press, 1970.

Smith, Dwight Moody. "Word." P. 1221 in *HarperCollins Bible Dictionary.* Edited by Paul J. Achtemeier. New York: HarperCollins Publishers, 1996.

Smith, Wilfred Cantwell. *Faith and Belief: The Difference between Them.* Oxford: Oneworld Publications, 1998.

Soulen, Richard N. and R. Kendall Soulen. *Handbook of Biblical Criticism.* 3d ed. Louisville: Westminster John Knox Press, 2001.

Spieckermann, Hermann. "Word of God, OT." P. 750 in *The Encyclopedia of Christianity*. Edited by Erwin Fahlbusch, Jan Milic Lochman, John Mbiti, Jaroslav Pelikan, Lukas Vischer. Grand Rapids, MI: William B. Eerdmans Publishing Company, 2008.

Spong, John Shelby. *Jesus for the Non-Religious*. New York: HarperOne, 2007.

Steiner, George. *After Babel: Aspects of Language and Translation*. New York: Oxford University Press, 1975.

Steinhauser, Paul. "Poll: Did Obama's Reaction to Gates Arrest Hurt Him?" CNNPolitics.com (August 4, 2009). http://www.cnn.com/2009/POLITICS/08/04/obama.gates.poll/.

Swinburne, Richard. *The Concept of Miracle*. New York: St. Martin's Press, 1970.

Thomas, Oliver "Buzz." *10 Things Your Minister Wants to Tell You*. New York: St. Martin's Press, 2007.

Tillich, Paul. *Dynamics of Faith*. New York: Perennial Classics, 2001.

———. *Systematic Theology*. Chicago: The University of Chicago Press, 1957.

———. *The Protestant Era*. Translated by James Luther Adams. Chicago: The University of Chicago Press, 1948.

Tiner, John Hudson. *Isaac Newton: Inventor, Scientist and Teacher*. Milford, MI: Mott Media, 1976.

Tracy, David. *The Analogical Imagination: Christian Theology and the Culture of Pluralism*. New York: Crossroad, 1981.

Trible, Phyllis. *God and the Rhetoric of Sexuality*. Philadelphia: Fortress Press, 1978.

Twelftree, Graham H. *Jesus the Miracle Worker: A Historical & Theological Study*. Downers Grove, IL: InterVarsity Press, 1999.

U.S. Religious Landscape Survey: Religious Beliefs and Practices: Diverse and Politically Relevant. Pew Forum on Religion and Public Life. June 2008. http://religions.pewforum.org/.

Vermes, Geza. "Introduction: Parallel History Preview." Pp. xvii–xxii in *Christianity and Rabbinic Judaism: A Parallel History of Their Origins and Early Development*. Edited by Hershel Shanks. Washington, DC: Biblical Archaeology Society, 1992.

Volf, Miroslav. *Exclusion and Embrace: A Theological Exploration of Identity, Otherness, and Reconciliation*. Nashville: Abingdon Press, 1996.

Waida, Manabu. "Miracles." P. 6049 in vol. 9 of *Encyclopedia of Religion*. Edited by Lindsay Jones. 2d ed. Farmington Hills, MI: Thomson Gale, 2005.

Westerhoff III, John H. *Living the Faith Community*. San Francisco: Harper & Row Publishers, 1985.

White, James F. *Introduction to Christian Worship*. 3d ed. Nashville: Abingdon Press, 2000.

————. *Sacraments as God's Self Giving*. Nashville: Abingdon Press, 1983.

————, and Susan J. White. *Church Architecture*. Nashville: Abingdon Press, 1988.

White, L. Michael. *From Jesus to Christianity: How Four Generations of Visionaries & Storytellers Created the New Testament and Christian Faith*. New York: HarperSanFrancisco, 2004.

Williamson, Clark M. and Ronald J. Allen. *The Teaching Minister*. Louisville: Westminster/John Knox Press, 1991.

Wink, Walter. *The Powers That Be: Theology for a New Millennium*. New York: Doubleday, 1998.

Wolpe, David. J. *Why Faith Matters*. New York: HarperCollins Publishers, 2008.

Wolter, Michael. "Word of God, NT." Pp. 751–52 in *The Encyclopedia of Christianity*. Edited by Erwin Fahlbusch, Jan Milic Lochman, John Mbiti, Jaroslav Pelikan, Lukas Vischer. Grand Rapids, MI: William B. Eerdmans Publishing Company, 2008.

Wylen, Stephen. M. *The Jews in the Time of Jesus*. New York: Paulist Press, 1996.

Zakovitch, Yair. "Miracle (OT)." P. 305 in vol. 14 of *The Anchor Bible Dictionary*. Edited by David Noel Freedman. New York: Doubleday, 1992.

Index

About the Author

Paul H. Jones is Professor of Religion at Transylvania University in Lexington, Kentucky. A graduate of Yale (B.A.) and Texas Christian University (M. Div.), with a Ph.D. from Vanderbilt University, Jones is the author of *Christ's Eucharistic Presence* (1994), and co-author of *500 Illustrations: Stories from Life for Preaching & Teaching* (1998) and *The Structure of Religion: Judaism and Christianity* (2005). He is a member of the American Academy of Religion, North American Academy of Liturgy, and Disciples of Christ Historical Society.

CPSIA information can be obtained at www.ICGtesting.com
Printed in the USA
BVOW010012280313

316661BV00006B/10/P